940.5481
GIL

GILPATRICK, KRISTIN
HERO NEXT DOOR

MUEHL PUBLIC LIBRARY
SEYMOUR, WI

Stories from Wisconsin's World War II Veterans

THE HERO NEXT DOOR™ RETURNS

Kristin Gilpatrick

Badger Books Inc.
Oregon, WI

© Copyright 2001 by Kristin Gilpatrick Halverson
Published by Badger Books Inc.
"The Hero Next Door" is a registered trademark
Cover design by Ann Christianson
Printed by McNaughton & Gunn of Saline, Mich.

First printing

ISBN 1-878569-76-7

All rights reserved. No part of this publication may be reproduced or transmitted in any form or by any means, electronic or mechanical, including photocopy, recording or information and retrieval system without permission in writing from the publisher. For information, contact:
Badger Books Inc.
P.O. 192, Oregon, WI 53575
Toll-free phone: (800) 928-2372
Web site: http://www.badgerbooks.com
E-Mail: books@badgerbooks.com

DEDICATION

To the *Heroes Next Door* who answered the call to share their stories with me. And, especially, to 82nd Airborne Paratrooper Jim Geach of Hurley, Wis., who lost his final battle just after publication of the first *Hero Next Door*, in which he is featured.

To my forever friend, my sister Shelly, and to the *Heroes Next Door* in my family.

And, especially, to the men and women of every American family who have gallantly and quietly served this country during its greatest times of turmoil and served their communities and families well ever since.

Thank you for your sacrifice.
Thank you for my freedom.

ACKNOWLEDGMENTS

There are so many who have helped and pushed me along the way to bringing this book to press. Among those to thank are:

• My parents Robert Gilpatrick and Barb and Craig Nichols who encouraged my love of writing and history and who taught me that there is nothing I cannot do or be.

• The veterans in my family who gave me a lifelong respect for my country and the people who fought for its freedoms.

• Sara Cox Landolt, Theresa Sweeney, Barb and Craig Nichols, Dee and Renee Halverson and all those who helped edit this book.

• Ann Christianson, the graphic designer who created the inspired cover for this and the first *Hero Next Door*™.

• The Credit Union Executives Society, which afforded me time and flexibility to continue my life's passion.

• Attorneys Gina Carter and Jim Peterson of LaFollette Godfrey & Kahn.

• My Little Sisters Kristy and Breona for their unending friendship.

• Friends Nancy Hilton and Pastor Bruce and Cynthia Burnside who support and push my dreams.

• The many readers of my first book who encouraged me to write a second.

• The Wisconsin Veterans Museum, especially researchers Richard Harris and Ivan Hannibal — and countless librarians and historians — who've helped me in my research.

- Norton Hubbard for the suggestion to add "Returns" to the title of this second book when I was stuck on simply "Part II."
- The "heroes next door" featured in this book. I am grateful that these veterans were willing to share their often-painful war memories so our next generation will have them to learn from. I feel deeply privileged to have come to know these men and women, not only as the heroes they will always be to me but as my friends as well.
- And, my husband Steve, who encouraged me to write the second book even before I thought of it. For putting up with my writer's block and doubtful moments, for selflessly doing so much for others, for bringing me hot chocolate and a hug when I needed it most, and especially for being a loving husband, an enthusiastic cheerleader, a supportive coach and a best friend. I am forever grateful to God for bringing us together because I know that I never really needed to look next door to find a hero; I get to spend my lifetime with mine.

TABLE OF CONTENTS

Introduction 9

EUROPEAN THEATER

COMBAT LINEMAN 16
Norton Hubbard

TEST PILOT 41
Jeannette Kapus

PATRIOT BROTHER..53
Virgil Murphy

GRATEFUL NAVIGATOR 71
George Durnford

MERCHANT 'MEDIC' 95
Lavern Meyer

DESERT NURSE 110
Marie Fredrick

LAND SEAMAN 119
Martin Gutekunst

PACIFIC THEATER

RED ARROW-MAN 159
Marvin Langeteig

YOUNG MARINE 187
Art Orlowski

'DRAFT DOGER' 200
Dave Brenzel

UNSINKABLE SEAMAN 244
George Watson

SUB SURVIVOR 255
Earl Baumgart

NEW GUINEA NIGHTINGALE 270
Marion Dorfmeister

REPLACEMENT MARINE 285
Gus Boener

INTRODUCTION

In my first book *The Hero Next Door*™, I told the stories of 14 men who fought across Pacific Ocean islands, on bloody beaches and in Europe's frozen forests. I believed that first book depicted the wide breadth of experiences and great distances covered in America's battle to save the world during1941-45. However, I also knew — even before I first put pen to paper — that one book could not include all the gallant efforts of all the Americans who fought that battle, at home and overseas. There are so many more stories to tell — stories the next generation needs to hear before they are wiped from the pages of our collective memories.

When that first book went to press, I already had the names of many veterans whose stories deserved to be told. In the year since that publication, many more stories have come forward. Nearly all of them were, once again, recommended to me not by the Wisconsinite who lived them but by his or her family, friends and neighbors because the veteran exemplifies the spirit of the *Hero Next Door* — men and women who humbly served their country well in war and peace.

The Hero Next Door Returns™ is a collection of 14 more of those stories, told by this small sampling of the scared but determined young Americans fighting for their lives — and buddies — while fighting for their country, in a place so far from home that mere mention of it hurt. While this next collection of stories

The Hero Next Door Returns

began as a way to capture some of the experiences missing from the first book, the veterans represented in the *Hero Next Door Returns* once again paint a broad brush stroke across World War II's canvas.

Their stories do not depict the traditional history book accounts of war, however — these are not the stories of generals and battle plans. Nor do their stories dare to represent the stories of the 300,000 Wisconsinites who served in World War II.

Their stories do, however, share the individual acts of bravery and sacrifice, borne by our brothers, sisters, uncles, grandfathers and neighbors — our *Heroes Next Door* — that combined to save the world.

Each man or woman who served this country was an important cog in the massive war machine that won World War II. Though each veteran I've spoken too insists they were "only doing their job," the job they were doing was securing freedom for America and the world. That was no small task, and no one American's part of that accomplishment deserves anything less than our deepest gratitude.

The veterans I know certainly have my deepest gratitude. And, I am especially honored to have come to know the men and women featured in this second book in the *Hero Next Door* series.

These stories are told from what each recalls of the small part they played in the most far-reaching war in American history. Nearly 60 years have passed since most of them were "over there." Some memories are foggy; others are too painful to remember. The veterans in this book each chose which tales of war to tell, what pictures to show and how much to tell. In most cases, the recollections they offer here are stories they've seldom told before. These are the stories they largely tucked away in their memories in order to get on with the second chance of life they were granted by returning home alive from war. They started families and businesses and gave their time to help their neighbors when they could.

After hearing from all of you at book signings in the last year, I know for certain that most of us sons, and granddaughters, and neighbors do not really know of the sacrifices the man or woman living in our family or down our street made a half a century ago. We do not know the *Hero Next Door.*

Let me introduce you to some of them.

— **Kristin Gilpatrick**
May 2001

THE WAR
IN EUROPE

THE WAR IN EUROPE

In this section you'll come to know a few of the Wisconsinites who fought with hundreds of thousands of Allied units to free the continent of Europe from Nazi German's deadly grasp. These *Heroes Next Door* include:

• **Norton Hubbard,** an Army signalman who scaled poles and dodged bullets to lay the thin line that held Allied communications together across Africa and Italy.

• **Jeannette Kapus,** a lady pilot who tested bombers and military tradition as a part of the Women's Airforce Service Pilots.

• **Virgil Murphy,** a radio operator with the 21st Weather Group whose brothers, wife and sisters-in-law all served in front of and behind the lines of the Allied war effort.

• **George "Dutch" Durnford,** a B-17 bomber navigator with the 15th Air Force in Italy who lost some friends—and much of his arm—as he and his crew struggled through hell to make it home alive.

• **Lavern Meyer,** a Merchant Marine pharmacist mate who tended his ships' crew and cargo as he sailed through dangerous waters to supply the war effort.

• **Marie Fredrick,** an Army nurse who endured the sandy desert heat to mend wounded soldiers coming through the 81st Station Hospital in Africa.

• **Martin Gutekunst,** a Navyman turned "soldier" who went in on Utah Beach in the Normandy Invasion before traveling to yet a second D-Day, a half a world away.

The Hero Next Door Returns

COMBAT LINEMAN
NORTON HUBBARD

It was a thin line that tied the American troops together in World War II—a line literally no thicker than a telephone wire. And, Norton Hubbard of Middleton, Wis., was among the men responsible for stringing it.

Hubbard was one of 400 to 500 men in a small, unattached Army signal battalion whose job it was to lay and repair thousands of miles of communication wire between headquarters and the field units from Northern Africa through Italy.

Following wire along mined fields, against sniper fire and between artillery blasts was not the job Hubbard had envisioned for himself when he enlisted in the Army Air Cadets after high school graduation in Hillsboro, Wis. in 1942. He assumed he'd be fighting from the skies above Europe not slugging his way across its fields and furrows.

When he and 48 other enlistees were inducted in Milwaukee on Sept. 27, 1942, they figured that since some of them had pilots' licenses already they'd all be Texas bound for air cadet training.

"It didn't quite work out that way. Instead, most of us woke up at Camp Atterbury, Ind., where we were assigned to the Signal Corps," part of a signal group the Army was developing to provide communications

Combat Lineman

from the base sections to the divisions in the field.

"They took the cadre out of Illinois Bell, and they were the officers and noncoms. Then they brought in this batch of yokels from Wisconsin that thought they were all going into the air force."

Despite their best efforts, the would-be airmen were signalmen for good. A decision Hubbard said he didn't like at the time but was grateful for later "after we saw the casualties the 8th Air Force was suffering in Europe."

"We were very fortunate we were in a hybrid company because we were back in the base section when we weren't stringing field wire on the line. I think the good Lord was with us when he transferred us to the Signal Corps because we wouldn't have made it in the air corps."

He was thankful too for the hard but experienced colonel who trained the Signal Corps. "We got assigned a new commanding officer, Colonel Banks, a short fellow with a butch haircut, who was infantry in W.W.I."

Though the group would be responsible for vital communications, Col. Banks spent little time training them on the intricacies of telephone equipment.

"Communications then was basically telephones; we weren't using field radios at that time and the magneto systems we had were so simple somebody in kindergarten could basically handle it. Instead, Col. Banks said 'we'll do basic infantry training—ranger training, commando training, whatever it takes to save your skin. If we'd get some signal training done too, that would be good.' About all we learned in those two to three months was to tie a square knot to splice wire together and climb poles because we were basically handling phone lines. We did a lot of hiking and one night had a maneuver after which two had broken legs and one a broken back. But, his training idea was good because he'd been in W.W. I and knew you had to be a tough number to last in combat."

By April 1943, the infantry-prepared signal corps

17

The Hero Next Door Returns

Used to climbing high above the ground as a lineman, Hubbard felt little fear straddling the top of the Leaning Tower of Pisa in 1945.

boarded the Louis Pasteur, a French luxury liner turned troop ship, bound for North Africa.

There were a few nervous moments even before they reached the African shore. "We had air cover for only about 150 miles out of New York and went the rest of the way across the Atlantic unescorted. When I was sitting at the rail we spotted a periscope and that made us nervous, thinking it was a German sub. It surfaced and we were relieved to see it was American. After he left, we changed direction every 11 minutes to avoid being a German sub target."

Combat Lineman

'HOT' WIRING

By the time the unit reached North Africa, the Allies had the Germans well on the run back toward the European continent.

"The show was just about over in Africa. They had lost a lot of signal people, especially in the Kasserine Pass and we went over as a unit but we were essentially their replacements. We were never part of one corps but were attached to different ones from time to time, such as the 5th, 7th and 2nd armies, including the 1st, 34th, 36th, 45th, 10th mountain and 3rd divisions. And, the British 8th Army required our services a few times.

"As this was a world war, if you named a nationality, we were with them. When you were with the British 8th you learned to listen to those Scotsmen talk very quick and fast. The southerners had an awful time keeping up with them. Sometimes it took a little hand signal to get the word across but there were not a lot of language problems."

Hubbard got his first taste of that world war perspective when the troop ship landed in Casablanca, Morocco, on the western coast of North Africa.

"We hiked nine miles out. It was so dry and hot you couldn't drive a tent peg if you wanted to, so we laid our blankets on the ground and tried to sleep but, after we'd been on the ocean so long, you still felt like you were rolling around."

That first night may have felt like an ocean voyage but there were no cool sea breezes to break the desert heat. "Climate was a challenge. The thermometers our medics had went up to 110 and broke the first day so I don't know how hot it got. We also learned the first night in the desert not to take our boots off. I woke up in the morning and grabbed my boots. I put my foot in one and, in the second one, I had a 20-30 inch snake! I shook that snake out and threw the boot in the air. Someone threw my boot back at me. I never took my boots off again, other than to change my socks, while

The Hero Next Door Returns

I was in Africa."

The desert had smaller critters to contend with too, disease-carrying mosquitoes for one. "I had a severe case of malaria at Tunis that lasted maybe a week. I remember lying in a tent and you could see an outline of my body when I got up from the blanket. They'd put 5-6 blankets on me and I still couldn't get warm . . . in the desert!"

Sgt. Hubbard was first put to work on mounted guard duty around the International Telephone & Telegraph building in Casablanca, where the (Allied) communications went out to the world.

"We had guards all the way around and sandbags from the gutter to the top of the second floor windows so no one could throw a grenade into a window."

Still, in war, no building was ever truly secure.

"One night, someone pushed a piece of parfait off the roof and almost got my guard at the main door. And, it was there that I shot at a man for the first time in my life.

"Marshall law was in effect and no one was supposed to be out at night. There was a large park affair out in front of the building and, about 2 a.m., I saw this shadow of a man coming across in the moonlight. He hid behind a big palm tree. I fired a couple of rounds into that tree. He took off and ran right toward the hotel. I never heard anything more from him. It was just like I was shooting at a sparrow or something. Shooting at him was a matter of survival because I didn't know what he was going to do."

There were a few other unusual interruptions as well.

"We did have one funny thing happen about 3 a.m. one night. We heard a noise that kept getting louder. Finally, here came an old donkey pulling the remains of a car with no tires. There was a plank on the frame and on top was a homemade casket. Behind were eight or nine mourners who were really moaning, making

Combat Lineman

an awful noise. When they turned the corner by our building, the casket fell off and landed in the street. All these mourners ran into the shadows and we thought maybe the casket was a bomb, but we just kept our cool and waited. One by one the mourners came out and listened at the casket to see if the body had come back to life. Then they picked it up and put it back on the old car frame."

After two weeks, the signal unit began establishing communications for the guards at the prison camp at Belshid outside of Casablanca about 30 miles. "Then we started rebuilding wire lines from city to city up to Fez and so on. When the war was over in North Africa, we moved on up to Oran and Algiers in Algeria. We got up to between Tunis and Bizerte in Tunisia and waited, thinking we were going into the invasion of Sicily. But, we weren't needed and instead established communications lines clear to Tripoli," along the coast of Libya. In all, Hubbard had traveled well over 1,500 miles across the desert to reach Tripoli.

According to *The Tech Services: The Signal Corps—The Outcome,* the signal corps in North Africa provided 1,103 miles of "wire and cable services between Casablanca and Constantine," and by the end of the combat in North Africa, the "American Army had *added* 5,000 miles of open wire line" across the desert.

In addition to hard work in the dry heat of the desert, their task was complicated by land mines, snipers and poor rations. "There was debris everywhere along the road, scattered all over. There was scrap iron everywhere!

"I was shot at by a sniper near Mateur. I was on a telegraph pole and he hit the insulator about a foot from my head on the other side of the pole. I dropped to the ground and went through a railroad tunnel and didn't go back. I figure it must have been an Arab as the Krauts were gone by then."

It wasn't all work, though. Boys, after all, will be boys. "One day, we were going along this road south of Tunis

The Hero Next Door Returns

and I had a bunch of wild boys in the back that were up to having fun. We met a convoy with big deuces all loaded with boxes of rations. They called to our driver and said 'get over next to that one!' So, we were six to eight inches apart when we met this truck. They had a hay bale hook and hooked a case off the back. Then we got down the road a ways and opened the case. You know what they had? Six #10 cans of sauerkraut for their efforts! Not to be outdone, we 12-13 fellows sat down and ate all that kraut up. I didn't even want to be in the same country with them after that!"

There was other unique food in the desert as well.

"We had desert chocolate bars that wouldn't melt. You could suck on bits of it like an all-day sucker. We got some desert butter too, and that wouldn't melt because, I think, it was half wax. Cooks could use it to fry eggs when we got some from an old Arab. Then, sometimes thoughout the war, we'd get a hold of some sugar and I'd make fudge. Of course, we didn't have good results with fudge in Africa because when we'd try to make it we couldn't melt the damn stuff. Still, we'd heat it up on a little can of aviation gas, and that stirred up mess tasted good!"

Some rations were better than others, however. "We drew rations from the British 8th a few days, which seemed like a month. You got three items, tea, hard tack and a can of bully corned beef from Argentina. You could take it in any sequence you wanted but it was the same three times a day.

"There were British from India who were very good fighters—some of the best—and could make the best tea. When it got to be 10 a.m. they stopped the convoy and held everybody up until they had their tea. They carried a little pail affair on the back and used American condensed milk, sugar and tea. They would be more than happy to share it with you if you were social. No matter how I tried to mix it, though, I just couldn't make tea like that."

Little did the Signal Corps know how good

Combat Lineman

sauerkraut, desert chocolate and Indian tea would seem when food became as scarce as rain in North Africa, once most supplies headed toward fighting in Italy—a new battleground Hubbard would soon join.

"We started getting ideas that we were going somewhere else. There were umpteen rumors of what was going to happen and one was that we were going north of Rome. We found out a year later, when we were north of Rome, that the Axis had believed these rumors and dug big holes so gliders couldn't land in the fields north of Rome."

In early September, 1943, the unit moved dockside in Bizerte and once again set about acquiring some extra "rations."

"The night before we went aboard ship we were bivouacked in Bizerte and rumor came back that there was a movie down at the docks. On the way down, two fellows from the south—original moonshiners—said they smelled something good in this little French boxcar. It was full of British ale! I never saw a boxcar emptied so fast in my life!"

As luck would have it that was the one and only night it rained in Africa. "It looked like rain so my tent mate Don and I dug a trench around our tent, even though we hadn't had rain the whole time we were in Africa. About 2:30 a.m. a downpour cut loose. I looked out to see what was going on and saw a boot go floating by. Everybody was soaked except us."

In the morning, as they loaded the vehicles to move down to the port, the night's raid and rain were evident when military police showed up to investigate the boxcar's missing stash. "There were bottles in all the slit trenches but there wasn't anybody who knew anything about it. Nobody saw or knew a thing!"

Only one man nearly got in trouble. "A guy from Georgia took a 5-gallon water can into town to get some wine. While he was gone, we went aboard the LST (landing ship, tank). He was an old moonshiner—probably 30—and was smart enough that when he saw we

23

The Hero Next Door Returns

were gone he reported to the hospital ill. He caught up with us in Italy about three months later."

ITALIAN LINES

From Bizerte, the signal corps rode the Mediterranean waves into an unknown future on land. "We didn't know where we were going then but we stayed topside because we found we didn't get as seasick. When we hit a storm on the LST, that flat-bottomed boat rolled like a cork, as did its passengers."

In fact the unit lost its most loyal member to the stormy ride. "We lost our pet dog, Doubletime, when he was washed overboard on the way to Salerno. He'd been picked up by somebody at Camp Atterbury; they found him as a puppy in some abandoned farm buildings and came in with him tucked in their shirt one day. He got special treatment; everybody took care of Doubletime. We smuggled him aboard the train and the ship; we smuggled him all the way across Africa. He was illegal as all get out but we managed to get Doubletime over there. Then he was on deck with us when the ship was rolling and he went overboard. He was sort of a mongrel beagle but he was friends with any GI. He was a great dog."

Hubbard nearly lost his good buddy Don as well. "We stayed up topside because our truck was topside and we lived in it. We didn't go down in the hold because if you get down where you can't see the horizon you'll get seasick. Don was feeling real queasy and this ship was rolling so much it was taking water on the deck. I was laughing at him and he said, 'I got to throw up.' He went to the rail—which on an LST was a wire rope fastened with stations every 20 feet—grabbed this cable in each hand and leaned over to heave. Just then, the ship rolled and all the slack in the cable came to him. He was several feet out into space and I thought, 'well, that's the last of Don.' But then the ship rolled back and he was still hanging on. He landed on his butt and slid 12-14 feet sitting up,

sliding right over to our truck. The back of his head hit the running board. He shook his head and got up. He was petrified but no longer seasick. I never saw anyone get over seasickness so fast in my life!"

Despite all the rolling, the LST made it to the invasion of Salerno in southern Italy (at the top of the instep of the boot-shaped country). "We had a pretty good skipper and he put us right up on shore. I jumped across to the sand and turned around and took a picture of the commanding officer coming off the ship. Then our interest was suddenly taken away because ME-109s were coming in and strafing the beach. The German 88mms started pounding and we looked for a hole in hell. Shortly after we were off the ship, and in a knoll a little ways away, an 88 entered the open doors of the LST and exploded back in there somewhere. It was quite a racket."

It was the first time Hubbard had experienced real combat. "It was like your first time at the circus. It's all here and it's noisy and you can't see it all. Every one moved fast until they found a place to hide from the fire from the Kraut O.P. (observation point). Everything and anything was a target. From Jeeps to trucks, any machine or man was eligible."

Though he was certainly concerned, from that day forward Hubbard was sure he'd find a way though hell and back home again. "I never had that feeling I was going to die; I always felt 'I'm going to make it through this.' It's an inner sense that says you're somehow going to make it."

At Salerno, though, Hubbard and the American Army weren't sure how, at first. The German position above the beach made fighting especially tough. "The beachhead was touch and go and questionable whether we were going to hold it. The British were coming up from the south and the 5th Army was trying to hold its own as German troops moved down.

"Fortunately, the British came along and took some pressure off. It was rather close; the Krauts were on

The Hero Next Door Returns

top and the infantry was in front, all we were doing was stringing lines, though we still didn't know where we were until we finally found a road sign that pointed to Salerno. Then, we knew we were in Italy."

The unit strung lines with W100 10B twisted field wire rolled out from the back of a Jeep or truck. "We had E.E.8 A. field magneto phones, which we hooked to at the end, that work on two flashlight batteries. If the batteries went dead, you could turn it around and talk into the earpiece (sound power)."

While infantry communications teams were stringing blue field wire from squad to squad; Hubbard's unit worked lines up to the company headquarters, operational center.

"We built open wire lines like we do here—two-crossarm lead strung almost the length of Italy—all built to Bell standards. Field wires we tied to whatever we could find. We didn't fix it; we just strung new wire. It was amazing how fast we could build wire lines. With the whole platoon we could probably build 10 miles in a day—pole crews, wire crews, test crews. We could put in 50-60 miles of field wire in a matter of hours. Each crew would drop off a wire terminal and leave somebody there to splice lines together. The next crew would pick him up, and they'd just leap frog up the road.

"We'd tie wire onto anything. I remember in one town square, there was an accurate statue of a man—as there were always statues in the town square. Well, this one still had its ... umm ... parts, so we just tied the wire right to that and kept going. There were soon dozens of wires tied to it."

Laying wire in the winter of 1943-44 was especially tough going as the Allies tried to push across Italy's many icy waterways and steep mountains, according to *The Tech Services: The Signal Corps—The Outcome (p. 52-53)*. As the Army neared Cassino "the problems of mounting communications increased in direct proportion to the worsening weather and terrain. The Ital-

Combat Lineman

ian mountains were passively as cold, unyielding, hard and dangerous as the active Germany enemy that ... (linemen) had to resort to mules, carts, jeeps, and even bicycles, or most frequently of all, were obliged to unroll huge spools of wire or cable by hand."

Getting across the many streams and rivers in the area was especially tough going, the book further notes. "Linemen waded and swam across the mountaneous torrents in order to establish communications. Signal Corps crewmen tied a length of wire around a volunteer's waist, bade him good luck and tried to cover him with fire support. Once over, the swimmer had to dig in and withstand whatever resistance the enemy provided, then set up for business."

While water and weather made the going tough, having to string aerial wires—so vehicles coming behind wouldn't tear it up—was probably the most dangerous.

"You'd go up a pole when under fire and have to tie the line to something. Normally, you have a safety belt you use, but we never put that belt on in the war. Instead, you just hooked one leg around the pole to hold on. That way, when you had to get down in a hurry, you just unhooked your leg and you were gone.

"Or, if the pole broke off, you could jump clear. I had three tip over with me on it while I was in Italy and I never got hurt. I never rode one down; I jumped off. However, with Bell Telephone after the war, I did ride one down one time. I cut a drop wire and the pole tipped over the fence into a field. I thought my foreman would have a heart attack, but I'd just gotten out of this kind of activity in the war and didn't think too much of it."

BREAKING LINES

When they weren't stringing new wire, Hubbard's 28- to 30-man signal unit fought sniper fire to repair the lines.

"The Nazis were constantly tampering with the wire.

The Hero Next Door Returns

Hubbard (right) and friends Gus and Charlie Moore posed on what was left of this railroad track — literally just the tracks as the bridge supporting it had been blown up.

What they'd do is run a needle through the twisted wire and short it out and then wait for whomever had to go up to pull the needle out and take them out. The snipers winged me in the ribs, which sent me tumbling over a bank where I twisted my knee. We found a medic at an infantry unit—because our unit didn't have one and just took care of our own as best we could. He just splinted it and said 'you can run around with a stiff leg for 30 days, then take it off and it should be all right.'"

When the fighting was heavy and lines were furiously being strung, food was scarce and there was little time to find anything beyond basic rations anyway.

"We had a lot of K rations, which is a box with sugar cubes, a fruit bar, stick of gum, and the strongest powder you'd mix in a canteen cup of water to make lemonade; it would take your tonsils out. There was chopped pork and egg yolk and some crackers. We had a B ration too that had a fruit bar that was almost 2-by-4-inches wide with the most concentrated vitamins, kind of like power bars today I suppose.

"We moved ahead every other day or so, living on whatever we could. We'd send a vehicle back down

Combat Lineman

to the beach when we could to the ration dump, which was a pile of boxes half as big as a house. You learned in a hurry what the codes on the outside meant. A certain color was fruit cocktail; another peanut butter. Most of it was C-rations but we didn't have anything to heat it with, we just ate it cold. After the quartermaster moved in, when a beachhead was secure, you had to sign for everything.

"We usually had somebody that was hurt ride along with the mess sergeant for supplies and there was a few extra cases of stuff that would get loaded in— 'moonlight requisitions' we called it. We got a pack of cigarettes with rations at noon and a lot of fellows started smoking. I just kept them and traded them and always ended up with the Raleighs and Twenty Grands left over."

Imagine the delight when the unit stumbled upon some extra rations in a railroad depot during the fighting around the town of Battipaglia, southeast of Salerno. "The baggage was still in the baggage room and we found a big, round jug about 30 inches in diameter of wine and carried it out on the loading platform for a picture. It was a darn fool stunt to pull as it very well could have been booby trapped."

By the time the front line of fighting was up against the German's Gustav Line at the Volturno River, the signal unit was six miles back at Aversa, Italy.

Even six miles back was not a safe place to be, however. "Our Navy was shelling the Gustav Line, which the Germans had established at the river. They were firing across above us and the danger of that is if they had a low shot they'd hit a tree and you'd get an air burst, which is deadly. When the first one of those shots went over, I was sitting in front of my tent and there was a slit trench between me and this fellow that was in the pup tent talking to me. When that first shot went over, I turned and fell into the slit trench but I fell on top of him. I don't know yet how he got there ahead of me!"

The Hero Next Door Returns

Artillery barrages were a frequent contention in Italy. "You'd often see what we called a creeping barrage. They'd fire and raise the sights and the next one would be 75 feet down and creep down the valley. So, when you'd see a creeping barrage, you'd wait until you'd see where it hit and then run towards it because the next one would be further away yet. We spent a lot of time running."

There was little room to run, however, when the Allies were tied up on the Volturno River north of Naples—a river "about as wide as the Wisconsin River at Sauk City. The Krauts were on the other side. They'd take a shot at anything they could see. They could see a lot, looking down from above. It was like shooting fish in a bathtub."

All in all Italy proved a tougher fight than the Allies envisioned. "We were in Italy a little over two years. At Aversa we figured we'd be in Rome for Thanksgiving but then we hit Cassino and didn't get into Rome until the next June."

Along the way, a beach invasion at Anzio was especially bad as Allied troops got bogged down in the narrow and deadly area that became known as Hell's Half Acre.

"Our unit got a replacement at Anzio, Norton W. Weathers from Georgia who had been blown out of a foxhole before they shipped him to us. Then, at Anzio, Tony Zajac picked up something and blew a hole in his stomach. When we took him to medics, you could see all his insides and we thought he was dead until four or five years ago he showed up at a reunion. Later, we got another replacement, Charlie Moore, who had been machine pistolled through his leg nine times and it didn't hit the femur."

Hubbard's signal unit lost just one man at Anzio. In total the Allies suffered some 59,000 casualties in the more than three months it took to push through Anzio towards Rome.

Fortunately, Hubbard's unit was in Anzio just two

Combat Lineman

days before being pulled back because "the area wasn't large enough to need us." They returned to the Anzio area shortly after the bulk of the fighting was over to start stringing communication lines. As Hubbard's unit moved inland further it came face to face with the biggest gun of the war.

"The Nazis had this big field gun they moved in and out of tunnels on railroad tracks. It was a 280mm gun formerly used to shell England from the French coast. The GIs named it 'Anzio Annie.' The air force could never catch it out in the open. We caught up with it at Civitavecchia, about 30 miles north of Rome. When our unit got to it, I told the boys don't go near it because we figured it was probably booby-trapped. I heard that the next day three guys were killed on it."

Fighting around Mount Cassino and its famous abbey from Feb. – May 18, 1944, wasn't any better. Cassino was part of the Germans' Gustav Line, a defensive boundary between Naples and Rome.

"We were on the back side of Mount Tracchio when they blew the abbey. I never saw so many airplanes in my life." And, the enemy was never too far away. "One time in Cassino, the Krauts had people in one room and we had people in the next who could hear them talking."

After the Allies finally took Cassino May 18, 1944, they started moving up the Lira Valley as the Germans retreated further north near Florence.

In between, Hubbard was dodging trouble of a high-ranking kind.

"We were stringing wire going to Caserta, which ended up being 5th Army headquarters later, and I climbed a pole near a bridge that was blown out near Capua. We had to get an aerial crossing of wire up across the road—because the tanks were coming through and would grind the wire up if it was on the ground. So, I went up the pole and flipped my helmet off because there was a bunch of wires already up there. I didn't know whether they were 'hot,' but a

The Hero Next Door Returns

metal helmet and electric wiring are not a good mix.

"Well, I put a clove hitch on the field wire and then heard, 'Soldier, Dismount!' I looked down and here is a Jeep with some general stars on the front of it. There was Gen. George Patton climbing out of his Jeep! I came down that pole fast, put the helmet on and saluted. He proceeded to chew me out but good. He said 'I got a notion to court marshall you but we need you,' then he took off and that was the end of it. He was a great but a fanatical general. If you were with George you got everything available but he demanded the utmost—he even wanted us to wear ties on the line. We didn't even have one, or if we did, I didn't know where it was!"

Hubbard didn't know where his issued weapon was either, for a while. "From the beach at Salerno on, we started picking up firearms. We were issued a firearm with a number that is charged to you, so it was a good idea to hang on to it. Don and I took ours and wrapped them up in some cosmoline and burlap, put them under the seat of the truck and forgot we'd done it. Later, we got called to Naples for a dress review that some general wanted and we couldn't find our guns! We had to just take some we found in the field. It was some time later that we went under the seat to get our chains and there were our guns!"

Hubbard also spent a short time in the 81st Station Hospital at Livorno, from Jan-March of 1944, with a re-twisted knee, though after he was later injured more severely, he could no longer remember how he hurt it. "I know I was in the orthopedic ward the whole time and my nurse was Mary Reiber from Tomah, Wis., and I knew her brother! They had some wonderful cough medicine there that was full of codeine. Johnson and I were on crutches and spent our time watching gun camera film the air corps brought back."

The unit finally made Rome on June 6, 1944, the same day as the D-Day invasion at Normandy. "But, we didn't stop until we were 28-30 miles north of it.

Combat Lineman

There was little damage in Rome itself because it was an open city, so we rolled through people waving and offering us wine and didn't stop."

By the fall of 1944 the Allies got stopped where the Germans had established an effective defense in the Appenine Mountains. "Winter in the mountains was very much like winter in Wisconsin but you could go 75 miles to the sea and it was like spring time. We spent most of the winter at the coast, at Livorno, where we spliced into an Italian cable that went across the bay from Genoa to Rome and on to Genova. We went out, the Navy fished it up, and we cut it in two and had a line from Livorno to Rome just like that. That immediately gave us 150 miles of communications."

A FATEFUL MISSTEP

By April 27, 1945, the Nazis were all but driven out of Italy and the end of the war was a few weeks away, at least for most everyone. For Hubbard, the worst of the war was just beginning.

"We had started north toward Bologna and were between two small towns, Loiano and Pianoro, when I got mixed up with a German shu mine and an Italian concussion grenade. We were in a field that looked like it had been plowed by a farmer because it had a creeping barrage go across it. The mine and grenade were hooked together and I happened to walk too close.

"I saw it and jerked my foot back but I was too close. It blew the whole end off of my climbing boots, which had a thick leather sole for climbing poles. That's what saved my foot, but it crushed the nerves, which didn't have feeling for a long time.

"The guys with me later said I flew 10-12 feet, got up and went back to look at where the mine was, but I don't remember that. I do remember I heard a noise and then everything got quiet because my eardrums had blown out. I remember looking down the hole and seeing smoke.

33

The Hero Next Door Returns

"They asked 'are you hurt' and I said 'no' but then they said 'yes' when they saw blood dripping out of all the holes in my legs."

A Jeep came by and the guys made the driver stop. "The driver didn't want me to get in the Jeep because I'd get blood all over it. But, after some arguing, he agreed to take me to the evacuation hospital in Bologna, which had moved into a soccer stadium that morning. By the time I got to Bologna I couldn't hold my head up any more. I remember I had to take a little step, about 4 inches high, to get into the building and couldn't raise my foot to do it. I was in tough shape, and the doctors knew they had to do something to save the body. I'd lost so much blood, they started pumping blood in me right away.

"I was bleeding enough from my legs, and everywhere. Blood was almost up to the top of my boot, and there was an inch-and-a-half deep pool of blood in the passenger side of the Jeep. At that time I didn't care if I lived or died. I really didn't, though I had no pain at all. I didn't begin to hurt until I came to after the operation.

"Two nurses started to cut my clothes off, put sulfa all over me and put me on an operating table and took x-rays on my back and side to tell where all the pieces were. There were three doctors on one side, three on the other. I remember hearing one doctor say 'I think we can save this left leg if we can get this knee cap sewed on.' That's when I went under."

When Hubbard awoke some nine hours later, the right side of his body was paralyzed. But he was relieved not only to be alive but because, "when I started feeling around, I realized they'd saved my leg!"

Hubbard was to be airlifted to the 24th General Hospital in Florence the next morning. "It was too foggy to fly. Instead, they put four of us in an ambulance for a bumpy ride that was 'bump, pass out,' 'bump, pass out,' all the way there."

The general hospital was set up in an art museum

Combat Lineman

on the riverbank in Florence. "I remember they set me down on the marble floor. My gun, which was still in my shoulder holster, slid out. That was the last I ever saw of it; somebody got a good souvenir."

Medical staff there "went to work on my arms and face to put things back together. On the third or fourth day they decided to sew up my legs and wheeled me in, and I asked if they'd mind if I watched. They put seven stitches in my left leg half way between my knee and hip where there was a hole as big as a baseball. About half way through I wished I hadn't watched, but I wasn't going to stop now."

In between operations, splinters from the shoe mine were working their way out of Hubbard's body. "They counted 93 holes in my skin but most were just bits of wood. As they fell out, they healed. Every day the nurse would roll me over and sweep the sheets off."

That was hard to bear, but Hubbard was more concerned one day when he regained consciousness after an operation only to discover he had total amnesia.

"I couldn't remember anything, even who I was or where I came from. It's a very unusual feeling not have any references—not as frightening as it is confusing. My dog tag finally got me started to remembering again. The nurse read my serial

Hubbard was feeling especially strong after his recovery in post-war Italy—strong enough to try to "straighten" the leaning tower of Pisa.

The Hero Next Door Returns

number and then I knew my name, rank and serial number, 16129312."

To fight infection, nurses "started giving me penicillin every three hours for three weeks. They wanted to give it to me in my buttocks but I said no because I wanted something to sleep on. I got it in the shoulder instead and I still have no feeling in my shoulders from all those shots."

The penicillin helped but there were still more battles for Hubbard to fight.

He had gone blind from three pieces of shrapnel in the right eye and soon couldn't see out of his left eye either. "It was something they thought was a sympathetic reaction of the nerves but the doctor didn't know if it would ever come back.

"Then, one day, I thought I could see the outline of a window. I shut my eye and peaked again and I could see the whole window! It was a thrill to be able to see again!"

By coincidence, Hubbard's good sign came the same day America cheered the news that Germany had surrendered. "They came through and everybody was hooting. Then, I got bold and thought, 'if I can see maybe I can stand.' So, I swung my legs off the bed. The pain was so great that I passed out!"

Little by little, Hubbard improved physically and even started remembering things. However, his memory took years to "fully" recover. Even today, there are bits of his time in Italy and his boyhood that escape him.

"While I was there I began remembering things. At first all I could remember of Madison was University Avenue and getting to the capitol. I remembered nothing more of it until I got home and toured around. To this day I still can't remember school graduation or the class play though I've seen pictures and know I was there."

Combat Lineman

BACK TO THE ACTION

By May 17, 1945, Hubbard was "well enough" to be shipped to a replacement depot for reassignment with the Army.

"At this time, anyone with broken bones was being sent home. While I could see bone in four different places, none of mine were broken. So, I went with bandages on my leg, arm and eye to a replacement depot, which is like a big grocery store. There were so many gunners, so many signalmen, etc. We had five to six numbers behind our name so we'd be eligible for anything."

But, he didn't want just anything; Hubbard wanted to be back with his unit. So, "when they called my name, I jumped out the other side and got picked up by a ration truck driver. We went through the Po Valley until I found where my squad was drawing rations and eventually found them."

Though the war was over; the dangers of war-torn Europe were not, as Hubbard discovered his first day back with his unit.

"A man from Tennessee was cleaning wire off poles to establish communications up and down the Po Valley. About a half block away, I was walking in a tiger tank track through a minefield. He stepped on a butterfly mine that was one of our own. When he saw his foot was missing he yelled. The explosion sent shrapnel and gravel flying and I hit the ground so hard I took the skin off my nose. He was a big fellow and four of us had to hold him while they gave him a shot of morphine. Because we had no medic and no more morphine, we got him into a town to a civilian hospital. A nun came to the door and we asked for more morphine. She said she didn't have any but then got an idea, went back in and came out with a 6-inch long needle. She gave him a shot and told us that it was actually distilled water. He didn't know that, and it worked real good for about 20 minutes. We continued the shots until we got to a G.I. hospital."

The Hero Next Door Returns

The unit remained in the valley about 10 days and ran into German soldiers "just as happy as we were that the war was over. There were horses by the acre, so many we didn't count any more. I've never seen so many machines and horses in all my life!"

By now, Hubbard technically had enough points to go home but the Army froze the unit for possible Pacific Theater duty. "We waited 30 days in Italy and spent the time traveling around by hitchhiking.

"One time I was in company headquarters and heard there'd be a chance for four people to go to Switzerland for a week or so. I made sure myself and three buddies got to go. We traveled all over Switzerland and, while in Luzerne, saw this lady coming up some steps. We tried French, German, Italian and then she says, 'fellas why don't you just speak English? She was a teacher interned in Switzerland during the war and she was happy to see us!"

Hubbard finally made it home, well to America anyway, on Columbus Day, Oct. 12, 1945, after being on a ship for 17 days and listening to the World Series en route. "The first thing we saw was the Ferris Wheel from Coney Island, just above the fog, and then we heard a train whistle. We got our first meal of all the steak and ice cream we wanted, but our stomachs were so shrunk that we could hardly eat it.

"I was in Fort Sheridan and got a 10-day pass and went home to help dad husk corn then went to Montgomery, Ala. to see my brother who was in the Air Force. I was there a few days when a pilot invited me along to New Orleans in his Pontiac convertible. That convertible didn't have wings but it should have!

"We went to a USO to find a place to sleep and two girls came up to us looking for men for a party. It turned out they were telephone operators that had a rented house on Bourbon Street. We had a wonderful Halloween party for three days.

"Then, I traveled to Tallahasee and Key West, Fla. I'm a traveling fanatic. Since the war, we've been all over

Combat Lineman

Norton and Marie Hubbard celebrate their 50th wedding anniversary with their four children, Marita Elizabeth Laufenberg, Finn Karl Hubbard, Leif Lindstrom Hubbard and Robin Ann Hubbard-Van Stelle — as well as their loyal friend Sitka.

North America several times and have visited the oil sands in Northeast Alberta recently. We've also spent a month down under visiting New Zealand and Australia. A year later, we spent a month in Northern Europe, Finland, Sweden and Norway and learned that life north of the Arctic Circle is certainly a different world!"

Besides traveling with his wife of 50 years Marie—and their four kids and 11 grandchildren—Hubbard enjoys his retirement from Bell Telephone. "After the war, they wanted me to go right to work, but I stayed home for Christmas, 1945, and went to work Dec. 27. I worked the first five years primarily out of my suitcase and ended up in engineering for 40 years."

In between, Hubbard worked as hard to serve his family and community well. He's belonged to the East Side Kiwanis for 34 years and ushered at St. Lukes Church in Middleton, Wis., for 30 years. He was a

The Hero Next Door Returns

middle school system treasurer for 10 years. He is a life member of the Disabled American Veterans Organization and The Military Order of the Purple Heart in Madison, serving as treasurer of the latter. He is a past member of the National Society of Professional Engineers and the Wisconsin Society of Professional Engineers (Southwest Chapter). He was a senior member of the Rock Valley Chapter of the American Institute of Industrial Engineers for several years and is a long-time member of the Telephone Pioneers. In addition, he has maintained the Hubbard Tree Farm on Evergreen Road in Middleton, Wis., for more than 50 years.

In his spare time, Hubbard built a quarter-mile toboggan run that takes him, his children and grandchildren through the woods and past the house he designed and built himself. A collector of the unique and historical, Hubbard still has much of the tools of his W.W. II trade tucked away—like his memories—in his home's cherished corners.

TEST PILOT
JEANNETTE KAPUS

It certainly wasn't the ladylike thing to do when Jeannette Kapus of Germantown, Wis., climbed into the cockpit of an airplane and took to the skies to serve her country in World War II. But, W.W.II—and daring female pilots like Kapus—redefined "ladylike" in a hurry.

Kapus was one of only 1,000 or so American women proudly wearing the wings of the Women's Airforce Service Pilots, or WASPs, who flew supplies and planes stateside to free up male pilots to take the controls in combat missions overseas.

She took to the skies on the advice of a fellow serviceman, her father. A World War I veteran, James Kapus was fascinated by the planes he'd seen fly overhead in France and urged his daughter to see how high she could soar.

In July 1941, when the Milwaukee native was working as a clerk-steno at the Rock Island Arsenal, Ill., her father made the fateful suggestion: "If you don't know what to do with your spare time, why don't you learn to fly?"

Kapus said, "Oh, Pops!" But, being the dutiful daughter, she complied. "I took an evening class at St. Ambrose College in Davenport, Iowa, in Civilian Pilot

The Hero Next Door Returns

Training and joined the Civil Air Patrol flying out of Cram Field, Davenport. The first time I was in a plane I knew I liked it."

A record-setting aviation career had been born of a father's dream.

Meanwhile, another female pilot, Aviatrix Jackie Cochran—the first woman to fly a bomber across the Atlantic Ocean—had dreams of her own. She was flying as a captain with the British Air Transport Auxiliary in England as part of the British and American war effort and thought if she could do it, the other 3,000 licensed American women pilots should be able to fly in support of their country too.

When she returned from England in 1942, Cochran presented a plan for General Hap Arnold, the U.S. Army Air Corps Commanding General, to train women pilots to meet Army needs. The plan she hatched soon became the WASPs. At the same time, a similar program using women pilots to ferry planes and supplies in the United States and Canada, called the Women's Auxiliary Ferrying Squadron, was started by pilot Nancy Harkness Love in New Castle, Del. It merged with the WASPs, under Cochran's direction, in 1943.

In all, the WASPs flew some 60 million miles across the U.S. from 1942 until their deactivation in December 1944—flying every type of aircraft made by the U.S. for W.W.II from P-39s and P-47 fighter planes to B-17 and B-29 bombers.

Some 25,000 women—from beauticians and mothers to stunt women and housewives—applied for the unladylike chance to fly for their country. Eventually 1,074 won their wings.

"We were all driven by a love of flying and a feeling of duty to serve the country for which our sons, brothers, husbands and friends were fighting," Kapus says of the reason she pursued the WASPs as soon as she was able. And, her thoughts were often on her own brother stationed overseas in England as a B-17 mechanic with the 547th Bomb Squadron.

Test Pilot

EARNING HER WINGS

"At first Jackie Cochran recruited women pilots with 1,000 hours or more—in at least a 65 horsepower airplane—then 500 hours and finally down to 35 hours. When they got there, I applied as I had 38:10 hours in by then."

With approved release from her defense job at the arsenal, Kapus was accepted for the 44-W4 WASP class Nov.1, 1943.

In addition to flying hours, WASPs had to (be 18 to 35 years old), have a high school education and a pilot's license, be at least five feet tall and pass a personal interview test. They then had to pass cadet training—sometimes in the cold and snow that befell Western Texas—and a three-phase military flight-testing program.

"We went through three, nine-week phases with military check pilots. It was the same as the Army's air cadets program. The first phase was Primary, consisting of 70 hours in either a PT-19 Fairchild (175 horsepower) or the PT-17 Stearman (220 hp). I arrived when the program was phasing in the Stearman and phasing out the Fairchild. I had 4:10 hours in the Fairchild and switched to the Stearman."

Learning to fly the Stearman nearly cost Kapus—and her father—her aerial dreams.

"About a month after I started my training, I was landing a Stearman—a bi-wing aircraft—when I 'ground-looped' the aircraft. The wind had caught my right wing and I slowly went around in a circle, scraping the left wing along the ground. That was grounds for a check ride by another instructor. It could have washed me out of the program but the instructor, Mr. Breese, felt I still had potential to become a WASP so I was retained."

Kapus passed the Intermediate Phase, requiring 35 hours on the BT-13 (450 hp), 35 hours on the AT-6, the Texan (650 hp), and instrument training time on

The Hero Next Door Returns

Jeannette Kapus at the controls during training.

the Vultee, which the girls nicknamed the "Vultee Vibrator" for its propensity to vibrate when it flew.

The Advance Phase really challenged the female pilots to see if they had what it took to fly big aircraft long distances. It required 70 hours of flight instruction in cross-country flying, including two, 1,000-mile solo trips—one over the western mountains, one in the southeast—through smoke and haze typical of those areas of the country. Then, to graduate, cadets flew a three- or four-day trip with overnight stops.

Kapus noted that, for their efforts, WASPs trainees received $150 a month; graduated WASPs earned $250.

Kapus joined the graduate ranks May 23, 1944. "I was elated. My mom came down to Sweetwater, Texas, and pinned my wings on me. She was as happy for me as I was."

The Kapuses had a right to be proud. Their daughter was among 52, from a class of 104, who graduated. Some dropped out; some were called home; and others were dismissed for drinking or poor performance, while 38 WASPs proved that even the homefront of W.W. II could be deadly. Margaret Seip of Wauwatosa, Wis., was killed in an air crash as was Kapus' friend Mary, in separate incidents.

"Just two weeks prior to graduation, one of my room-

Test Pilot

mates Mary Howson and a student from another class crashed when they both turned into the downwind leg of approach to the field. Mary made a right hand turn as the other student made a left hand turn, neither seeing the other."

After graduation, Kapus traded her white shirt and beige trousers for a Santiago blue uniform and was assigned to Courtland Army Air Base in Alabama, a basic training base flying BT-13s. Kapus would be flying the big birds as an engineering test pilot.

"Originally, WASPs were ferrying aircraft around the U.S. and Canada but as the war progressed that changed. Some began towing aerial gunnery targets in support of gunnery training, flying simulated strafing missions and smoke-laying missions. We learned to fly by instrumentation. I was placed in ferrying and engineering test flying. Test flying meant that I tested aircraft when replacement parts were put on, like a new wing, engine or aileron. So, if they put a new wing on a plane I had to go up and see if it would really fly."

Kapus' duties also included flying personnel to doctor's appointments and meetings at other bases or ferrying aircraft like the Fairchild and Stearman—which had been 'mothballed' at her base—to airplane graveyards in Laurel, Miss., and Muskogee, Okla. Then, when the air base became a bomber training base in September 1944, Kapus had the chance to copilot a B-17 to pick up B-24 parts and maintenance materials.

Later in the war, some of her fellow WASPs got to fly the new B-29, a bomber that some of their male counterpart pilots were skeptical of at first. "Some would not fly them and said they wouldn't be safe. So, Gen. Arnold got a couple of WASPs to fly to bases around the country. The pilots there would gather around the new B-29 when it landed wondering what fool they got to fly the thing. Then, out would pop two girls. Well, if girls could fly it ..."

45

The Hero Next Door Returns
TESTING THE SKIES

Though she enjoyed the ferrying runs, it was the hours Kapus logged as a test pilot that she found the most thrilling, and the most dangerous.

As part of a test flight Kapus had to first bring the aircraft up to fast time, flying it full throttle—as fast as the plane would go—for 10 minutes and then backing off and flying around for another 50 minutes, testing its maneuverability before landing.

One "fast time" nearly proved to be Kapus' "last time."

"A mechanic on a BT-13 asked if he could go up flying with me because he'd never been in a plane. I had to go up to test an engine with 'fast time' so I said he could come along. I tested it in fast time but when I wanted to bring the throttle back by pulling on it like I usually did, it wouldn't come back and we kept flying fast time. I had us both try to pull it back but it still wouldn't come.

"I called the tower to alert them to our problem and they cleared the area of aircraft and called for a 'hash wagon' to stand by. They instructed me to bring the aircraft in, cut the engine as I passed over the fence at the end of the field and land it."

Kapus and her now not-so-eager passenger landed unscathed, though the mechanic said he would never fly again!

"I checked later with the maintenance section to find out what happened to that throttle. It seems the attending mechanic—which I don't know if he was the same mechanic that flew with me or not—had not locked the battery guard, causing it to slip off the battery and jam the throttle in the wide-open position."

The second time Kapus faced a problem, she was not at the controls.

"A navigator on a B-24 asked me for a ride and said he had flown smaller aircraft and would like to try his hand at a BT-13. I took the aircraft up for a fast time check and, when I was through checking it, he asked

46

Test Pilot

The lady pilots fall out for training.

if he could fly it. We took the aircraft up to 9,000 feet and flew around. Then, he inadvertently put the aircraft into a spin to the right. At this point, he threw his hands up in the air and said 'it's all yours!'"

Kapus was able to correct for the spin but nearly over-corrected when the aircraft started to spin to the left. "If you go into a spin, you've got to keep the nose down. If you go into a flat spin you're all but done for. I managed to keep the nose down but overcorrected a bit and spun to the left. I got it under control though and we came out of it OK."

Even more experienced pilots could wind up in an aeronautical jam, however, like on a night run Kapus and a major made to take two BT-13s to Winston-Salem, N.C.

"Our weather officer didn't want to let us go as it was dark and raining. We didn't have radar then on these planes so visibility was even more important. When visibility was bad, like it was that night, I'd have to stay on the major's wing and watch for his wing light to keep me in position. But, we took off and flew two aircraft over the Appalachian Mountains together as it started to rain.

"That night visibility was quite bad and I didn't re-

The Hero Next Door Returns

ally think we should go up either but the major said 'we're going,' so we went. I stayed right on his wing; I didn't want to let his wing light out of my sight. Only after we flew together in the one aircraft back did he admit that conditions were bad and we maybe shouldn't have flown."

BLAZING A LEGACY

Kapus' time with the WASPs took a negative turn just when all the war news was so positive and victory seemed certain. On Dec. 20, 1944, the Army Air Force deactivated the WASPs. The women were informed that victory was nearly assured and enough male pilots were returning from combat so the WASPs' services were no longer needed.

After their deactivation announcement, Gen. Arnold, summed up the importance of the WASP program in a speech to the last WASP graduation class in 1944:

"Frankly, I didn't know in 1941 whether a slip of a young girl could fight the controls of a B-17 in the heavy weather they would naturally encounter in operational flying. Those of us who had been flying 20 or 30 years knew that flying an airplane was something you do not learn overnight.

"Now, in 1944, more than two years since WASP first started flying with the Air Corps, we can come to only one conclusion—the entire operation has been a success. It is on the record that women can fly as well as men.

"The WASP have completed their mission. Their job has been successful. But, as usual in war, the cost has been heavy. Thirty-eight WASP have died while helping their country move toward the moment of final victory. The Air Forces will long remember their service and their final sacrifice."

As a result of their service, Kapus says the military learned some basic differences about male and female pilots. "One curious fact had come out of training women pilots. The instructors told us that women were faster on instruments than men, more smooth and gentle in flying characteristics in general. On the

Test Pilot

male side of the ledger goes credit for less mechanical flying and better memory for details."

Even more importantly, the WASP program had taught the military—and America—much about the capabilities of its women. "We proved that women were effective, safe, physically fit, dedicated and in every way peers to our brother pilots. As Eleanor Roosevelt once said, we proved we were 'a weapon to be used' to win the war."

The WASPs' legacy is remembered by the female fighter, helicopter and transport pilots—even astronauts—who fill the military ranks today. And, Kapus is especially proud of the nearly 1,000 hours she flew to help blaze a trail in the American sky for them to follow.

SPINNING ALONG

But, she's prouder still of a trail she blazed for herself—into the aviation record books—after the war.

Kapus set the national female spin record in an aircraft, a record she still reportedly holds as of this printing.

While working a civil service job as a secretary at the Wisconsin Intelligence Agency in Milwaukee—where she typed up interviews of former POWs to gain information for war crime trials—Kapus was teaching flying on nights and weekends as an instructor at Curtiss-Wright Airport (now Timmerman Field) in Milwaukee.

In 1949 a military organization, AMVETS, asked if she could break the spin record set at 48 spins by Rosemary Sponner, a local pilot, at a big event in Manitowoc, Wis. "I agreed after discussing it with my parents. My mom wasn't happy about it but my Pops was all for it."

Still, even Kapus wasn't sure she was up to the challenge. Though she did compete in All Women Transcontinental Air Races from time to time, she hadn't done more than three or four spins at once for quite

The Hero Next Door Returns

a while. "So, I asked a fellow instructor Rex Chalker to teach me again about spins. He did, and several times we went up and did eight to 10 spins at a time."

It was still a far ways from 48, but Kapus was ready to go for the record.

"On the day of the event, I took a light aircraft, a Cub J-3 (65 hp) up to 9,000 feet. Then, I watched the field below for my signal—a Jeep going around in a large circle—to begin my spin. I was to count the number of spins I made while Rex, another AMVETS member and an FAA representative, counted along from the ground.

"I started my spin and used the river that flowed into Lake Michigan as my check point. At approximately 1,000 feet I started my recovery. After I landed, I told the three men that I had counted 64 spins. They had the same number."

She'd broken the record, and then some. Unofficially, she broke it again at an event at the South Shore Yacht Club, Milwaukee, when she did 73 spins.

BACK INTO SERVICE

In the meantime, Kapus had re-enlisted in the military. The WASPs had been offered a commission in the U.S. Air Force when the Army Air Corps became a separate command in 1948.

"I accepted a 2nd lieutenancy and joined the Air Force Reserves. In 1952, I requested active duty as a pilot. What a dreamer I was! My request for active duty was accepted but my request to be a pilot was denied. I was told 'only MALE personnel are rated' to be pilots. So, I went on active duty as a personnel officer."

Without her wings, Kapus' mother Viola worried her daughter would be little more than a "camp follower." Though she certainly followed the Air Force to camps around the globe—from Scotland to France to West Pakistan—she did so in the lead of men.

"In the Air Force there were many times I was the only woman—I was one among 40 fellas at OBMC (of-

Test Pilot

ficer basic military class) and the only girl in 18 at personnel school. Everywhere it was a man's game and I learned how to play it. I was, most of the time, seen as 'just one of the guys.'

"How the men reacted to and whether or not they respected me depended, of course, upon the man. Some were real supportive; others, well, were not. But, once I was in the Air Force, I had a high enough rank that if they gave me any trouble I'd just bellow at them—'I'm the boss!'—and they had to do it."

Not all men were difficult though. Kapus dated several during her years of service but never found one she wanted to marry. "In a way, in my personnel job especially, I felt like I was married to all of them!"

Kapus spent 20 years in active duty in the Air Force, moving up the ranks to lieutenant colonel by the time she retired in 1972. Though she kept up her pilot's license for quite a while, flying in various aero-clubs on weekends, Kapus never flew in a military cockpit again.

After retirement, Kapus hung up her wings for good and became involved in many military organizations, including the American Legion. She is also past commander of Chapter #23 of The Reserves Officers Association, and local chapters of the The Retired Officers Association and the Military Order of World Wars, serving as state commander for the latter two. Meanwhile, she also went to work as a real estate agent for seven years until her mother's health required more of her attention and she worked at home as a travel agent. Kapus retired for good in 1980.

In recognition of her flying accomplishments, Kapus was awarded the Billy Mitchell Award by the Billy Mitchell Chapter of the Air Force Association in 1981.

In recognition of the sacrifices her fellow women pilots made in W.W.II, Kapus donated her WASP uniform to the Wisconsin Veterans Museum in Madison, Wis., along with the photo of the four WASPs who were stationed with her in Alabama.

The Hero Next Door Returns

Jeanette Kapus, at right, with her fellow WASPs and friends Ruth Petery, Betty Stagg and Daisy Vaugh. This picture, along with Kapus' flight suit, were donated to the Wisconsin Veterans Museum in Madison.

"It seems we women are always being challenged for everything and I think we should always accept the challenge," she adds noting that accepting the challenge of flying an airplane in service to her country has made Kapus very proud. "I look at all we as women and we as a country accomplished in World War II. And, even today, when I see a parade, I cry."

When she looks back on all she accomplished, as a pilot and a woman, Kapus pauses in comical reflection. After all, "I still can't believe my whole life hinged on a two-word answer to a simple question: "Why don't you learn to fly?" WHY NOT?

PATRIOT BROTHER
VIRGIL MURPHY

When Wisconsin's men and women went to war, thousands of Native American men and women went with them. Like many Wisconsin families, the Murphy family of the Stockbridge-Munsee Indian Reservation, near Bowler, Wis., eventually sent all of its sons—and some of its daughters-in-law—to war.

Virgil Murphy was one of four brothers who, along with a foster brother, answered the patriotic call to serve their country during W.W. II. Murphy actually began his service before the U.S. entered the war, enlisting in the Army Sept. 5, 1940, after serving in the Civilian Conservation Corps for two years following high school at Crandon, Wis.

At basic training, Murphy raised his hand when they asked for those who could type. "I thought, oh boy, you're probably volunteering for latrine duty. In fact, they sent us all up on recruiting duty and said they'd put us as close to home as they could, which turned out to be a good

Virgil Murphy and Ernestine (Quinney) Murphy.

The Hero Next Door Returns

deal. I was stationed in Milwaukee and traveled the state recruiting people for the Army."

As part of his duties, Murphy helped process new recruits who came to Milwaukee for their physicals and process paperwork before recruits were shipped to basic training. "We had a contingent of doctors that they went through, standing there one after the other, for shots and physicals. By the time they got to the end of all that, there was all the paperwork to do. We had to type up everything.

"We had 300 to 500 inducted every day and had to have everything done by the end of each day when we sent them on a troop train because a whole new group would be coming in the next morning.

"It was impressive to see so many people, so much paperwork. But, what impressed me the most was that these people *wanted* to go. They wanted to fight for their country. Sometimes, if there was some physical reason they couldn't enlist, you'd see grown men sit down and cry. The patriotism was just incredible back then; everybody was behind America. Everybody wanted to pitch in and do what they could to help their country."

For Murphy, pitching in meant driving in cars—followed by trucks of supplies—from Milwaukee to Michigan's Upper Peninsula, west to Eau Claire, south and east again in a regular, round-robin recruiting tour. It was a pace that only intensified as the U.S. drew closer to the war.

Murphy was on the road—in Eau Claire, Wis. —when the Japanese ensured the U.S. would go to war by bombing Pearl Harbor, Hawaii, Dec. 7, 1941.

"We often stayed in rented rooms in people's homes and, when we got to our home in Eau Claire, everybody was congregated around the radio. They said the Japanese had just bombed Pearl Harbor. Everybody was a bit shocked, and I remember we thought about it an awful lot; everybody was discussing it."

By the time Murphy returned to Milwaukee a few

Patriot Brother

days later, the U.S. had declared war on Japan as well as Germany and Italy. Though more and more men and women were volunteering, the pace at the processing office "didn't change too much while I was there, as we could only handle a certain amount at a time."

But, there were changes. "I had been living in a room of an older couple's home, and they rented rooms to quite a few different men. Well, I got back to the house and the lady told me that the day they declared war, the military came and picked up a German man living in the room next to ours. Apparently, they were rounding up suspected spies. All I could think was that here we could have been talking in our room about how many recruits came through that day and that guy would have been listening in."

Things had changed at home too. Murphy's mother Leila soon had a large map of the world on the wall of her kitchen as son after son followed Virgil into the service.

"When I was home to get my mom's signature on my enlistment papers (which you had to have if you weren't yet 21), my foster brother Lonnie Whisman decided to join the Army engineers. My older brother soon got married but, as the war went on, later joined the Merchant Marines. My younger brothers enlisted as soon as they were out of high school. Everett joined the Navy and Roger became a paratrooper with the 82nd Airborne (504th Regiment, headquarters company, heavy artillery)—facing combat from North Africa to Italy and Holland.

"With all of us all over the world, my mother would draw on that map with different colored pencils where we'd been and, I imagine, she spent a lot of time praying for us all to make it home again."

The praying paid off; all her boys returned home alive and well. "The good Lord was just taking care of us, but then I often think about the guys that got killed—sometimes two or three or five brothers from

The Hero Next Door Returns

the same family—and I know we were lucky too."

'WEATHERMAN'

Murphy escaped actual combat but did face the danger of serving in a war zone. He could have served his country equally well at the Milwaukee recruiting office but, "after three or so years there, it had become too much like a civilian job," so he volunteered to serve in the Army Air Corps and went to radio operator training in Sioux Falls, S.D.

Murphy became a ground radio operator with the 40th Mobile Communications Squadron, which was attached to the 21st Weather Group that was part of the 9th Bombardment Group.

As part of the communications squadron, Murphy and other radio operators were scattered at small six- to eight-man outposts within an approximate 50-mile radius of the weather station, located amid the devastation but far behind the front lines of war-torn Europe. The squadron was responsible for gathering and communicating information for the 21st Weather Group so its weathermen could then predict precisely what the weather would be like over different Allied bombing targets and/or the weather advancing troops would face.

Such predictions were especially critical for invasions, like the massive D-day invasion of Normandy, France on June 5-6, 1944. Severe weather threatened just before and just after the invasion, and Murphy's squadron helped communicate the small window of weather opportunity that made the war—and history—changing invasion possible.

However, Murphy surely didn't know what he was communicating at the time. "Everything was in a code of letters and numbers that made no sense. We'd get the coded message and pass it along to the weather guys who decoded it and made their predictions. Most of it was done by radio but occasionally—like when we got to France where there was electricity—we

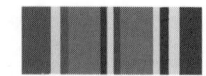

Patriot Brother

Virgil Murphy saw the devastation war brought upon the city of St. Lo, France, when his squadron moved through there to set up communications after the Allies broke out of St. Lo (near the Normandy beaches) and started beating the Germans back across France.

could use teletypes."

As the head of one of the detachments, Tech Sgt. Murphy would take his group to different sites every two weeks or so. Once set up, they'd take six hour shifts on the headsets, continually listening for Allied communications and passing the information on. "Some times were busier than others. Yet, some times there was nothing being communicated so, if there were two of us side-by-side on headsets, we could sit and play cribbage while we listened."

Until June of 1944, Murphy's squadron was setting up throughout the English countryside—"a place I really enjoyed. The first place we were at, Lavenham, was an old, old city with cobblestone streets. All the rain made the hills so green. It was a beautiful place and people were very friendly. You'd go into these

The Hero Next Door Returns

pubs and they'd have music boxes, which you'd put these big copper pennies in to play these really tin-sounding old tunes.

"One time a bunch of us went into town because it was one guy's birthday and we wanted to get him a cake. We found a bakery but the lady didn't have any sugar (it was rationed), so she said 'if you find me some sugar, I'll bake you a cake.' We did, she did, and it was great!"

Murphy especially liked the people of Great Britain. He made friends with some of the women serving in the British Land Army who invited him back to their home to meet their housemother. "She was an elderly Irish woman. When she met me she said 'you're the first Murphy I've ever seen who didn't have red hair!' That made me laugh because she didn't know that while I was half Irish, I was also half Indian."

There was less and less time to spend with new friends, however, after the squadron transferred to Colchester where the 1st Army Base launched its medium-range bombers. "That's where we really started monitoring communications."

The site of the massive Allied bombing effort made a big impression on the small town serviceman. "Every day, every minute, you could look up and the sky was just full of bombers, as far as you could see!"

All those planes drew a lot of attention, especially enemy attention, which made even behind the lines not the safest place to be. "The Germans began sending buzz bombs at us, which you could hear coming for miles. When you'd hear them coming, you'd hit the ground."

The bombings had an effect on the soldiers. "Every Sunday I went to church and there were usually just a few guys there. Well, one Saturday night they bombed the field and the next day when I went to church the place was full. The chaplain said we'd have to credit the Germans for filling the pews!"

Several weeks after the D-day landings, Murphy's

Patriot Brother

squadron moved into France and just kept moving, following behind the front-line troops. While he was glad he was not up front in the action, Murphy worried about the brother he knew was likely facing the worst of it with the 82nd Airborne.

"You'd hear about things happening here or there and knew the 82nd was in it and, sure, I worried about him. My job was hard sometimes with all the traveling and seeing the devastation in places, but we were behind the lines so there was nothing grueling, nothing like I knew Roger had."

In a world war filled with hundreds of thousands of soldiers, however, it would be impossible for Murphy to check up on Roger in person. Except, of course, that even at its biggest, it's still a small world.

In all, the brothers were able to contact each other three times while overseas, meeting twice.

"While I was in England I got a letter from Roger saying he was in England too and had gotten a pass for a certain day and would meet me at Piccadilly Circus in London if I could get a pass too. I mailed him back that I would put in for one. In fact, I got one and was all ready to go, but we never met. The day he picked was the day we launched the invasion of France!"

As Murphy later traveled through France, he and those in his squadron made it a point to ask any 82nd paratroopers they saw if they knew Roger Murphy. Then, one day in Belgium, the inquiries paid off. "My friend brought over this guy who knew Roger and told us he was in the hospital at the edge of town. So, I went right to the MPs (military police) and told them. They said that, since they were patrolling that direction anyway, I could ride along. When I got to the hospital, they said 'no visitors were allowed,' and I thought I'd miss my brother again. But then this guy said, 'look let's say I didn't see you and you walked down that hallway and happened to find who you were looking for?' ... so, he didn't see me and I went into this room.

59

The Hero Next Door Returns

Some guys were listening to the re-broadcast of a football game and I walked right past them. My brother was there, and I didn't even recognize him! Then I heard someone yell my name. It was a great reunion!"

Roger Murphy was hospitalized near Rheims with trench foot (a condition where perpetually wet, frozen feet eventually turned black). "Every time I was off-duty, I'd go and visit him. That was the fall of 1944 and by Thanksgiving he was back at the front and soon in the Battle of the Bulge. As we heard more and more about it—how cold it was and the way the Germans overran our position—I worried about him. But, I had my job to do too."

After the Battle of the Bulge in early 1945, Virgil Murphy was stationed near the outskirts of Paris when his commanding officer flew in for an inspection. "When he saw me he said that he'd run into my brother and that he was hurt and, as soon as we came back seven to 10 days later, he'd give me a three-day pass to see him."

Roger Murphy was in tough shape but not from injuries sustained in combat. His arm was in a sling from a practice jump accident. Murphy visited for three days, and then Roger got a three-day pass to go back with his brother and spend some more time together before he was sent back to war—this time to Germany.

SEASONED JUMPER

Though never wounded in combat since joining the paratroopers Feb. 24, 1942, Roger Murphy had his share of bumps and bruises—and the kinds of war wounds that don't show—from his time as a paratrooper dropping behind enemy lines to fight.

The arm injury was just one of several times he had been hospitalized. "I was injured three times in jumping accidents. In the one-month jump school we had after basic training about three-fourths of us were hurt because they were experimenting with how high we could jump from and how much equipment we could

Patriot Brother

jump with.

"My worst injury was actually on a non-combat jump we did onto a parade ground for General George Patton in North Africa," he recalled. "About 600 of us jumped, but a sudden ground wind kicked up just as we jumped; about 400 of us were hurt. I was temporarily paralyzed I hurt my back so badly, but I was soon able to walk and talk so they sent me back to work. I was jumping into combat just a few weeks later. I re-injured my back later when I fell in a foxhole while carrying an 81mm mortar up to the front," recalls Roger Murphy whom fellow paratroopers "nicknamed 'Dead Pan' because they said I never learned smiled. I was pretty serious and when I said something, I meant it. I never smiled until after I was married," he adds. "We saw a lot of combat but most of what I did in the war I just want to forget. Every mission we had about a 75 percent casualty rate. You'd make a few friends and the next day they were gone. It's not something you want to remember."

Some of the ugliest fighting the 504th regiment saw was in Italy, where troopers would often go three or four days without sleep, fight the enemy in fierce hand-to-hand combat and "many, many of our men died."

The battles for Italy's Salerno and Anzio beaches were especially tough. The 600-man regiment is credited helping the Allies gain a firm grip on Salerno in September 1943, by seizing and holding nearby high ground at Altavilla. The 504th held position despite "intense enemy artillery and small arms fire" and a fierce enemy counter-attack Sept. 17 that cut off the paratroopers overnight, reports *Devils in Baggy Pants: The Combat Record of the 504th Parachute Infantry Regiment.*

Roger Murphy would sometimes help man an 81mm mortar. In one Italian battle, he recalls, paratroopers "laid out mortars that killed about 300 Germans."

Seldom was fighting worse than at Anzio, Italy, however, when Roger Murphy landed not by air but by water—from a landing craft—on Jan. 22, 1944. After

The Hero Next Door Returns

Virgil and Roger (left) Murphy while back in the U.S.

making the beach, the paratroopers began struggling through heavy fire and German counter-attacks to take and hold the beach area that would be the regiment's home for eight weeks.

At Anzio, *The Combat Record* reports, many companies in the 504th (which started with about 75 men each) were down to 20 or 30 after one particular day of fighting, on Feb. 5, 1944. After a week-long, initial assault, paratroopers found themselves digging trenches in a defensive position as the invasion stalled on the beach for nearly three months before the Allies finally pushed through.

"For the first time, 504 men were digging dugouts and living in them for weeks at a time; barbed wire entanglements and mine fields in unusual depth covered all areas where the enemy might conceivably tread," *The Combat Record* notes. "... All in all, this was not the type of combat for which the 504 was psychologically suited. In fact, it was absolutely contrary to the way paratroopers had always been taught to fight."

Surviving paratroopers left the beachhead when they were called back to Naples March 23, leaving 120 of their own killed, 410 wounded and 60 missing at Anzio.

Though never injured in combat, the fighting took

Patriot Brother

its toll. When the regiment left Italy on April 10, 1944, Roger weighed 132 pounds. After months of English fish and chips—as the battle-weary regiment waited in reserves during the D-Day invasion—Roger Murphy was up to 200 pounds. After his return to combat, he was soon back down to 145.

As the Allies pushed the Germans back across Holland, the 504th was called to jump again into combat, participating in the bloody battle for the Dutch town of Nijmegen and its critical bridge as part of Operation Market Garden Sept. 23, 1944. After jumping in, paratroopers had to cross the river in small boat, and Murphy recalls, "only about nine of the 24 first wave boats made it to the other side."

After the bridge was secure, Roger Murphy and the 504th quickly became ground troops and, by winter, found themselves in the fierce fight to hold back the last, and coldest, German offensive—the Battle of the Bulge—in late December of 1944.

By this time, the 504th were well-seasoned veterans whose reputation preceded them. The regiment had already won several Presidential Unit Citations for their heroic stands against the enemy. And, perhaps, it was the enemy that summed up the action of the 504th and paratroopers like Roger Murphy best. *The Combat Record* contains this passage from the diary of a German officer who opposed the 504 at Anzio: *"American parachutists—devils in baggy pants—are less than 100 meters from my outpost line. I can't sleep at night; they pop up from nowhere and we never know when or how they will strike next. Seems like the black-hearted devils are everywhere..."*

REUNITED

As the American Army pushed into Hitler's Germany, Roger Murphy received word that he would not be joining yet another battle. The seasoned jumper had enough points to go home, and he wasted no time. Out of the original 600 men Murphy went to Africa

The Hero Next Door Returns

with in 1943, he only knows of six others who survived the war without being killed or suffering wounds that took them out of action. "I had had hepatitis, malaria and trench foot and got hurt in practice jumps, but I was never wounded in combat. I didn't know if it was luck or divine providence, but it felt good to go home."

In the meantime, Virgil Murphy was also excited to be heading back to the United States, though he hadn't heard whether his brothers had returned home before him as he made his journey back across the Atlantic Ocean aboard the QUEEN ELIZABETH in the spring of 1945. "I was soon at Fort Sheridan waiting to be processed for discharge when a friend of our family's came up and said 'I just saw your brother.'"

Dorothy Murphy

"I was supposed to get discharged that morning but I had overslept and had to sign my records through again. I had just done that when I saw that friend of ours," Roger recalls.

"So, Roger waited for me to be discharged and we went home together. Oh boy! Was our mother happy! She could finally stop drawing lines on the kitchen wall!"

LOVE IN UNIFORM

One of the hardest parts of war had been being away from that kitchen. But, letters from home helped lessen the loneliness.

Murphy was especially cheered by letters from his childhood friend and fellow serviceman Ernestine Quinney, who was serving in the Navy's secret and confidential files department in Washington, D.C., with the U.S. Women Marines. Friendly letters soon blossomed into love and, by the time Murphy was discharged in late summer of 1945, the two had decided to marry and tied the knot Nov. 20, 1945.

Patriot Brother

Virgil and Ernestine Murphy (left) and Roger Murphy and Ernestine's friend Louise Little posed on the Murphy's wedding day in Nov. 20, 1945.

Roger Murphy had similar thoughts about his "penpal" Dorothy Laurence who was discharged from the U.S. Women's Army Corps (WACs) a few months after Roger came home. They were married in July of 1946.

While Roger was fighting in Europe, Dorothy had

The Hero Next Door Returns

been serving in the WACs since 1943 and was eventually stationed in New Guinea in the South Pacific where she helped write and send war telegrams.

All the while, she kept writing Roger, her one-time high school date. "We started out just a long ways away and ended up a half a world away from each other—him in Europe and me in the South Pacific. We both kept all of each other's letters. It was definitely a long-distance romance!"

Roger beat his future wife back to the states by several months. And, much like how Roger had met Virgil at the discharge station, Dorothy had her own coincidences. "In New Guinea I ran into a grade school classmate and another man from near my hometown, which is amazing enough. Then, the day I was discharged, there was my twin brother who'd been in the Army. We went home together! Put that story with Roger and Virgil's, and that's a real coincidence!"

After a brief time in Sturgeon Bay, Roger and Dorothy started a life together in Milwaukee where Roger worked for American Motors until he retired, and Dorothy worked part-time for Milwaukee Sprayer Manufacturing while she raised their two sons. The couple now has six grandchildren. Roger remains active in several paratrooper associations, and they both belong to the VFW and are active in the local American Legion post as well as their church.

In the meantime, the service continued to separate Virgil and Ernestine right from the beginning, since the new bride had not yet been discharged from the U.S. Women Marines. "When Virgil came to put me on the train to go back to the service I was in my uniform and he was seeing me off. The man at the train station said that, through all the war, he'd never seen that—a fellow waving goodbye to a girl in uniform!"

Though they'd known each other since childhood, Ernestine had attended Indian high school in South Dakota and was working in a Milwaukee brewery when she volunteered for duty in the U.S. Women Marines

Patriot Brother

in 1943 (shortly after Virgil had left the Milwaukee recruiting office). "There was a lot of patriotism and I decided I wanted to join the service and do what I could to help the war effort. I liked that the requirements for the Women Marines were more stringent and that I would get to travel, but mostly, I joined the Marines because I never liked the color brown. I didn't look good in khaki!"

The recruit endured her basic training at Camp Lejune, N.C. "That was the hardest part of being in the military, and I think a lot of people would say that Boot Camp is a tough thing. We got 'gigged' for every little thing like how, when we marched on the dusty parade ground, the blinds in our barracks would get dusty and then never pass inspection. There was a lot of marching, drills and physical fitness, a lot of calisthentics. We'd crawl through barrels and jump ropes to the other side of ponds and got yelled at a lot. But, after basic training, I enjoyed the military."

While her future husband was handling communications in Europe, Ernestine was at first serving in the non-commissioned officer office at a Navy base in Norman, Okla. Within a year, she was filing personnel documents in Washington, D.C.

"We were handling the Air Corps records, and I had them for guys with names toward the end of the alphabet. When the Air Corps would send a transfer notice or killed-in-action report, we either filed it in that man's file or took the card to a different room if he'd been killed. That always made me feel sad.

"I had a friend Keith Wickman and, because I had that section of the alphabet, I always knew where he was and that he was surviving the war."

The Women Marines worked alongside security-cleared civilians. As with her husband (and Roger and Dorothy Murphy), the subject of their Indian heritage was never a big issue with anyone they served with in W.W. II. "There, of course, are always going to be some prejudiced people but I never had any problems. I

The Hero Next Door Returns

worked next to one girl and we chatted all the time and were good friends. She was curious about me being an Indian, so I always used to tease her about how I never had shoes until I joined the military, things like that.

"About the only incident was one time, when we were getting ready to go out, I spilled some nail polish on one of the girls and she yelled, 'you damn dirty Indian!' Well, I stood up—and my knees were shaking—and said 'I may be Indian but I'm not dirty and if you ever say that again ...' and she just sat with her head down and she never said anything like that again and we remained friends after that. That was the only time something like that happened."

Being a woman serving in a man's field presented a few problems on occasion but nothing exceptional. "We lived in barracks separate from the men's area, although we could fraternize when we went into town and often had dates. We couldn't date enlisted men in the Marines but could date Marine officers or men from other branches of service. I didn't drink or party, but we did go on a lot of dates. We just went out and had a good time, but it was never anything serious."

There were no real difficulties with most of the men she encountered, "and I believe we were mostly respected for the work we were doing. However, we did have a cook (a fellow Women Marine) who didn't show up one time. It turned out she was in jail because she'd gotten into a fight with a civilian lady who didn't like that women were in the service. She was mad because we women being in the service meant that her husband had to go overseas."

Ernestine continued to serve in the U.S. Women Marines months after she was married. She returned home happy to begin a new post-war life, working from time to time as she raised a family. Ernestine eventually began working for the tribal health clinic in 1976 and retired in 1990, though she continued to spend a lot of time helping others, serving as a senior com-

Patriot Brother

panion and helping with the tribal senior center and at the Presbyterian church she and Virgil belong to. They both also belong to the local Veterans of Foreign Wars chapter.

BACK TO SERVICE

By 1947, Virgil Murphy had decided to reenlist in the service, this time joining the Air Force to help make ends meet as the Murphys began their family. His first child, a daughter, was born while he was in the service. Murphy spent four more years in Air Force control tower communications, serving first in Japan and then in Korea during the beginning of the Korean War. He was again discharged in 1951.

Soon, the Murphys had a second daughter and then took in foster children and later adopted a girl and boy in their foster care. Today, they have 12 grandchildren and seven great grandchildren.

Through the years, Murphy worked for several grocery chains and eventually took a job with Gulf Oil Co., retiring in 1982 to live on the reservation of the Stockbridge-Munsee Indians, a band of the Mohicans, near Shawno, Wis. He was all set to enjoy quiet pursuits of retirement when members of the tribal council approached him in the early 1990s to serve a one-year term as vice chairman.

In that one year, "we had quite a squabble here that ended up with the chairman being impeached and me becoming chairman to finish out her term and then ending up with me being elected chairman for two years. After that, I served one year as a councilman."

When he retired from the council, representatives of all 11 Wisconsin Indian tribes attended his party. The mayor of Shawno gave Murphy the keys to the city and Sen. Johnson announced that Murphy's name had been officially mentioned in the *National Congressional Record.*

The Murphys even got invited to President Clinton's second inauguration. "We were very excited to go but

The Hero Next Door Returns

then, about that time, they laid off 50 people on the reservation. We just couldn't see how we could go to this lavish thing when all these people had lost their jobs!" Murphy explains.

For all his accolades, Murphy was most proud when his tribesmen recognized all he'd done to help guide the tribe through difficult times—voting Murphy their Elder of the Year in 1998. The plaque they gave him says it best:

You have walked the forests of life, a quiet, gentle man who loves the good things that you have found here. Your gentleness has been an example to us as we try to follow your paths. You have stood firm before our youth, have comforted our elderly and been an example to all the rest of us.

When troubles came, you reluctantly set aside your quiet life and moved out in front of us, taking the lead. The time for gentleness seemed over but years of walking life's forests prevailed and your counsel was patience and peace. We did not want to disappoint you so we listened and, in the end, we prevailed.

Your name is not written on the winds of the forgotten—gentle Mohican—it is written forever on the hearts of we who followed you.

GRATEFUL NAVIGATOR
GEORGE 'DUTCH' DURNFORD

Victory in war comes at a high price. No one knows that better than George "Dutch" Durnford of Monona, Wis. Durnford lost his elbow and much of the use of his left arm when the B-17 he was flying in as a navigator was hit by German flak on its way from Italy to bomb Berlin, Germany.

But, his sacrifices cost far less than those of others, he insists. Two of the six men injured on that bombing run—the bombardier and right waist gunner—paid the highest possible price for the Allied cause. They gave their lives in the skies above Europe.

They were not alone. When the Allied Air Forces finally could claim victory in the skies on April 16, 1945, they reported that 160,000 Allied Airmen—including 79,265 Americans—had paid for victory with their lives, according to *Time Life Books: The Air War In Europe*, p. 191.

Not that any of the airmen really thought they would be the ones to bear the worst of war. That sort of thing always happened to someone else, you figured, you hoped.

The Hero Next Door Returns

A CALL TO WINGS

Actually, Durnford didn't even think he'd be a navigator on a B-17, anyway. When the Richland Center, Wis., native enlisted in the Army Air Corps in February 1943, he thought he'd be a pilot.

"I was working at the Mason Hangar Construction Company when they were building the Badger Ammunitions Plant in Baraboo and knew I was either going to get drafted and end up wherever they sent me, or I could enlist and get some choice over where I'd serve. Walking past the post office, I saw a poster that said 'you can be an aviation cadet.' I wasn't sure I wanted to be one but that sounded like a good idea."

Durnford was on track to marry his high school sweetheart Carolyn LeMoine when he enlisted and wasn't too eager to head into combat. But, "in W.W.II we just felt that Hitler had to be stopped and felt like somebody had to do it. For my oration my senior year in high school forensics I did 'Building Patriots of America' so I was somewhat of a patriot before the war."

The patriot was soon pilot-training bound and, after scoring quite high on his entrance exams, was in pre-flight training at Gibbs Field in Fort Stockton, Texas in 1943, when Carolyn caught up with him. "We were to be married there the day after I soloed. Well, the day I soloed I wasn't doing too well and my instructor said, 'you've sure got your mind on something else,' and I sure did!"

Carolyn stayed by Durnford's side throughout cadet training and followed him to secondary training at San Angelo, Texas and advanced training at Foster Field in Victoria, Texas.

It was there that Durnford's Air Corps duties took an unexpected turn. "I was going on a night cross-country mission and had an accident on the runway. Both of us cadets were up for elimination (from the pilot training). After three or four days, they told me

Grateful Navigator

to go back to Monroe, La., for navigator training. By then they didn't need as many pilots because the Luftwaffe had been all but knocked out. And, not becoming a pilot, I guess I didn't miss much. I found out later that, though we'd been training for fighters, all the cadets I knew ended up on bombers anyway. It's just one of those things and I ended up a navigator—the one responsible for providing the directions and course for the pilot to follow—instead."

Becoming a navigator was no easy task, however. "I never studied so much in my life. They called me a 'worry wart' and I did worry because I didn't want to get pulled from *this* now. And, I was so grateful to Carolyn because she kept my spirits up."

Durnford studied the four basic types of navigation he would need to use on bombing runs to varying degrees, depending on weather and combat circumstances. These included: Pilotage (using topography and maps), Dead Reckoning (using instrumentation), Radio Navigation (using vectors from different stations), and Celestial Navigation (using a sextant and astrodome) to determine where you are.

"I mostly used dead reckoning but would use anything available when I had to. I never did consider myself a very good navigator, though, and didn't feel I was trained enough because you didn't have a lot of time in school. You're pretty green when you go over and are you ever cocky as a second lieutenant! But, then, you have one mission and you settle down a lot!"

As a navigator, Durnford was the last to join the nine-man B-17 crew of pilot Bill Hill, because "pilots are naturally picky about the navigator they get since the navigator has to be able to prove to the crew that he knows what he's doing and can get them home."

The crew left for Italy in October 1944. "We were going to fly over and I remember I had to plan a northern route, a southern route, and a central route while the rest of the crew was out partying. In the end, we

73

The Hero Next Door Returns

went over on a Liberty ship.

"I'd never been overseas before and I was in awe of everything. I was apprehensive about what was ahead but excited at the same time." And, Durnford was especially nervous about what he was leaving behind. Not long before he shipped out, he and Carolyn discovered they were expecting their first child, a baby she'd likely have without him.

BOMBING RUNS

Durnford arrived at the 15th Air Force base in Foggia, Italy, in November 1944, as part of the 775th Bomb Squadron of the 463rd Bomb Group, 5th Wing, otherwise known as Allyn's Irish Orphans after the commander Lt. Col. Robert H. Allyn from Winthrop, Iowa.

In all, Durnford flew less than 10 missions in combat—to bomb oil refineries and such in places like Ruhland, Germany and Vienna, Austria.

"My first mission was to Linz, Austria, Hitler's hometown. I was flying as a replacement navigator for a different crew. There was a lot of antiaircraft fire and I was scared. Anyone who says they weren't scared was a nut or lying.

"When we got over the target, my oxygen froze and I went down. The bombardier and navigator rode in the nose together and when the bombardier saw me go down (pass out), he looked me over. In all that heavy clothing, he figured out what happened and he had the presence of mind to squeeze my oxygen mask. Once I was back on oxygen, I came to.

"We had to leave formation though and go back to base on our own which was pretty scary for a navigator's first mission—and with another crew—but we made it."

Though air combat was plenty to be nervous about, Durnford always felt secure in the plane itself and ever grateful to the men that put and held it together. "One thing I think is remarkable is the tremendous care the airplanes got from the ground crews. The ground

Grateful Navigator

crews were absolutely terrific. When you stop to think of it, we were flying in the winter as it was, and then flying at 25,000 feet where it's way below zero, all with loads so heavy that it's amazing we ever got off the ground. So, I have a lot of respect for the ground crews that got us ready and kept us flying. They did a lot more for the war effort than I ever did."

Still, combat in a cold bomber flying in formation toward a target was "awful, awful" for all on board but, for a navigator charged with guiding the crew back should the plane have to leave formation, there could be added pressure. "I was scared and apprehensive about my capabilities in case we were alone and had to get back."

Fortunately, Durnford adds, he never carried the added weight of being a navigator on the lead plane, who was responsible for hundreds of planes arriving at the right target. "As a navigator flying in formation, you just have to keep track and know where you are in case you have to get back on your own. And, you also always had Plan A and then Plan B—two flight plans, one for what we were supposed to destroy and one for our backup target. Interestingly, you never went right to the target. You had to zigzag to it like ships did to avoid submarines. That way, the enemy would not know right where you were headed."

Such diversionary tactics did not always work. From his seat in the nose, the navigator had a good view of the carnage victory left behind.

"One time coming up off target I looked to the left and could see things coming out of a plane but I didn't know what it was. Later I heard that the crew of that plane was on their 25th mission—their last before getting to go home—and they went down."

Their shared combat experiences welded the crew together like brothers. "It's interesting that, for a lot of air crews, it gets to be like a family. You get very close and it's amazing what you do for each other in stressful, crisis situations. In civilian life we may well

The Hero Next Door Returns

Dutch Durnford, left, and his pilot Bill Hill, take a break outside their tent at the Foggia, Italy, air base.

have not even become friends, but when you're tossed together into combat like that, well, you'd lay down your life for each other."

Nothing had truly prepared the crew for the record-breaking bombing run they were called to participate in on March 24, 1945. Some 28 of Allyn's Irish Orphans

were called to join a 1,500 mile bombing run on the Daimler Benz Tank Works in Berlin—the longest bombing run in the history of the European air war. Because the distance was nearly as great as the danger, the Air Corps had set up a makeshift "hospital" and emergency runway in Zara, Yugoslavia, for planes too banged up to make it home to Italy.

When it was over, few of the 775th Bomb Squadron's planes returned from that distant target intact. Many—including Durnford's B-17—would use that emergency airstrip; some didn't make it that far.

By this time Durnford's crew had a new co-pilot 1st Lt. Stanley R. Juracich. The previous co-pilot (Martin), had been lost while flying as a replacement pilot for another crew. "He had done less than half of his required missions and it was supposed to be a milk run but he flew into a mountain over Naples." Bill Hill, their pilot, moved to the co-pilot position for the Berlin bombing run as he was a junior officer to Juracich.

"I remember we were all quite surprised to learn at the briefing what the target was and very apprehensive, of course. Then, we were told to go back and get some sleep. Yeah. Right! I can't say I didn't sleep at all but it was a nervous sleep."

WAR WOUNDS

Durnford had reason to be nervous. Before plane #402 even reached that distant target, two of its crew would lay dying, Durnford would all but lose his arm, and three others would suffer the wounds of war.

In excerpts from his diary of the bombing run (published in 1946 in *Allyn's Irish Orphans: 775th Bomb Squadron of the 463rd Bomb Group*), pilot Juracich records the hell his B-17 survived.

"Everything went along smoothly until... over the town of Komotau, just a little west of Brux, all Hell broke loose without warning. We had not expected to run into flak so no one in my crew had their flak suits on. We were [in] the lead squadron in the lead group leading the air force

The Hero Next Door Returns

and had no flak counter measures in use. The flak we ran into was the deadliest our group had ever encountered. We were 'cold turkey' to the flak gunners below and they really poured it on us.

"The first bursts to hit us wounded the engineer Sgt. Roper in the leg. He tugged on my sleeve and by sign language conveyed he was wounded. His mike switch wasn't operating so he couldn't use the interphone. In the meantime, we were being hit continuously."

It was in those initial bursts that Durnford and the bombardier—both riding in the nose—took the brunt of the flak.

"Somebody hollered, 'FLAK!' and I was reaching for my flak jacket to put it on when I got hit in the arm. I was hit in my right arm first and I put my left arm across my chest to feel what happened. That's when I got hit again. Had my arm not been there, it would have hit me in the chest instead. I was told that I was one of the few guys that ever got hit by two antiaircraft shells and lived to tell about it.

"The shot took out my elbow and triceps muscles and six inches of humerus were shot up past repair. My left arm was shattered.

"When I was first hit, I thought my arm was shot off because all I could see was the jagged edges flak makes when it tears into you. Then I noticed I could feel my fingers wriggling and I thought, 'Golly!' Knowing I still had an arm was an exhilarating feeling!

"Our tailgunner and Roper, our upper turret gunner, were right there after I was hit. Roper kept putting tourniquets on and off me."

The same flak that hit Durnford with such force mortally wounded his friend Donaldson, the bombardier. "He got hit right in the chest. Donaldson was bleeding from the mouth and about the last really conscious thing he did was point to let me know our oxygen was shot out."

All that had happened in the nose was but one part of the hell raging inside the B-17 the pilot recalled.

Grateful Navigator

"Left Waist Gunner Sgt. S.B. Scott called and said Right Waist Gunner Keith was seriously hurt. Another flak hit in the nose and shook the whole ship and smashed the window in my face. I was flying from the right seat. The hit cut the right oxygen line and smashed the walk around bottle in the nose.

"Both oxygen systems in the waist were also cut. I sent the engineer to the nose to take care of the wounded men and tried to find a way out of formation and down. I nearly passed out from lack of oxygen but managed to hook onto the top turret in time. We were boxed in by planes on all sides and flak below.

"Diving with nearly full power, I cleared the formation and flak, descending from 23,000 to 16,000 feet. I leveled off at 16,000 in order to keep out of range of light flak and headed for Yugoslavia."

Meanwhile, in the nose, Roper and co-pilot Lt. Hill continued giving first aid to Durnford and Donaldson. "Roper gave me some morphine but I didn't even know he did it." Meanwhile, Sgt. Teague, the ball turret gunner, came up from his damaged turret to help others do what they could for Keith, the right waist gunner, Juracich recalled.

"Upon emerging, Teague put on a 'flak helmet' and al-

George "Dutch" Durnford stands on the wing of his plane during pilot training.

The Hero Next Door Returns

most immediately was hit on the head by flak. He was knocked down and his helmet knocked off, but he himself was not hurt. The wounded right waist gunner's chute was damaged by flak so Teague put his own on Keith and later got one for himself out of the emergency pack. Tail gunner Gersting, Radio Operator E.F. Evans and left waist gunner Scott helped Teague to take care of Keith. When they had administered first aid, Gersting went back to his position, Evans came to the nose to help Lt. Hill and Roper while Teague and Scott remained in the waist to look after Keith and man the waist guns. Roper came up to help me salvo (jettison) the bombs and never once bothered about his wounded leg."

Men didn't suffer the only flak damage, Juracich added.

"The co-pilot's oxygen system [was] shot out and oxygen bottle in nose smashed, both oxygen hoses in waist cut. No. 4 engine controls shot away, one rudder cable shot away, ball turret glass smashed, turret door shot off, ammunition covers shot away, holes in the fuselage from the nose to the tail and in wings from one tip to another. The fuel tanks sealed themselves up so we didn't lose much fuel."

As the plane headed for that emergency airstrip in Zara, Yugoslavia, Keith died.

"Donaldson was in bad shape and I 'poured coal to the plane' to get to Zara as fast as possible. Lt. Durnford, wounded as he was, attempted to navigate but had it extremely difficult because his maps were in shambles and his vision was blurred. He navigated mostly from memory and did an excellent job."

Durnford's efforts—despite his own tremendous pain and loss of blood—would later earn him one of only four Silver Stars awarded to men of the 775th Bomb Squadron.

"I never understood why I got that because I don't remember being very helpful navigating. I'm proud of the fact that I did try very hard to do something but everything—my maps and everything—were so

bloody. I just kind of put my arm up on the table and did what I could to read them. But, I think I got a lot more credit than I deserved and I wished they'd interviewed me about it. I would have had a lot of great things to say about Roper, our pilot Bill Hill and the other guys. They were the heroes."

His crew recalled Durnford's heroic attempts to guide them to that emergency airstrip differently—a testament summarized in his Silver Star citation by Major Gen. Twining. *"Despite intense pain, shock and loss of blood, realizing his crippled aircraft could not reach the objective, Lt. Durnford gave his pilot the necessary course to an emergency field. Displaying outstanding fortitude and determination, although suffering from his severe wound, Lt. Durnford, continued to guide his pilot..."*

With Durnford's help and the pilots' skill, the crippled B-17 made a tough but solid landing at Zara. "Though, a lot of credit goes to the durability of the B-17, I was told later that there were over 200 holes in the body of the plane and we had lost the left inboard engine."

Just getting to Zara beat the odds of war, and yet, Durnford was sure that somehow they would make it. "I remember I was very grateful to be alive and had faith we'd get back all right. I have to be honest. I wasn't really religious, though I grew up in a church, but think I probably exhibited more faith on that mission than any time in my life. Everything I learned came to the surface. Faith is very real; I found that out.

"I had faith especially in the pilots, particularly in the guy we'd been flying with Bill Hill. I think Hill did just a tremendous job! I've always felt kind of funny that I never got to say anything about what a good job he did, except to him when I wrote his family when he retired that I always felt he'd done much more than me to get us back."

Despite his ultimate confidence in their return, Durnford has always wondered why the lone, crippled plane was not attacked by German fighters.

"When we were getting down to land in Yugoslavia,

The Hero Next Door Returns

off our wings, we could see some fighter planes and were wondering why we weren't attacked. They were our planes and were escorting us back and they tipped their wings. I remember looking out and seeing the pilot off our right wing smiling."

Juracich reported that, after landing, they quickly took men and equipment from the plane. *"We removed our equipment and both nose and waist of the ship were in shambles and covered with blood. Keith's body was also removed. Keith had bled to death from an artery that was cut near the crotch."*

Durnford remembers the "evacuation" well. "I remember them lifting me out of the plane, under my armpits and down through the hatch and putting me on a stretcher and taking me into this makeshift clinic. I do remember lying there and looking around at all these Yugoslavian people looking at me. They looked like peasant-type people and I remember the looks of compassion on their faces. I never forgot that, and when the recent Bosnia problems came around, I had the opportunity to send a little of that compassion back there."

That night, the crew flew back to Bari, Italy, via a C-47, with Keith's body, Donaldson and Durnford and the crew's "walking wounded—Roper, Hill (who hurt his back while giving first aid) and Teague (who suffered from a windblast that damaged his eyes)—on board.

"Donaldson and I flew on the plane together. He was still alive. He was across from me on the stretcher and I seem to remember that we were holding each other's hands through the flight. Then, I felt his hand drop (10 minutes before they landed). I knew he was gone."

RECOVERING

While the rest of the crew attended a funeral for Keith and Donaldson before heading back to Foggia, Durnford began a 17-month-long recuperative process

Grateful Navigator

that took him to eight hospitals in four countries, from the 300th General Hospital in Naples to hospitals in Miami Beach, Clinton, Iowa, California and finally to George Wright Hospital in the state of Washington.

But, Durnford remains grateful that he not only survived the war but did so with injuries that "could have been worse."

"I was so fortunate. They told me later that I had the best orthopedic surgeon in Europe. Even today orthopedics I go to can't believe he could do what he did with my arm. My muscles are tied to the bone in my lower arm and don't go all the way up, yet I can still use my hand and never had any trouble or pain with it.

"I really am so grateful. I didn't have my flak jacket on and put my arm up and got hit by the shell in both my arms or it would have gone into my chest. Knowing the situation you just can't help but be grateful. And, as I often say, every time we make a judgment about something it's always relative. Usually we say how much better it could have been instead of seeing how much worse it could have been. I look at how much worse it could have been and I have a deep appreciation for the faculties given me to use.

"I think the world of my arm because here I am 77 years old and Donaldson and some of these other guys never had the opportunity. What do I have to complain about?"

During his hospital stays, Durnford ran across many who had it worse and some who never did make it home. He especially remembers the suffering of one man—an enemy German soldier actually.

"I was walking down the hallway in the 300th General Hospital in Naples, Italy, and saw a German on a gurney in the hall crying. He had his hand out. He was badly wounded and his head was all open so you could see his brain. I asked an orderly to do something with him and he said there wasn't any room for him and, besides, he was going to be dead by morn-

The Hero Next Door Returns

Home—minus all the comforts—for Dutch Durnford was the 15th Air Force Base in Foggia, Italy.

ing anyway. And, he was dead by morning. But, I took his hand and held it. Though I couldn't understand what he was saying, I could understand him. There's an interesting language with that sort of thing."

On the way back to the U.S., Durnford spent more recovery time in a hospital in Casablanca, Africa. "That's where I saw this fellow coming down the hall with a day orderly. He had pot marks all over. He lost both arms, one below the elbow, one above and he looked so awful, but he was smiling. I said something, but he couldn't answer me. The orderly said he was blind and deaf in one ear and explained he thought he was smiling because he was so grateful for the help people were giving him—as he couldn't do anything for himself—and had no other way to convey his appreciation. Later, I found out he'd been in a demolition outfit and something exploded in his hands. That really affected me in terms of the human side of war."

Not all of his hospital time was difficult, however. Shortly after he was wounded Durnford got the best news of his life. As Durnford lay recovering in an Italian hospital, his wife had given birth to their first child,

Grateful Navigator

a son named Roger, on April 5, 1945. "She was expecting when I left for overseas which was hard on both of us. I didn't see my son until I got back to the states that summer but it's strange that the three of us were in the hospital—half a world apart—at the same time."

And later, in Clinton, Iowa, Durnford got to briefly meet one of W.W. II's great air war heroes—and one of his own personal heroes—then Gen. James Doolittle. "He was a little guy but so nice and I have been a fan of his ever since. He had come to see another airman and when he came to my ward he asked if there were any airmen there and I said I was. He asked where I'd been wounded and I said on the mission to Berlin and he said, 'Oh, I never knew those guys ever went that far and he smiled and winked.'

"I was really in awe and that put me at ease. He was already one my heroes from the war because on his April, 1942, mission to bomb Tokyo they were flying a bombing mission off a carrier—which had never been done before—and they had to fly earlier than they wanted so it was farther and they knew they wouldn't make it back to the ship. And, he was the first one to fly off. He wasn't in one of the back crews; he was up front. Jeepers! What a person, but he was something special!"

Durnford spent most of his hospital time waiting between one experiment on his arm after another.

"I really don't know why I spent a lot of time in various hospitals. You wouldn't think something like that would take so much time but they tried lots of different things to give me an elbow and nothing really worked. They told me I could have a flail arm or a stiffened arm and I chose the flail arm because my doctor thought I might be able to get a little use out of it.

"In all, however, I felt I was treated very well in all the hospitals I was in. A lot of the orderlies really appreciated that I'd given so much and were very helpful."

The Hero Next Door Returns

Because of the seriousness of his injury, Durnford was actually retired from the Air Corps—to receive retirement/disability benefits—on Aug. 15, 1946, in Washington State.

"When I was retired I thought it was interesting that I was called before a panel like it was a trial and they brought in witnesses to attest to my wounds. Even for 20 years after the war, I had to keep going back every year to prove it was a permanent injury."

Though he had visited home between hospitals his first year back, now Durnford could finally return to Wisconsin for good.

READJUSTING

"My mother and my wife Carolyn were elated at my return and I was happy to finally see my son, though Roger had been born with infantile eczema—which he grew out of—but it was difficult to see him hurting so badly."

Durnford had some healing to do as well. Emotionally he would travel to a special childhood place—"a place where troubles go"— near Richland Center.

"I'd go up on this hill there and reflect and that helped me readjust." But, physically, there was plenty to adjust to as well. "I couldn't do a lot of things I used to enjoy. I was a drummer before the war too but couldn't do that any more, and I also loved to swim but my arm in the water is no good at all. Still, some things I figured ways to do. I used to play golf and played one handed for many years. I loved to bowl and continued to bowl."

And, while he was adjusting, Durnford got on with his life and his family.

"People today ask me how my family reacted to my injury. Well, my family was just wonderful, just like there wasn't anything different."

Durnford enrolled in Beloit College in the fall of 1946, as a political science and economics major, graduating in 1950. He and Carolyn ran a restaurant

Grateful Navigator

and general store for nine years in Beloit and then decided "that was not the life for us."

"A real good friend, Professor Clarence VonEschen, who chaired the education department at Beloit College, suggested I'd be a good teacher and I went back for my teaching certificate. He'd been chair of the Monona Grove High School evaluation committee and sent my references there. At that time, teachers were more scarce. The same day I interviewed, I got the job."

By the time the family moved to Monona, the Durnfords had three children, Roger and twins Jayne and Jaque. He taught mostly economics at Monona Grove High School for the next 26 years, chairing the social studies department for more than 20 of those years. Durnford retired from teaching in 1985, but his legacy lives on.

"I always used a lot of phrases, like 'everything we make a judgment about is relative.' And, after every class period, I always said 'be good to each other.' It's nice to see how many students remember that!"

In between working and raising a family, Durnford and his wife explored a passion for collecting more than 500 exquisite pieces of American Brilliant cut glass made between 1880 and 1920. He served as a director of the board of the American Cut Glass Association and is still a member of its identification committee.

Then, tragedy struck again. Durnford's wife and brother Dale—a paratrooper with the 82nd Airborne Division in Europe who served nearly the entire War in Europe in combat—died close together, both from long-term illnesses. "As far as contributions to the war effort, I always felt Dale did more than I did."

About a year after Carolyn died, Durnford realized he'd fallen in love with his brother's widow Lylas—and she with him. They were married Jan. 1, 2001 to the happy amusement of their children and grandchildren. "It tangles the family tree a bit, but every-

The Hero Next Door Returns

one thinks it's wonderful and I do too."

PAYING THE PRICE

Over the years, Durnford had little contact with many of his former crew members, though by coincidence Bill Hill, a native of Minnesota, became the head of the Wisconsin Council of Economics after the war and, as an economics teacher, Durnford got to work with him on occasion.

In the year 2000, some of his war-time "family" finally contacted him.

"After 55 years, the tailgunner Fred Gersting called. He didn't sound any different and I knew pretty quick who he was. He's trying to track down everybody and got a hold of our upper turret gunner E.G. Roper in Texas. Our tailgunner lives in West Virginia. The first thing each one asked me was what happened to my arm. It looked so bad they thought, for sure, I'd lost it and were amazed to learn I still had most of it."

The reunited crew's conversations are always bittersweet for it's hard to wipe away the memories of a bombardier, co-pilot and right waist gunner they'd lost earlier and the two men they'd lost on that final Berlin run together.

"The important message for the next generation to learn from what we went through is to understand the price that was paid by all these guys that can't speak for themselves. I think that's our responsibility as survivors of it."

And, in an attempt to better convey to others the price his friend Donaldson and so many others paid, Durnford wrote a conversation of his own—the kind of discussion that might have taken place between Donaldson and "Death" when it came calling.

"For years I was trying to find a way to express how I felt about war and about our Donaldson and all the other Donaldsons. About 25 years after the war, I was downstairs at home and this just came to me. I put it on tape, played it for my students and many organi-

zations over the years and never changed a word."

THE LAST RITES OF WAR

Hello there, young man. I understand your name is Donaldson, bombardier on this plane. You can't see me, man, 'cuz I'm really nothing to see, in the usual sense anyway. But I'm here all right, real close you can be sure. My name is "war death" and it's my job to count out guys like you. I'm the one that sends you into life on the other side.

Sometimes I'm in a bad mood and act pretty rough. Then, other times, I can be kind of gentle. Yeah, I'm near you all right. We communicate through thoughts, your last thoughts. You might say this communication is your last rites, your last rites of war.

What's say? "Do I keep a record of it?"

Oh, sure, sure. We keep a record of every one of you guys. They're written down between the lines of all official reports and newspaper stories and historical accounts of the war. The only trouble is that human beings haven't learned to read them.

I did tell you didn't I that my name is "war death." Yeah. I come from a large family of deaths—Natural 1 Death, Natural 2 Death, Violent 1 Death, Accidental 3 Death—they're just a few of the family. Some of the family has passed on, and others are about ready to go too or at least retire. But, it looks like I'm going to have to stick around a long time yet. So far, I don't think my life's meant much. Doesn't seem to have done any good in the world.

Say, man, you really got hit bad, didn't ya? Sure doesn't look to me like, like you're going to make it. Wow! What a hole in your chest! That must have been a close hit by a big one. Yeah. No place to hide up here in this nose of this damn airplane either is there? Colder than hell too.

Course it's fine with me if you don't make it. Oh, nothing personal, you understand. Well, it's just I have

The Hero Next Door Returns

to make a high enough quota to make an impression on my employer. And, once in a while, I really make it big and get another page in the history books. But, then, that's getting to be a little old too, pretty much the same old stuff. Fact is, it's hard to see any real purpose for me anymore.

You're really hurtin' aren't you man? Like I said, I can't say I'm sorry 'cuz it's, well, it's part of my bag. Hey. By the way, I keep calling you "man." How old are you anyway? Nineteen? Well, I'll be. Of course, it's hard to tell with the blood and pain and all that. It doesn't really matter to me, though; I call all you guys "man" 'cuz, well, in war that's the way it is.

Don't look at the idea of me like that man. I didn't shoot ya. I just came when they called your number. And, like I said, I don't really see why, but they just won't let me quit, you know, like pass on peacefully, you might say.

Yeah. Don't expect much help from Durnford over there. He's got his hands full. Hmm, that's a good one! The way his arms are shot up, he's gonna have a hell of a time using his hands, but it looks like he's going to make it all right. Ahh, that is if he and Hill can get the plane back. Hey, I hadn't thought of that ... maybe you'll all end out down below in those Alps. Wow! You suppose?

Well, in any case, I'm getting two of you guys on this plane on this trip.

Oh, you didn't know about Keith, the right waist gunner, huh? Sure, he got a big hit in his right leg, right up by his groin. No way to stop the bleeding either. I'll get him for sure; he's losing blood faster than you're gaining miles.

Hey, man, and you should see the look on his face, scared to hell! That ought to please the heart of any enemy and test his inhumanity.

You know, sometimes I'm further ahead when a guy lives 'cuz he might deliver some other guys to me that way. Ahh, but not Keith. What a cocky guy he was

Grateful Navigator

The early crew Durnford flew with included (from left) front row: Lts. W.J. Hill, pilot; E.L. Martin, co-pilot (later killed), Durnford, and Jarvis Murphy; back row: Sgts. A.G. Roper, E.F. Evans, Jas. Keith (later KIA), and S.B. Scott, F.W. Gersting. Not shown is W.F. Donaldson (later KIA).

when he came over here to combat. You know a lot of them act that way on the outside. But, you know, he was always scared to death on every mission. I don't even think he even fired a shot out of that 50-caliber machine gun of his. Some people might call him a coward laying back there crying and not wanting to die. But, maybe he should just be called human ... a very human boy. What do they write the parents of a guy like that? "Died bravely?"

Hey, now. Listen to me, gettin' soft. Can't afford to do that in my business. You know, once in a while, I even find me giving in a little. But, actually I'm only as bad as the people whose purposes I serve. I'm not really the culprit responsible for all this at all. Just being used.

Hey, ahh, Donaldson, old man. Ha. Can you imagine that, now I'm calling you "old man?" Well, as a matter of fact, life is about over for you. Hmm, old at 19. How about that? I suppose some bastard would think that's funny.

The Hero Next Door Returns

Hey! Don't try to raise up man, you're not going any place. Oh, well, that is ... you know what I mean. And, don't try to speak because you don't have to speak to me. And I know you don't have to speak to your boss upstairs either. We both understand, in our own ways.

Right, right, I know, you'd like to make it. Ahh, but even if you can't you're thinking it wouldn't be so bad if it wasn't so far from home, or maybe your mom could hold your hand. No, you're not being a baby. That's not unusual at all; it's just honest.

You know, your eyes tell me a lot too, man. You're wondering if your dying is going to accomplish something. Well, all I can say is that I've been around for a long time at this kind of thing and so far it's never meant a hell of a lot. Sure, your hometown will, you know, have a paper that will have a little notice in it. And, your family will really care—and maybe a few others—for a little while. Yeah, but, who's kidding who, man? Your fighting is more a process than a cause, and processes are just to be used and are not important after they serve their purpose.

I know, I know. You've always been taught to believe that you get what you pay for. And you figure you're paying a real high price. Well, I agree with you, man, but like I say, that's the best I can do. That's been my experience. But, then, I suppose there's always a chance that it'll be different this time.

Hey man. I told you not to try to talk. You're choking on your own blood!

I know. I know. You've got faith. Good for you, buddy, good for you. OK. OK. You know that's the trouble with you guys; you've all got faith.

Yeah. Now, man, your mind is really going way out! You know it's amazing to me how fast and how much you guys think of in such a short time before you die. Your whole world, your whole life, is going before your mind's eye isn't it? And, you really feel mixed up. I can understand that. Thinking about me and thinking of making it right with the guy up above too—you

Grateful Navigator

might say, communicating with death and peace at the same time.

Ahh, don't worry about that candy you swiped from Olson's Grocery when you were 10 years old. Ahh, and for crying out loud, who hasn't smoked before their parents knew it! Man, you sure never had time to do too many things wrong. And, I agree with ya. It would be kind of nice to know what life might have had in store for you—a wife, perhaps a bunch of kids who now can't be born, maybe even a real contribution to humanity, in your own way. We'll never know will we?

Sure, go ahead and cry. I know you can't help it. And, like I said before, it's a very human thing to do.

One thing I do know from experience, man, is that the guy upstairs has a special love for you guys and feels a great sadness for your sacrifice. He looks on your tears and lifts your burdens to the highest part of his heart. You can be sure of that.

Yeah. Usually human beings can never fully communicate their deepest feelings—you know, things like hate and fear and sorrow and love. They're expressed all right but, never quite complete. 'Cuz humans are always hung up with masks and facades and defensive mechanism. But now, man, it's all you and it's all honest, and that's what makes it right.

In a little while you won't have to cry anymore.

. . . Now, that's a pretty tough question, huh. You wonder if the ones who live through this war will be able to communicate—or even try to communicate—to the next generation about what's happened here and all over the world in this damn war? You think maybe that they can try to get what's right for the price that's been paid.

Well, I can't say, man, but that question has been asked by a lot of you guys, a lot of times.

You feel cold Donaldson? Hey, Donaldson! Donaldson?

I guess you're ready now, man.

The Hero Next Door Returns

Welcome past the long mirror of war, Donaldson. You have been assigned to a special high place of peace, now and forever, man. Now and forever, you'll feel the warm breath of God."

MERCHANT 'MEDIC'
LA VERN MEYER

If there were waves to be found when LaVern Meyer was born on Nov. 11, 1920, they were among the snowdrifts of his family's Hillpoint, Wis., farm. The biggest steam boilers Meyer grew up with powered the trains he helped unload as a desk clerk and baggage boy at the Hotel Huntley in Reedsburg.

So, it was hardly "natural" that the Reedsburg High School graduate would find his way aboard some of the biggest ships and across some of the wettest and wildest waters of W.W.II. By 1946, Meyer had sailed through the Suez Canal, across the Atlantic Ocean and back again, around the Red and Mediterranean seas and to ports from Aruba to Yemen and England to New Orleans.

Meyer found the sea when he first began looking for alternatives to being drafted in 1942. "I was working in Chicago as a draftsman for Sola Electric Co., a manufacturer of florescent light parts, and the draft board was breathing down my neck. I figured if I waited to be drafted I'd end up in a foxhole and that didn't sound too safe to me. So, I tried to get into the Navy Air Corps, but they were backlogged.

"They were taking some Chicago men each month into the Merchant Marine" (under the direction, be-

The Hero Next Door Returns

ginning in W.W.II, of the U.S. Coast Guard as the service transporting war materials across the sea). "I'd thought of that as a backup plan and had already applied. In the end, it turned out the Merchant Marines had the highest mortality rate of any of the branches of service. For a lot of Merchant Marines—but thankfully not for me—it wasn't really safer than a foxhole after all."

On Aug. 24, 1942, Meyer joined tens of thousands of other Americans who served from 1939-1946 in what C.L. Salzberger called the "unsung service" in his book *The American Heritage Picture History of World War II*. Meyer was among the Merchant Marine seamen who sailed the perilous waters of the war to deliver the materials, men and machines needed to win it. Some 733 U.S.-flag merchant marine ships were recorded lost in W.W. II as a result of enemy action alone, costing 6,000 Merchant Marines their lives, reports John Bunker in *Heroes in Dungarees*.

Given those statistics, "the amazing thing was that seamen could always be found to man ships with cargoes of explosives that would blow them to glory if torpedoed, or to serve on tankers where they were likely to be incinerated if hit. Not all the heroes of the war got medals," Salzberger writes.

Most Merchant Marines, like Meyer, were just small town boys doing their part to win a big war.

"I had never been on a ship, and not to see anything but water for weeks was an experience you never imagined in Reedsburg High School. I had no idea what seamanship life was going to be. That's why they send young people to war because they acclimate faster to unusual conditions and, of course, we believed nothing could actually happen to us."

GETTING READY

Meyer began training for life on the high seas at the U.S. Merchant Service Training Station at Hoffman Island in the New York City harbor when he received

Merchant Medic

his certificate of service as an "ordinary seaman." "I remember all our barracks were named for old time sailing ships, and I was assigned to the Flying Cloud barracks."

Then, Meyer was given a choice. He could go into the Merchant Marine as an "ordinary seaman" (deckhand) and work his way up to be an "able seaman," earning different duty and pay. Or he could go to additional training for a specialist rank aboard ship. "Though I wasn't really interested in medical things at the time, I decided to pursue being a pharmacist mate, which is like a ship's medic. I trained at Sheepshead Bay in Brooklyn and sort of interned for awhile at the U.S. Public Health Hospital in Staten Island."

There, Meyer learned how to give shots, administer first aid, keep medical records and keep his equipment sterile—essentially take care of a 40-plus man crew thousands of miles out to sea.

While much of the training resembled the boot camp toughening of other branches of the service, "instead of calisthenics, we had lifeboat training where they taught us how to survive. They taught us how to jump off a ship and, if we didn't have lifejackets, how to survive by inflating our dungarees by throwing them fast over our heads.

"They also taught us—in a huge, indoor swimming pool—how to breathe when the oil or gasoline on the water was on fire. We would practice this with real fire and we'd come up flailing our arms to create a small air pocket, take a breath and go under again and keep doing that. That probably was one of the most trying parts, where you had a little apprehension. They kept telling us the torpedo threat was not that great but we'd get thinking, 'then why are we practicing this?'"

SHIPPING OUT

By late 1943, the small town boy was ready to really get his feet wet in the Merchant Marines as he boarded

The Hero Next Door Returns

the SS PINE RIDGE as a junior assistant purser and pharmacist mate in New York City on Oct. 15. His first trip would be across the cold, unforgiving waters of the North Atlantic and back. It was a journey he'd make several more times as he spent the next three years traveling up to five months at a time on three different merchant ships (the SS PINE RIDGE, SS LINCOLN STEFFENS and SS JOHN H. REAGAN).

Never having been on a ship before, Meyer had little idea of what moving on the water would feel like. Luckily, he seemed to have natural "sea legs."

"I never did get seasick but some guys got real seasick. On the PINE RIDGE we had an electrical engineer who suffered from seasickness terribly bad and constantly. We finally set up a hammock for him in the area where we stored canned goods because it was a cool place. The hammock would sway with the motion of the ship, which would ease his seasickness. Still, I don't know how he made it in the Merchant Marines but he did his job."

Veteran Merchant Marines—called "old salts"—showed little sympathy. "Some 'old salts' would give instructions to us sailors who came on board. They'd tell the guys that got seasick, 'if you feel your stomach is a little upset, take a piece of raw bacon, tie a string to it and go over to the rail. Put the bacon down your throat and pull it out real fast. That should take care of it.' Of course, these are the same 'old salts' who had us gullible new guys all standing vigilant watch as we passed the Rock of Gibraltar to see the Prudential Life Insurance sign painted on it!"

The typical merchant ship Meyer served on had a crew of 40-plus in addition to a 20-man Navy gun crew—added to merchant ships in late 1941, after so many Merchant Marines were lost even before America was officially at war. "There was one 5-inch gun in the stern, a 3 ½-inch gun in the bow and four 50-caliber antiaircraft guns."

Most of the time, Meyer's ships traveled in convoy

Merchant Medic

with some 50 ships, under protection of about five destroyers and others that escorted them. "In a convoy, all ships went as fast as the slowest ship in the water "usually about 5-7 knots an hour. The only radio contact we had with other ships was the walkie-talkie type. When we were in convoy we usually had destroyer escort, and the majority of my duty was done in destroyer escort convoys."

On the PINE RIDGE —a turbo electric tanker that used oil to make steam and steam to make the electricity that drove it—there would be no such protection. As "a little more modern" ship that could go 15-17 knots an hour, it was fast enough to travel alone as it did on every voyage Meyer took on it.

Unfortunately, alone wasn't always such a great way to travel across the Atlantic Ocean—where German U-boat submarines waited. In 1943 alone 40 American merchant ships were sunk in the North Atlantic, Bunker reports in *Heroes in Dungarees*. "A voyage across the North Atlantic seldom avoided submarine alerts and was frequently spiced with actual attacks by U-boats ... (especially through) the first half of 1943."

The lurking danger made a solo passage across the frigid seas that much colder.

"Though we were alone, as we went to Gander, New Foundland and left there for Greenland, we were covered by air once a day until we got near Greenland. Then, a plane from Greenland would come and check on us, then Iceland would check and finally, Shannon, Ireland. The idea was, if a torpedo hit us, they'd be checking on us so those of us who made it into a lifeboat—where we had an S.O.S. signal—would soon be rescued."

Those who didn't make it into the lifeboat would quickly succumb to the frozen waters of the North Atlantic. The North Atlantic proved one of the most treacherous stretches of the watery highway the Merchant Marine sailed—dangerous not as much for German sub attacks as for frigid swells and stormy

99

The Hero Next Door Returns

weather. "The North Atlantic, one of the stormiest, dreariest seas on earth, was the most dangerous," Salzberger notes.

Its cold winds would cover ships in snowy ice and thrash frigid waves upon their decks. Still, every towering swell had a silver lining. When the seas were rough, German subs couldn't find a target.

"We were told our chance of a German sub trying to sink us in the North Atlantic—where the water was rough most of the time, even when it was calm—was almost impossible. First our route was not in ordinary shipping lanes and, even if they did put a bead on us, the torpedo couldn't be fired very accurately in the rough water."

Chances of running into German subs increased on other routes, however, such as near the American and French and English coasts, in the Mediterranean Sea and as they traveled to South America for supplies. In *Heroes in Dungarees*, Bunker reports that in the last 19 days of January of 1942 alone, German U-boats sunk 250,000 tons of shipping along the East Coast of the U.S. And, in the first six months of 1942, all Allied Nations lost 383 ships in the waters from the Caribbean, to the Gulf of Mexico, along the U.S. East Coast and all the way to Canada.

Rough weather—like submarines—could cause havock anywhere, and Meyer recalls riding out the worst of it in a hurricane off of North Carolina.

"We got into a hurricane when we were coming back with manganese ore from Africa. The wind and sea were so strong it ripped the life rafts and lifeboats off from one side of the ship and many times the decks were awash. The captain said we needed to go out of our way to get out of the worst of it. We only put enough power on the engines to steer and turned so the heavy seas would hit us at a quarter angle. In that 24-hour storm, we went only 25 miles."

MERCHANT MEDICINE

Meyer sailed through it all unscathed, administering to the aches and accidental pains of his fellow seamen along the way, though much of his medical duty was preventative.

"Mainly, I administered vaccines and kept medical and personnel records up to date. We had to boil syringes and needles and know how to handle rubber gloves and keep everything sterile. Then, before a trip, I had to go to the U.S. Public Health Hospital and pick up vaccines to administer to the crew. I could usually tell where we were going by what vaccines we needed.

"I treated a lot of cuts from the accidents that just tend to happen aboard a ship. Whether we're tying up a ship or lowering the anchor, men could pinch fingers or cut or burn themselves. I was sort of like a walk-in clinic, I suppose."

Still, out on ocean—especially when they traveled alone—there was nobody for Meyer to consult with. "Luckily, we had young people that were quite healthy and agile and never ran into anything that would injure a lot of men at once."

But, Meyer did encounter a few medical challenges.

Among the things the pharmacist mate found himself giving such shots for were venereal diseases—especially gonorrhea—picked up by a few of the Merchant Marines when they'd stop in different ports. "After shore leave one or two guys each trip would come in with gonorrhea. That was probably the main venereal disease I treated. We had penicillin but it was new and in true mold form, which we kept in a vial in the refrigerator, along with a vial of sterile water to mix it with. It was not as potent as it is now, so we had to give a shot of it every four hours. I'd have to have the people on watch at night wake me up every four hours to give these guys their shots."

Occasionally, Meyer tended to more serious kinds of medical needs of the Merchant Marines and Navy

The Hero Next Door Returns

gun crew. "I had one case of a broken leg where a steel cable broke loose, whip-lashed the seaman and broke his leg. That was probably the most serious injury I dealt with, though we had a case of appendicitis. However, we were traveling alone and had to leave him in a foreign port to take care of it. If we'd been traveling with a convoy we could have transported him to a Navy ship that had a doctor and hospital facilities."

In his four years at sea, Meyer's crews suffered just one fatality, a man who died from an undetermined illness. "He was buried at sea, which was hard on us all and I had to make a big, long report on it to furnish the relatives and public health hospital."

PERSONNEL PURSER

Most of Meyer's time was spent on other duties, however, as he also worked as the ship's purser, responsible for keeping crew payroll lists and cargo inventories.

"I had the job of working with the Recruiting and Manning Organization, and we had to make copies and testify that the men assigned were the men aboard. If they took off, I had to report it to the RMO.

"Merchant Marines had a few more choices as to what ships they sailed on and when. You could take 30 days of leave each year and could decide when to take it. But, once you were assigned to a ship, you were on that ship. We also got hazard pay when we'd got to the European and Mediterranean area—a bonus of $5 per day while we were in the war area. So, we had some more choices in the Merchant Marine, but they had to be favorable choices or we'd be reclassified by the draft board in a hurry."

In tandem with keeping track of the crew, Meyer kept track of the payroll and operated the "Slop Chest," a miniature general store where Merchant Marines could charge against their wages to buy their trademark dungarees as well as cigarettes, tobacco, shaving supplies and the like.

The men also drew against wages to have money, if possible, whenever they made a port where they could go ashore. "If we went to England and there were four or five days, they could draw against their wages. I'd have to go ashore and meet the representative of our shipping company—there was always one in every port—and have him convert the money."

Meyer also kept track of the Merchant Marine IDs when the ship made port. "In a foreign port, they'd all turn in their 'passports' and we'd put them in the ship's safe. We had a crew list with the passport numbers and these were valuable things to get a hold of.

"I was really sort of a bookkeeper, and I'm most proud of the experience I got onboard ship that I could carry through into the business world where I became a purchasing person first for Badger Ordinance Works and then for the State of Wisconsin."

Between his duties, Meyer found other ways to pass time atop the waves.

"I didn't have regular hours onboard ship and spent a lot of time playing cribbage with the radio operator who only had to listen to messages since he wasn't allowed to send any except in emergencies. We played for a penny a point and I think he owed me something like $30. We listened to the BBC on the ship's radio, read letters from home if we got any when we came into a port and read a lot of anything we could get our hands on. But mostly, time at sea doesn't go very fast."

CARGO COUNTER

In addition to serving as payroll clerk, Meyer helped manifest the cargo. Typical cargo was often 100-octane gasoline below deck in the tanks and a cargo of P-51 fighters. "For example, we went to Trinidad off the coast of Venezuela and loaded up with aviation gas and then went to a U.S. port and loaded on P-51

The Hero Next Door Returns

planes and then went on to Liverpool, England to deliver it all.

"I remember, too, one trip where we went down to Aruba with a tanker for 120,000 barrels of fuel. We were basically a floating bomb and couldn't smoke anywhere on the ship itself, except way out on the fantail or stern and only during daylight hours. At night, we could show no lights at all. If we were out on deck at night we had to go through an entryway of canvas curtains to get back inside. Portholes were welded shut and the glass was painted so no light would shine through."

One captain was extra-particular about his cargo and the man in charge of it. "Sigval Lien was my captain on the JOHN REAGAN. He was retired before the war and had his masters license for three different types of ships. He was in his early 70s and really an 'old salt.' He was an excellent captain—just the kind you'd want when the going was tough—but he didn't care anything about keeping track of cargo and other bookwork. He sort of depended on me to manifest the cargo and pay the crew and he seemed to want me on his ship. One time, I had to fly down to New Orleans to catch his ship when I was home on leave because he'd sent for me.

"I'll always remember that—after he'd go down to the officer's dining room and eat his lunch and then go up to his room near the center of the ship—he'd put a cigar in his mouth but not light it. Then, he'd take out his sextant and go up on the bridge and take the noon sighting. If the sun wasn't shining, he, the 1st mate and the 2nd mate would agree how far the ship had gone by dead reckoning until the next day, when they could use true noon by Greenwich-Meridian Time to adjust us a bit if necessary. He'd do all this and never light that cigar. By the time he was finished, the cigar would be gone just the same and its juice would be running down his lips and onto his brown shirt."

The "old salt" captain also didn't like to sail a ship

Merchant Medic

that was anything but full of cargo of some kind. "He just couldn't see going over to Europe and coming back empty. So, one time when we unloaded in Oran, we went down to South Africa to refuel and then went up the coast of Africa further and picked up some manganese ore to take to Boston."

Cargo was just as often even more unusual, as it was on one trip to Iran—reached by traveling from the U.S. to Africa and then around South Africa and up into the Persian Gulf, a 32,528 mile round trip that meant about 243 days at sea and 97 days in port (*Heroes in Dungarees*). "We went up the Tibers River and unloaded two locomotives that were part of what was called a 'lease-lend' to Russia. We also transported lots of rolls of shoe leather in hide form and lots of alloy metals in the front holds."

The most unusual cargo had to be some 1,500 prisoners Meyer's ship picked up one time from LeHavre, France, shortly after the Battle of the Bulge. "The prisoners had marched from Antwerp to LeHavre. We had 500 bunks in the center hold of the ship and 1,500 prisoners on board who had to sleep in shifts. They used the steam from the ship to cook with and saltwater-soluble soap to bathe in. When we saw that they ranged in age from 14-70, we couldn't have gotten a better indication that we were winning the war and it was almost over. Hitler was throwing his last measure at us, and I felt sorry for them.

"When they came aboard they were just filthy. They had marched something like 25-30 miles a day and just had their bed rolls and no change of clothes. Many were wounded and their dressings were almost rotting off, but they did have their own medics to deal with most of it. We were asked to share our medicines, however. I retained enough to take care of our crew—which came first—and gave them some bandages and salves and what we had extra. As far as I know, they all survived the trip."

Meyer—who grew up in a German family and barely

The Hero Next Door Returns

spoke English until grade school—conversed with some of the medics. "They were so glad they were prisoners and were being taken care of. They didn't show much loyalty to Hitler."

While the prisoners proved the most unusual cargo, the Wisconsin farm boy was witness to many unusual and exotic sights so far from home.

"I still think the most unusual thing I saw was in French Equatorial Africa on the Duala River. They were bringing cattle from the interior on barges and going to put them onboard a French ship. How they unloaded them from the barges was a sight. They all looked like Texas longhorns and they put a rope around the horns and lifted the cattle up and up. Then they swung them around and down into the hold. These cattle looked a little surprised but not too upset about swinging in the air like that!

"I also remember that the captain took us out to dinner at quite an exclusive French restaurant there where we were served by black men dressed in tuxedoes and ties. What struck me is that they were barefoot. They were dressed up like that but then barefoot; I'd just never seen something like that before."

PERILOUS DUTY

There were other sights and sounds that Meyer would just as soon forget.

"I remember the ping of the depth charges going off when you're down in the engine room. Because of all the metal around you, and because you're under water down there, when the depth charges go off it really doesn't sound like an explosion. It felt like, and you were surrounded by, this 'ping' sound.

"We had the depth charges to roll overboard if we suspected there were German subs nearby. I was down in the engine room a couple of times when that happened because either a sub was sighted or the destroyer escorts told us to drop depth charges on one side or another to guard against subs. Believe

Merchant Medic

me, when they did that when you were in the engine room of the ship you felt like the ship got hit with a sledge hammer!"

Most often the danger was the unheard—and unspoken—kind that lurks just below the surface somewhere, out there.

"In convoy a lot of times a ship would have engine trouble and leave the convoy or fall behind the convoy until they could repair the problem and catch up or make it to a port for repairs on their own. The convoy had to keep going but would occasionally send a destroyer back to check on the ship." Damaged ships would be easy prey for German subs and other problems. "When we'd go out to have a cigarette we'd often take guesses, asking each other 'do you think they'll make it back by dark.' Some didn't make it back at all. We actually saw a ship picked off by a German submarine about 10 miles out from us. "

Other dangers also lurked quietly in the water, especially along the European coast where mines floated partially submerged, even after the war's end.

"One of my most nerve-wracking voyages was after the war ended when we went to Hull, England with a load of wheat from Albany, N.Y., and took it across the North Sea to Hamburg, Germany. They hadn't removed all the mines from the North Sea so we went across real slowly—about 3 miles per hour—with two minesweepers out front carrying a cable between them to hopefully catch any mines."

Perhaps the closest Meyer came to the peril so many Merchant Marines had faced before him was on a run to Oran through the Straits of Gibraltar between Africa and Spain in the Mediterranean Sea.

This time danger flew above the waves.

"We came through the Straits of Gibraltar slowly because we were in convoy and because only two (big) ships could go through at a time. Sometimes it could take a whole day to get through and we'd assemble along the African shore and wait for every-

The Hero Next Door Returns

one to go through. We were waiting outside Oran, Algeria, when Italian planes suddenly came in and attacked our convoy.

"All the ships had smoke pots to light and dump overboard, which we did. It practically covered our convoy in a cloud. The planes did drop some torpedoes but didn't make any hits. The worst of it was that we could only hear the planes and not see them. You didn't know where they were or where they were going, only that they were there and after you. Yeah. That was ... well, that was scary."

ON SOLID GROUND

Meyer traded in his sealegs for good in June of 1946 and went to work for the International Harvester Co. in Madison. He caught the Love Bug when he met LaVona Hilgendorf "which pretty much took care of any desire to stay in the Merchant Marine." They were married in 1947 and eventually had a son and daughter before LaVona died 26 years later.

Meyer remarried in 1981 to Rozelle Lukenbach, who understood all too well the sacrifices of a war veteran. Her first husband Max had been a reconnaissance pilot off the Kitty Hawk Aircraft Carrier during the Vietnam War. He was flying with Glenn Daigle, his navigator, on one mission in 1965 when they were shot down. Her husband was killed but his friend Glenn survived seven years in captivity as a POW.

Meyer enjoys a good life—and especially his two grandsons. He is proud of his career as a purchasing manager. Still, he admits, he would have liked to pursue some other things he learned in the Merchant Marine.

"When I got out I would have loved to have gone to medical school because I wanted to learn more. But, I could never afford it, and as Merchant Marines, we didn't qualify for the G.I. Bill." *(Meyer and the rest of the Merchant Marines eventually did qualify for the G.I.*

Merchant Medic

Bill and other benefits afforded military veterans—about 45 years after W.W. II—when the United States recognized the Merchant Marines as part of the U.S. Armed Forces.) "I was glad that the military services recognized the value of the Merchant Marine in W.W. II and we can now get some of the benefits other service people have, but 45 years was a long time."

Yet, the Merchant Marines was its own education. "I never did go to college, but I got a lot of practical education through life, and you could say I got a college education in the Merchant Marine. All the places and things I saw, and responsibilities I had, you just can't get in textbooks."

The Hero Next Door Returns

DESERT NURSE
MARIE FREDRICK

Anna Marie Yager Fredrick already knew she wanted to nurse others by the time America began heavily recruiting volunteers to nurse its wounded servicemen in 1942. A graduate of nursing school in 1939, Fredrick had worked at Michael Reese Hospital in Chicago and was working for a Racine, Wis., eye, ear, nose and throat doctor when she answered her country's call in 1943.

"Everyone was saying they needed nurses so badly and a lot my friends were already in it so I enlisted." She volunteered for overseas duty and nursed America's fighting men in America, Africa, and Italy, from Feb. 1, 1943 to April, 1945.

Like so many Wisconsin volunteers, the Lyons, Wis., native and Burlington High School graduate traveled to Fort McCoy, Wis., with "no idea of where military service would take me." When the nurses were transported to "the swamps" of Camp Shanks, N.Y., she knew she'd be bound for the European Theater.

When the 29-year-old nurse made the ocean crossing to the European Theater—destination Africa—she was one of the few on board not to get seasick, though she'd never been on a large boat before. They landed in Oran, Algeria, in North Africa, at a place called Goat Hill in 1943, and were welcomed by a desolate sight.

"There was nothing there—not just no tents or anything, but no trees either, nothing. Everybody was in a quandary of where to put us nurses, so we were shoved here and there while they figured it out. We lived in tents and they eventually set up a place for us to eat."

This was the beginning of the 81st Station Hospital, a sort of field station hospital where Fredrick would serve with 26 nurses. They went to work treating the desert wounded almost immediately.

"We got wounded fresh from the field, almost like an emergency room. They might be coming all night. Most injuries we saw were to legs and eyes and arms. Fortunately, I was quite well prepared for the work before I left because I was quite a bit older and had more years as a nurse than a lot of the girls."

The wounded came in at any time and every time. "We'd look down the road and see a bunch of ambulances headed our way, though we'd usually get six to eight wounded at a time. We tried to work shifts so we'd have a break but that didn't really work. Sometimes you'd be so tired you could hardly stand."

Fredrick worked mostly as a post-operative nurse, working among the cots full of wounded in the tent hospital and trying to keep the patients' wounds clean of sand and desert pests. "Those that could, talked about home and girlfriends and families. But, it was hard to see the wounded men; it's still hard to think about."

Many of the wounded couldn't be patched with stitches and bandages. According to *GI Nightingales* (page 80) psychological wounds were common as the fighting "produced an unexpected number of psychiatric disorders but 58 to 63 percent were actually 'battle fatigue' and returned to duty."

The 81st was eventually moved to Bizerte, Tunisia, in North Africa, after the Allies secured it in early May,

The Hero Next Door Returns

The nurses created entertainment of their own, sometimes throwing parties.

1943. But that proved not the best location either. "They were bombing our hospital then, even though we had the Red Cross symbol on it. Fortunately, they missed our tent but one hit just outside it and made a big hole."

Besides the threat of being wounded or worse, nurses working in Africa had others hardships to bear. "We did our washing in our helmets and somehow found a scrubbing board to make it easier but it was fairly primitive conditions you could say. Daily comfort was always a challenge and everybody was living where they didn't know how to cope.

"We slept four to a tent and the cots we slept on were hardly comfortable. There was never enough water and the desert was very cold at night. We only had mud for flooring until the Navy fixed that for us. One of the nurses went with a Navy guy and he built us a wood floor."

The desert was also host to a few unwelcome camp visitors. "We didn't really have any rats but there were awful spiders. Actually, we got pretty good at killing them."

Tiny creatures took their toll on morale and health

as well. Many nurses came down with various illness, especially malaria.

Fredrick too suffered the mosquito-borne fever. "Even though we took Atabrine and salt tablets, I still had malaria for several days and just burned up with fever."

To make matters worse, water was always scarce and food supplies were barely adequate. "And, what food we had was terrible. I can't even remember one thing we ate."

Well, except for one thing—four things really, Fredrick smiles.

"We were always hungry and longing for old friends and happy places, warm, safe places. I wrote to my parents about how great it would be to taste some real potatoes instead of the grey-around-the-edges variety we got in Africa.

"When a package arrived for me from home a while later, there were four medium-sized raw potatoes. I

Washing day in North Africa required plenty of determination, a sense of humor and a little ingenuity.

The Hero Next Door Returns

couldn't believe my eyes!

"We peeled them and fried them in butter from the mess hall on our oil drum stove. What flavor! What aroma! What a wonderful treat! I can still almost taste them. We lived in those bad conditions so it took very little to make us happy—even just four Wisconsin Russet potatoes would do the trick!"

THOUGHTS OF A NIGHT NURSE

Such reminders of home were always bittersweet ... and especially thick in the quiet of a desert night shift when Fredrick penned this short poem—that captured the feelings of a nurse serving so far from home—to her parents:

It's two o'clock in the morning
My wards are quiet again
My patients are deep in slumber
Until I know not when.

I sit at my desk a moment
And think as I have before
Of my home and friends and loved ones
And of times before the war.

I wonder just what they're doing
Perhaps they've gone to a show
Or visiting friends or neighbors
They are all people I know.

They may be spending the evening
At home – it's just eight o'clock there
Sewing, smoking and chatting
As the day's events they share.

OH! How I'd love to join them
My mom and dad and sis
To think I left that Heaven

Desert Nurse

To come to a place like this.

It's cold and rainy and dreary
The floors are covered with mud
And I am getting so sleepy
My head bobs down with a thud.

Why that's no way to be thinking
I say to myself – see here!
Your job's to help these soldiers
To nurse them and bring them cheer.

They too need a little kindness
For the things they've been thru
And they all want to go back
To their houses just as much as you.

And so I put my thoughts of home
And all my dreams away
To pray that soon the time will come
When I'll be there to stay.

DESERT DIVERSIONS

Not all of Africa was so difficult. There were good times too, she recalls.

Fredrick spent some time with "the love of my life at the time," an officer who worked elsewhere as a linguist. Together, when they could find downtime, they toured the area a short distance from the hospital and away from the fighting, visiting the Carthegean ruins and Tunis where she was amazed to see camels driving turnstiles to help bring up water. "We saw ditched German tanks and remnants of fighting in the desert lots of times."

And, the troops were treated to top performers, including comedian Bob Hope and singer Frances Langford.

"We worked and we played a little; when we got some time off we went to the beach. Some of the girls par-

The Hero Next Door Returns

Fredrick, at right, gathers for a picture with a patient and others at the station hospital.

tied too but I was never a drinker."

All the nurses found there were plenty of diversions in the sheer number of men to every woman in the area.

"We were a rarity over there and the guys really flocked around and there were a lot of nice ones. It was kind of cute. Even when we were at Fort McCoy waiting to board a bus, one guy was in every seat on the bus. They had been sitting two to a seat but one got up so that each guy would have a chance a girl would sit with him!"

However, fraternization was deterred. "We weren't supposed to date enlisted men but some girls found ways around that. One of them even married one."

ITALIAN SURGERY

Fredrick was in Africa a little over one year before the hospital followed the Allies' push into Italy where sand and mud accommodations gave way to sturdier, more permanent buildings.

It was a bit of welcome comfort that Fredrick would see little of.

"I arrived in Italy not feeling well and they did exploratory surgery. I had a spinal (shot) so I could sit in on the action ... but I didn't make it long before I asked to be put under. They found I suffered a perforated ulcer, which I guessed could have been triggered by some of the medication we all had to take.

"I was operated on in an art gallery. I think I must be the only nurse who had ulcer surgery in an art gallery!"

But even art, like patients, wasn't safe in war. "While I was there recuperating, there were bombings and the plaster fell off the wall. All I could do was lie there."

Fredrick developed peritonitis and was transferred to a hospital ship bound for the United States. "I was a sight to behold. I weighed about 80 pounds with bleached blond hair and had yellow skin and was so weak I could hardly stand."

Shortly after she arrived home she learned her father had died just a few weeks before.

STATESIDE RECUPERATION

Fredrick's recuperation was a long one. Her medical records show her sick in the Walter Reed General Hospital in Washington, D.C., from Dec. 21, 1944 to April 16, 1945, with a few weeks sick leave granted in between. She was discharged in late April, 1945, when she was nearly fully recuperated, though she had additional surgery at the Mayo Clinic in Rochester, Minn., and still has some lasting effects from the ordeal.

Fredrick worked for a time as a school nurse in Illinois before returning to Wisconsin where she met a

The Hero Next Door Returns

veteran of the Pacific Theater, Lawrence Fredrick, an anti-aircraft gunner, on a blind date. They were married in 1952 and have two children, Steve, born in 1954 and Pauline in 1957.

Though she gave up her work as a nurse to raise her family, Fredrick never gave up serving others. To date, she has logged over 5,000 volunteer hours at the Oconomowoc hospital and continues to knit newborn baby caps for the hospital's newest arrivals.

In between, she and the "true love of her life" have been able to travel near and far away from their home base, taking in Europe and the Scandinavian countries.

And, Fredrick has kept in contact with the "true friends for life" she made in the African desert so many decades ago.

"Since the war, we've kept a round-robin letter going, but it's getting shorter and shorter as more and more of us are passing away. The friendships I made in Africa have lasted more than 55 years and they're still some of the best friends I've ever had. These friendships were the best part of my time in Africa.

"And, I'm proud of my friends. I'm proud that we were able to get so many patients to a general hospital and that most of those made it home. It wasn't always easy work, but I'm proud of the women who served our country so well as nurses."

Land Seaman

LAND SEAMAN
MARTIN GUTEKUNST

When the Navy started to teach its new seaman recruit Martin Gutekunst how to dig trenches, he should have suspected that his duties would carry him far from the water ... and into two of the most extensive land invasions in W.W. II, one at Normandy, France, June 6, 1944, the other at Okinawa, Japan, April 1, 1945.

Gutekunst ended up far indeed from the service he chose when he was drafted in spring of 1943. "At first, my lottery number was high so I thought the conflict would end before my turn. By 1943, most single men had been drafted. When I received my "greetings" the Milwaukee Boiler Manufacturing company I worked for got me a deferment because it had defense contracts."

A few months later the deferment ended and he was drafted. "I was anxious to join though because so many of my friends preceded me into the service and their mothers often reminded me that their sons were in service and I was not!"

The Fond du Lac County native and 1935 Kewaskum High School graduate was inducted May 14, 1943, with two years of an engineering education at the University of Wisconsin-Milwaukee. When asked what mili-

The Hero Next Door Returns

tary branch he preferred to serve in, Gutekunst said the Army Air Corps. "So, naturally, the man in charge directed me to a table full of men in blue uniforms who informed me 'you are in the Navy.'"

The aspiring airman soon shipped to Great Lakes Naval Academy near Chicago for boot camp, learning the skills he'd need to work much closer to the ground than he hoped, in U.S. Navy Visual Communications.

On Dec. 1, 1943, Gutekunst and his signal schoolmates traveled by rail to Camp Bradford, Va., an amphibious base used as a stopover and invasion landing training center. The Seaman 1st Class learned visual communications using signal lights and semaphore flags. He also learned to dig trenches and discovered that the Navy "does not guarantee three meals a day in mess halls, nor indoor toilets, nor a dry bed at night."

Gutekunst's group of 20 or so signalmen joined up with another 100 men, all trained in radio or visual communications, to form JASCO (the joint assault signal company).

By Dec. 27, 1943, Gutekunst was in New York City and celebrated New Year's Eve in a browned-out Times Square. On Jan. 7, 1944, the party was over and the signalmen boarded the MAURETANIA troop ship.

Even his first day on the water did not pass without incident. "We didn't even get out of the harbor. We were rammed by a freighter, which dented our starboard bow, and we were delayed 24 hours."

That incident only delayed the inevitable tumultuous ride to the war waiting for him across the Atlantic.

"We were the last on board and slept in hammocks in "C" deck. The ship creaked in North Atlantic storms and the British food was lousy. The jam-packed ship caused the toilet facilities to overload before we even left the harbor. Home was never like this."

The ships tried to avoid German submarines by run-

Land Seaman

ning a zig zag course but Gutekunst remained worried about the danger lurking below the waves, especially after the Navy plane escort departed a few days into the journey. "I was worried for a while, well, at least until the North Atlantic storms became so violent I was too seasick to care."

The signalmen reached Liverpool, England on Jan. 17 and boarded a train to Salcombe arriving late at night Jan. 19. The base was already in blackout conditions.

"You could have flashlights with an 1/8-inch hole and the barracks had a double entry so no light could escape. They were very strict on blackout conditions so German bombers wouldn't spot our location. However, there were many times we had to empty the barracks when bombing raid sirens went off."

The weather didn't make the darkened nights any more comfortable.

"It rained most of the time so trudging through the mud became common place. Our gear, including our mattress, did not arrive until three weeks later, though sleeping on bare springs was perhaps good preparation for things to come."

The Navy's communications radio/signalmen group was a small dot in the immense gathering of combat ground and air troops in England and the seamen felt a bit adrift.

"Many of us were complaining about our unit's lack of purpose. We had little amphibious training, so we spent much time playing cards, preferably Sheepshead if we could find three Wisconsin men."

After transferring to Fowey, some in Gutekunst's group trained with the North Africa and Italy-seasoned 2nd Navy Beach Battalion. But most of the JASCO group, including Gutekunst, "did everything but train for what was to come. I painted hotels and other buildings ... and enjoyed the English countryside, traveling to London where one 8-year-old boy—unaccustomed to seeing Americans in sailor uniforms—even

121

The Hero Next Door Returns

asked for my autograph. Also, one man in our group was a magician by trade; we almost went nuts having all these tricks pulled on us. The U.S.O. provided entertainment on a few occasions too. The Navy also sponsored dances, though with no racial integration at that time, the Navy had black nights and white nights for the dances to avoid a confrontation."

In late April of 1944, "some high ranking Navy officers visited the camp and were shocked to find so many trained signal and radiomen painting hotels."

Gutekunst's JASCO unit was quickly reassigned to beach battalions in alphabetical order. Those with last names E through I were transferred to the 2nd Beach Battalion and Gutekunst was temporarily assigned to the Navy's SeaBee combat demolition unit assault force "U."

The 10-man unit was sent back to Salcombe for demolition unit training on May 15. They were added at the last minute to provide communications for the demolition teams, under the direction of Navy SeaBee Lt. Smith. "And I don't think I ever knew his first name. We all went by last names over there, even though when they got to my name they murdered it."

"The Army and Navy demolition personnel were all highly trained and experienced in civilian life as explosive experts. Most came from the mines in the Western U.S. Our 10 communications personnel were assigned one each to each of 10 demolition teams. Each team had five Navy and five Army engineers."

Though communications would be his primary responsibility, Gutekunst did receive some explosives training.

"They had a huge supply of the explosive called C-2, which is similar to a Fels Naptha soap bar in consistency and appearance and is safe to handle. It burned if lit with a match but would not explode unless properly detonated. We helped put the C-2 in specially designed canvas containers that we eventually carried on our backs in the D-Day landing."

Land Seaman

GOING IN

From May 26 until June 2 Gutekunst and nearly 3 million Allied soldiers, sailors and airmen were readied for the assault on France, according to C. L. Sulzberger in *The American Heritage Picture History of W.W.II*. Sulzberger reports that "the actual attack was accomplished by 176,475 men, 20,111 vehicles, 1,500 tanks and 12,000 planes."

On June 2, 1944, "we received the now famous message from Gen. Eisenhower and his message and stature gave us all encouragement. Morale was very high when we boarded LST (landing ship, tank) 282 for the invasion of Normandy."

As the last troops to board, the team bunked in the cargo deck and, once again, relentless storms turned the voyage into a seasick ride. In between, Lt. Smith briefed the teams on the landing area and type of obstacles to destroy. "That's when we found out that we were going to be right up front, right after the first wave, on Utah Beach."

Gutekunst checked over his portable radio so the 130-pound seaman would be able to transmit messages from Lt. Smith to the leaders of the other nine teams. "My portable radio weighed over 50 pounds so I was excused from carrying a 50- to 75-pound bag of explosives on my back. All the other personnel on our team had that privilege."

It was still dark when the demolition team assembled on D-Day June 6, 1944, and boarded the LCVP (landing craft, vehicle, personnel) as they listened to the Navy's big guns trying to soften up the beach targets prior to landing.

"We climbed down the rope ladders while the LST and LCVP were going in opposite vertical directions in the waves. I got my foot caught between the two and I didn't notice it hurt until two days later. Lt. Smith saw what happened and asked if I was OK or if I wanted to go back aboard the LST. I said 'no.' It wasn't brav-

The Hero Next Door Returns

Gutekunst stands at his signal tower on Okinawa in 1945.

ery; I just wanted to get to dry land."

In addition to the 50-pound radio, Gutekunst boarded the LCVP with his issued rain gear, Eisenhower jacket, helmet (which featured a blue stripe above the lower rim to distinguish him from Army troops), paratrooper boots, gas mask, carbines and K rations. The son of a Lutheran pastor, the 5-foot, 7-inch seaman also carried a miniature New Testament and Psalms book. "My faith was very strong and very important to me. I carried that Bible with me everywhere. It did help you deal with it. After a while, you're just doing your job and you can't stop and think about your mortality."

Once aboard the LCVP Gutekunst joined others circling the landing pattern and watching the fireworks ashore as planes were shot down and Navy guns pelted the beach. "We were watching all the action before we landed and there was a lot of bombing. There was an awful lot of noise; you couldn't even hear the person next to you. There also appeared to

Land Seaman

be some confusion on instructions for our turn to proceed. The entire landing force was not at the correct landing site, which caused the confusion because the photos we'd seen ahead of time did not correspond to what we now saw at the site.

"After perhaps an hour Lt. Smith determined we had better land and said, 'well, let's go in!' Lt. Smith's decision was a wise one because we had to land soon in order to take out the obstacles while the tide was still low and it was only low for about six hours. If we didn't get them out of there in time, the tide came up so fast—up to about 30 feet—that some obstacles could have been underwater and then it would have been a lot more difficult to get rid of them."

The group landed on Utah Beach about 6:30 a.m. amidst "a lot of gun fire from our ships and the German 88-milimeter. Navy rocket fire was erratic, and though I was not an expert at this, it appeared that some of these rockets landed on our own troops. I remember seeing a cluster of troops, then an explosion, and then no troops."

The demolition teams were to remove the obstacles (mines planted on tall poles to take out ships at high tide) in the way of later ships coming in at high tide.

"All the obstacles consisted of telephone poles about 20 feet high with taller mines on top and steel "X" frames. They were built to destroy landing craft at high tide. The teams, under Lt. Smith's instructions, strung wire from one obstacle to another, placed the explosives and, when ready, electrically detonated them."

All the while the teams were drawing and dodging fire. "At one time we received a report that the team adjacent to ours was hit and that all five Army engineers were killed and the five Navy men were injured, though how seriously I don't know."

That was one of only a few reports Gutekunst would receive. "My radio wouldn't function. So, Lt. Smith said to ditch it and help string wire. We continued on that

The Hero Next Door Returns

way until all the obstacles were destroyed. The gun fire was constant and the tide kept rising so it was essential to complete our efforts hastily."

Communications were mostly done with flares and "by yelling as loud as you could because there was so much noise you couldn't hear an officer except when you were right next to him. So, when we were ready to blast, someone would send a flare up to warn everyone."

While demolition crews largely stayed clear of their own explosives, many were killed or wounded by enemy fire. There was little time to help them on D-Day. "The seriously wounded or killed had to be abandoned because the rapidly rising tide made it impossible to give assistance. In a short time, abandoned Jeeps and other mechanical equipment were completely submerged. The Army had to wait for the receding tide to recover bodies and vehicles."

Beach obstacles were pretty much all demolished by the end of D-Day, so Demolition Team "U" dug in at the sea wall for the night. "I recall shrapnel hitting my helmet, which left a slight dent. Later I was using my helmet to dig the foxhole in the sand when shrapnel hit the helmet liner, but there was no damage. Speed in getting to a safer spot in that foxhole was the objective, so I was willing to sacrifice temporary danger without the steel helmet."

It was at the sea wall where Gutekunst encountered his first German troops. "The Army infantry first wave that landed before us took them prisoner, so they were no danger to us at that point. It was a pleasant sight to see German prisoners. The troops we met there I noticed were mostly Polish or young Germans." They encountered more experienced German soldiers further inland and at other beaches like Omaha (the American invasion force beach where fighting against crack Nazi infantry divisions proved the most fierce).

Some Germans he later saw had been taken prisoner by the demolition teams themselves. "A number

Land Seaman

of more adventurous and brave Navy demolition men walked up the beaches and got the Germans in bunkers to surrender. I heard they received special awards for their heroics."

Lt. Smith also ordered the team to help carry injured men on stretchers to the LCVPs for evacuation. "One of those wounded happened to be my buddy Steve Karatzas who was in the team that was hit. I later met Steve again in Oceanside, Calif., in the fall of 1944, and he said his doctors were still removing bone splinters from him that came from one or more of the men injured or killed around him that day.

"The first aid station (where he'd pick up the stretchers of wounded to carry) was situated just a few yards from my fox hole. Shortly after the evacuation of the injured, a shell hit that spot. I don't know if anyone was hit."

Gutekunst himself narrowly escaped a shell on the beach. "The night of D-Day I slept in my foxhole, using my helmet for a pillow. Because I thought that location too vulnerable, on D-Day-plus-one I dug a foxhole about 100 yards inland. Fortunately, on D-Day-plus 2, I again

Martin with his brother and mother on leave after the Normandy invasion. Martin is wearing the same uniform he wore to storm Utah Beach.

127

The Hero Next Door Returns

moved to the sea wall. That night, a shell hit the area I had been in the previous night, and left a huge crater."

The next day, their beach work done, the Army demolition men in Gutekunst's team moved inland while the Navy personnel remained on the beach. "While I stayed in my foxhole, an Army lieutenant came to me and ordered me to follow the Army infantry inland. Fortunately, Lt. Smith heard the order and pointed to the blue identification stripe. I was off the hook, though we were still under heavy fire by Nazi troops from their bunkers. But we didn't envy the Army guys going inland."

Many of Gutekunst's memories from those first three days of the Normandy invasion remain as vivid as they are difficult to recall.

"It was a sad thing on D-Day-plus-one to see all the bodies on the beach and those washed in with the tide. After a few days, we saw the bodies of the glider troops and paratroopers that missed their drop points and landed in a swamp and died. The decaying flesh created an awful stench. I was just numbed by it. You feel compassion of course but you're at a point where there's nothing you can do. You're almost in a daze after awhile. In fact a fellow I helped carry told me I looked like I was in a daze and I sure was. "

There was nothing Gutekunst could do but watch when American troops fired on their own.

"Twice in the first few days when American pilots strayed over the area—dipping their wings so we could see the distinctive markings—our troops shot down the planes. In one instance a number of men shot at two pilots after they bailed out and were coming down in parachutes. I asked one of the men why he shot at the pilot and he said it could have been a German. Fortunately, in both cases, the pilots appeared to escape serious injury."

Gutekunst and the Navy men rejoined the 2nd Beach Battalion on the third day and moved about half-mile

Land Seaman

inland.

"Until the rest of the 2nd Beach Battalion landed after D-Day we had only the K-rations we landed with. A better meal could be found by scavenging the beach starting on D-Day-plus-one. The landing craft that were sunk had cases of food in them and the tide washed the boxes ashore. All we had to do was pray the 88s didn't hit us while we looked for our favorite dish.

"After D-Day-plus-three, when the rest of the battalion landed, we had C-rations and they set up a field mess hall. I recall trading various C-ration cans of meat for the Wisconsin cheese I loved. Later, I recall cooking some precooked Boston beans in my mess kit on an open fire but, unfortunately, the blowing sand didn't help the seasoning."

Gutekunst stayed on Utah Beach for one month after landing, though the duty got considerably lighter as the days, and the threat of Nazi firepower, passed.

"We had little duty. We stood watch at the 2nd Beach Battalion headquarters at the sea wall. We could see many German gun emplacements protected by their concrete walls and roofs. These were placed for miles along the sea wall. We did snoop around the bunkers and found some that appeared booby-trapped. They all had scenery painted on the walls representing the area you would see if looking from that direction. Amazingly none of our bombing destroyed the bunkers we saw!

"Our beach area was hit by the German 88s for more than two weeks. By this time we knew the sound of those 88mm guns. They have a weird whistle, a sound that I recalled for years afterward. I observed that the one you hear you don't have to worry about because I'd watch a shell explode on the beach and a few seconds later actually hear the sound."

Day by day there was less threat of Nazi fire but still enough to be concerned.

"The total blackout meant Nazis dropped flares from their planes to try and find us. Flares remain sus-

The Hero Next Door Returns

pended for a considerable amount of time. The entire harbor was well lighted, though we didn't see any Nazi planes bombing our ships. Their bombings were aimed at land targets.

"Most of the time after those first few days, we saw the explosions in the distance. We were always alerted and warned in advance of enemy planes to get in our foxholes. One night, though, after the alert some of us didn't feel like jumping into the foxhole—because by this time most explosions were so far away. Then we heard the whistle of a dropping bomb. We made a mad dash for that foxhole!

"The Luftwaffe also did some strafing. I personally did not observe any one get hit but I heard one of the demolition men was killed by strafing. Another man died when he dug his foxhole too deep and was asphyxiated when sand collapsed around him. He was a 17-year-old who had been in the Navy for only two months."

Land mines were always a danger as well since the Germans had planted them throughout the beach and inland areas. "The Army de-mined areas but, after a few days, the white tape used to mark a de-mined area became so numerous you didn't know which side of the tape was safe. In fact, one vehicle path that had been used for three weeks had a mine explode when a lightweight truck passed over it—one man was blown up; the other was OK."

"The blackout also made it difficult to find our way from our camp to the beach office. Security guards checked everyone walking in the area at night and I was always concerned I'd forget the code word with consequences unknown."

For all that danger though Gutekunst survived D-Day and the days that followed almost uninjured. "The only injury I sustained happened in mess duty when opening a metal coffee can with a can opener. The pressure caused the coffee to squirt into my eyes and someone had to lead me to an Army field hospital to

Land Seaman

have my eyes washed out."

Perhaps the most memorable part of Gutekunst's time on Utah Beach was bearing witness to the sheer expansive power of the Allied invasion forces.

"The massive number of troops and supplies landing on Utah Beach astounded all of us, and our last look at the beachhead deserves comment. The thousands of ships of all types in the harbor were mind boggling. The Yankee ingenuity, the superior U.S. equipment, all left a lasting impression."

And yet, even in such massiveness, it is always a small world.

"On one occasion I hitched a ride from the beach to our area on an Army duck. The driver's voice was unmistakably that of a Petermann, Orville Petermann, from my hometown in New Fane, Wis. We celebrated our reunion with a meal of C-rations." Later, at a Petermann reunion in 1948, the two would share a meal with his cousin Lloyd—a grand feast by comparison—again with thanks that they had survived.

In letters home to his widowed mother from "somewhere in France," in June of 1944, Gutekunst described his Utah Beach perils, in the "not-so-bad" way most men described such details to their worried mothers back home.

June 14: *"I'm lying peacefully in my pup tent writing. Of course, I have my foxhole handy for all occasions. It sure is a lot better than when we came in on "D" Day. I still don't know how I missed the shrapnel but I guess it just shows how the Lord will protect in time of danger. ... I'm getting along very well in the outdoor life, getting enough to eat and enough sleep so all is well."*

June 19: *"Two weeks have gone by already over here in France. I'm still not suffering although my old bed would be more comfortable and those meals would be more appetizing. When I get back, I'll have to sleep in the backyard and sprinkle sand in my food to feel at home. ... Everything is OK so don't worry about me but pray and thank the Lord for protecting me."*

The Hero Next Door Returns

June 22: *"All's well over here in France. I haven't had any mail yet so I should get a lot of lowdown when it does come. Today, I took a bath in my helmet. I had a tough time getting in but made it OK. I have to do translating (Gutekunst grew up speaking German in Wisconsin) for a lot of fellows when they find some German literature. I never knew there were so many big words. It's a little different from the New Fane German."*

Gutekunst left the "not-so-bad" beach he described to his mother on July 6, 1944, bound for England, and eventually the U.S. for further training. But like that first day at sea the year before, Gutekunst's last day in the European Theater did not pass without incident.

"The night before we left, we had a final air raid, though we didn't suffer any damage. However, earlier that day, we had cleaned our area and burned our rubbish in one of the men's foxholes. So, when the sirens started that night, that man was almost frantic!"

Gutekunst thought as well to find a souvenir to take with him from Utah Beach. "Somewhere along the line I spotted a German helmet I wanted. I picked it up and there was a gunshot hole in it. When I turned it over, I saw part of the skull still in it. I gave up on helmets after that."

He left Utah Beach with more memories for souvenirs than he cared to carry.

A HERO'S WELCOME

Gutekunst traveled back to the U.S. through England and re-crossed the English Channel on the way. "The effects of the June storms were quite visible. Hundreds of small craft up to bigger ships were damaged and a large number had washed up to the sea wall.

"We received a hero's welcome back in England. The civilians were elated that the war was now progressing in the Allies' favor."

Gutekunst had little idea where the Navy communi-

Land Seaman

cations men would be going next and was happy to hear later in July that his next stop would be the U.S.A.

"We went aboard the AQUATANIA troop ship in late July from Glasgow, Scotland. Our 2nd Beach Battalion, a number of SeaBee personnel and some Normandy casualties were aboard. We had a calm crossing of the Atlantic to New York. As we approached everyone was on deck watching for the Statue of Liberty. There was a lot of excitement and noise until we saw the Statue of Liberty. Then there was complete silence as we passed by. It was a moment of respect and honor, which I am sure none of us will ever forget.

"Then at the dock a band was playing and I didn't even realize at first that it was for us. We were treated like heroes wherever we went, especially back home in Milwaukee. I didn't realize that everybody in the U.S.A. considered this operation a major, world-history-making event. After all, men and women were fighting every bit as much in many areas of the world before and after D-Day at Normandy without so much acclaim."

Gutekunst was given a 30-day leave and discovered he would soon join those men and women fighting in other parts of the world. He was to report to Oceanside, Calif. The battalion would split up and, at last, its troops would know their final destination ... they were going back into combat in a different ocean—the Pacific.

'FUN' IN THE SUN

Oceanside was a far better seaside view than the one Gutekunst had in Normandy. "We had a lot of liberty. There was nothing of interest in the city of Long Beach so we spent many nights watching old movies on the base. We legally had liberty every other weekend, but we often took liberty 'over the hill.' You just followed a well-worn path past the guards at the gate to a place where the fence was low enough to step over. Weekends when I stayed on base I'd appear for

The Hero Next Door Returns

muster along with a half dozen other men from a company of 100 answering 'here' for every name called. No one was ever reported; shore patrol never checked for passes. There were so many Navy and Marine personnel hitch-hiking you had to learn the technique of where to stand and how to sneak ahead of someone else."

Most of the time hitchhikers went into Los Angeles but Mexico and San Diego were also on the agenda. "I attended the Rose Bowl game Jan. 1, 1945, but the Rose Parade had been canceled."

Gutekunst's days of fun in the sun were short, however. The 100-man company—half radiomen, half signalmen—had combat landings to train for. "The beach had considerable LCVP traffic which created high sandbars. These sandbars, like in Normandy, made landings close to shore difficult. Sometimes the LCVP pilot could have gone in closer but, as the captain of the ship, it was his call. Consequently, many of these 'dry landings' resulted in a lot of soaking wet men."

Gutekunst also had classroom training for how an invasion force by sea operates. "As I recall, ships line up back from the shore prior to H-Hour to provide an organized movement. The LCVPs are launched from their mother ships and men in the first waves crawl down rope ladders to their LCVPs. After loading, each group of six or eight LCVPs forms a circle and keeps in a circle. There may be hundreds of these circle groups, each in their designated pattern. At H-Hour, the first wave peals off and heads inland. Shore personnel land first and vehicles on landing craft follow later. Heavy equipment follows even later."

In theory, it's a smooth, well-organized operation. In combat? Well, Gutekunst already knew landings had a way of turning organized design into functional chaos.

So, when their unit was broken again into new groups of 10 (five radio, five signal men)—with orders to ship all gear home except for skivvies, shorts, 1 pair dress whites, black shoes and personal items—Gutekunst knew such organized chaos would be waiting right around the corner.

The unit was temporarily transferred to the 6th Marines. "We had even been given Marine fatigues; I guess to confuse the enemy. But when we marched, everyone could tell we weren't Marines."

On Sept. 15, 1944, Gutekunst wrote to his family about his renewed combat concerns and tried to reassure them—and perhaps himself—that combat wouldn't be as bad the second time around.

"Dear Kinfolk: ... our future is very vague. ... We are in a Marine JASCO and I don't know when we will leave the area. Don't even know if it might be this week. It won't be too safe but I won't land in the first wave again. I don't look forward to any action with much desire for it, but I'll have to do it as the last time. Trust in the Lord."

On Jan. 4, 1945, Gutekunst and the out-of-step "Marines" in his group boarded the USS MANAFEE PA202 with no idea where they would be heading. "Certainly we were not looking forward to another invasion. As we approached land, one of the men recognized Diamond Head volcano on Oahu, Hawaii and we were soon hoping the Navy would lose us there for the duration."

The commissioned officers accompanying Gutekunst's units seem to disappear when they docked in paradise, Jan. 10. "The result was equally humorous and frustrating. We arrived in time for noon mess but our gear with our dress whites had not arrived from the ship. Since we were Navy personnel wearing Marine fatigues, we were not admitted into the Navy mess hall. The uniform of the day was Navy dungarees or dress whites. We also could not enter the ship's store to buy uniforms or get in to see the officer of the day without wearing the uniform of the day!"

Finally, the mess hall took pity on the mis-dressed servicemen and gave them special dispensation to

The Hero Next Door Returns

Gutekunst's friend Pete Long gets a shave on Okinawa.

enter. Still, the crews needed the right digs and ended up sending three volunteers to the ship's store to secure new uniforms, at each man's own expense.

"The Navy had many rules and regulations in Hawaii, and just as many Shore Patrols to enforce them! One time three of us were walking near the Royal Hawaiian Hotel and a Jeep with two SPs (shore patrol) came up. One SP jumped out and issued us 'tickets' for not having our hats squared properly. However, I don't think the SP was interested in following us to our next destination in the South Pacific to prosecute us!"

In fact, nothing came of the infraction but a good laugh. "We had to turn the citation in to the officer of the day back at camp. He said, 'what am I supposed to do? Put you in the brig!' It ended as a joke."

Except for a few regulatory entanglements, Gutekunst loved the tropical island. "Hawaii was everything I ever dreamed. Ever since geography class in grade school I thought Hawaii was the ultimate travel goal. At the time the Royal Hawaiian Hotel was majestic and isolated, compared to that area today. The hotel was primarily used as a rest and rehabilitation center for Navy submarine crews. We stayed in an isolated tent camp near Waimanalo where the surf was wonderful. We rode the surf using our belly in place of a surfboard. Except for losing a little skin, nothing more happened. It wasn't until years later that I learned that area had some of Hawaii's more dangerous surf."

Gutekunst had to abandon that paradise just a few weeks after he arrived. On Jan. 25, yet newer groups of 10—now separated from the 6th Marine designation—boarded the USS TETON GC14, a communications flagship. The 10-man groups were now called Beach Party Teams and Gutekunst was in BPT 38 under the direction of Lt. Spencer. "I never identified the meaning of the letters BPT to people back home because I thought they'd all envy me being in a beach party!"

ISLAND HOPPING

The communications groups were heading to a different Pacific island—this one more like hell than paradise. They were on their way to Okinawa, the last leap in the island hop the Allies had been conducting on their way to mainland Japan.

The ride there was no cruise. "The quarters were as tight as I've ever seen. Those on C deck were so tight that space between bunk layers was almost nonexistent. It was so small that men in the two lower bunks had to sleep on their backs or bellies. To turn over, you had to slide out of the bunk and slide in the other direction you wanted!

"Besides that, C deck was below the waterline. The hatches at the top of the ladder were secured during an alert. The thought of a direct hit and no escape passage was quite frightening."

To add insult to worry, the 10-man groups almost

The Hero Next Door Returns

couldn't get paid. "Because we'd been assigned temporarily to the ship, our records stayed in Hawaii and no records meant no pay. Finally, our officers convinced the pay officer that we were physically on board. Medical records, however, were no problem. Those, of course, came with us so we had to endure all the shots."

But the worst part of the trip was boredom. "We had absolutely no duties or responsibilities aboard ship for quite a few days. It was boring, even though we had a library—Perry Mason was my favorite—could play cards, watch old movies, sit on deck and watch flying fish or listen to scuttlebutt (rumors). In fact, for entertainment one morning, another man and I decided to create a rumor. By evening it had made the rounds on the ship and I heard it. I almost believed it myself until I realized who had started it!"

To help alleviate boredom, some signalmen practiced blinker signals using an unused light and shining it on the bulkhead. "We got quite proficient by using four or five syllable words from books. I can still read Morse code in blinker light. In fact, I used to use it to the consternation of our three children as Easter treasure hunt clues."

The groups' officer was able to eventually get the group assigned to bridge duty for four hours at a stretch. "No messages could be sent at night due to blackouts but it made life more interesting."

The sailors serving on the ship had little time to be as bored as their guests, however, Gutekunst is quick to add. "They were on duty every day of the week, morning to night with all types of make-work projects. The ships decks had so many layers of paint I swear it almost sank!"

The USS TETON hopped along the Pacific island chain, which the Allies had already re-conquered, stopping at the Marshall, Caroline, and Peleliu islands between Feb. 6 and 15. The stops weren't much of a respite for the sea-bored troops, however. "All these

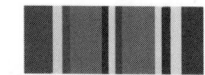

Land Seaman

islands were so desolate that it was hard to visualize them as strategic military bases. But it wasn't all bad. They did provide free beer to us on some of the island beaches, since it was against Navy regulations to serve alcohol on board."

The ship dropped anchor at its "final" destination, the Philippines, on Feb. 21. "We landed in Leyte at the spot where Gen. MacArthur had made his historic return earlier. I didn't see any reporters waiting for us when we landed though.

"My impressions of the Philippines at that time were that it was poor and smelly. I remember seeing women plowing with oxen." And in letters home he described the natives as "small and dirty," saying: *"I did see a couple of gals one day when I took a Jeep ride. They didn't look bad but then, I guess, I've been out here too long to be a judge. Their homes are like those you see in encyclopedias—straw roofs and loaded with lice. It's hard to tell the difference between the house and the barn because they look and smell alike. They work all their land, which is very poor. Farms are small and tombs take up most of the area. ... Prices are very high; they sell bananas for 25 cents a piece and small pineapples for 50 cents each. I sure wish I were back in England now for liberty."*

While in the Philippines, Gutekunst lived in tents a short distance from Tacloban where he practiced signal duty at a shore station tower. "Two people worked on a shift. One read the blinker signal; the other recorded. On one shift I was paired with an Army corporal and I began to gripe about having to be there, until he told me about his experience. He decided to get his one year of service in as was permitted in 1940 when he joined. When his year was up he was sent back to the U.S. His ship was actually in sight of San Francisco when the Japanese bombed Pearl Harbor. The ship turned 180 degrees and headed for Hawaii, and he went on to a number of combat experiences. He was not complaining, just resigned to his fate some

The Hero Next Door Returns

five years later, so I stopped griping for a short time at least."

Soon the troops began preparing for another D-Day, and Gutekunst volunteered to make wooden containers for transporting the signal equipment. "It was very interesting and rewarding work for me. The Army Air Corps graciously provided the lumber and hand tools—over the fence, no requisitions, no red tape. We had to hitch a ride to our ship and haul the items aboard."

Bootlegging supplies was not the problem; gaining access to the tools needed to assemble Navy equipment onboard a Navy ship proved more frustrating. "We needed to use the carpenter shop's table saw and welding machine but were continually denied until our officer went up the chain of command and down again to get permission."

The containers had to be portable enough to hand carry but big enough to hold the signal equipment, which included everything from the signal light to a gasoline driven motor generator for a power supply. "The box for our light had to be built with a dual purpose, not only would it be a closed container that would carry the light securely bolted inside, it would also later serve as the base upon which the light would be bolted."

Gutekunst's landing equipment list soon included five Jeeps, though he certainly didn't have to make containers for those! He was glad to hear they'd be bringing Jeeps because, with the equipment that large he knew he'd be going in later and "would not have the same type of conditions we had as the first waves in Normandy."

D-DAY 'DEJAVUE'

From the Philippines, Gutekunst and his team boarded the command LST in a convoy bound for another beach invasion, though which Pacific island beach remained a mystery for some time. "Many rumors as to the exact location of our next combat were spread and the Philippine civilians knew a lot more about where we were going than we did. They said it would be Okinawa and they proved to be correct."

Okinawa, a 700-square-mile island located some 350 miles from Japan, was a strategic necessity for the Allies if they hoped to invade mainland Japan—and all indications were such a bloody invasion would yet again be necessary.

But first, they had to capture that strategic island.

Gutekunst was on his way with tens of thousands of Army soldiers and Marines to do just that. The Navy communications man was onboard a flagship with Admiral Hall and his staff. "He had Army, Marines and Nisei in his staff. The Nisei were Japanese Americans who provided intelligence information and acted as translators. Everyone respected them, though they were segregated but I believe that was for security reasons."

Gutekunst spent Easter Sunday of 1945 watching the pre-invasion bombing and initial invasion from the deck of that LST offshore from Okinawa.

The watery mountain of men, ships and equipment was an awesome sight.

"When we first arrived off the coast March 31, 1945, there were hundreds of ships of all types. It was dark and all observed complete blackout. We, aboard BPT38, were told to stay below deck, but we didn't want to get caught in our compartment with the hatches secured. So, despite orders, we stayed on deck in case we were hit.

"Soon the firing started and it was Normandy all over. Ships were hit, including the ship I knew Lloyd Petermann, from my hometown, was on and I wondered if he was OK. The sky was filled with tracers and exploding shells."

There was much less resistance at first on this D-Day. There was so little resistance the first days of April 1945 that "five hours after the first Marines were

The Hero Next Door Returns

ashore, they had captured one vital air strip and not a shot had been fired," reports C. L. Sulzberger in *The American Heritage Picture History of W.W. II.*

On D-Day-plus 2, Gutekunst and his team went ashore on the so-far-quiet beach, lugging all their heavy communication equipment onto the beachhead. "We had to take all our gear with us, our signal light, generator, etc.."

The worst part of Gutekunst's second D-Day proved logistical. "The beach had so much coral that LCVPs could not go close enough. Because of the amount of heavy gear we had, we had to stop at a floating dock section, unload and reload onto a vehicle that looked like a tank but could float and had tracks that could overcome the coral.

"Okinawa did not have the high tides that Utah Beach did, so the type of landing craft we used (LCVPs) were not as effective in Okinawa. Also, since they first went in at night it was too dark to see many of the obstacles. Getting supplies and troops was more difficult in Okinawa. The terrain in general, though, was very flat with many rice fields, especially near the beach where the terrain was almost a wasteland.

"We dug in near the beach and set up radio communications but no visual station. We set up pup tents and alternately slept in fox holes and on the ground in tents."

Then, on April 6 and 7, the Japanese resistance finally struck. "700 enemy aircraft, including some 350 kamikazes, pounded the American beachheads and task forces assembled off shore," Sulzberger further detailed. The bloodshed continued as soldiers and Marines moved inland. It took 82 stubborn days of fighting to clear the island. (Though months afterwards Japanese hiding in caves were still found.)

Still, mild or fierce, fighting of any kind still brings hard memories with it.

"One thing that's always bothered me is something that happened in the first days on the beach. There

Land Seaman

were some Navy personnel down the beach a ways from our position. Our Navy guns shot down some fighters. When one plane was shot down there was further tragedy. The small boats in the harbor continued shooting their 20mm guns after the plane was hit and was dropping to the ground. They followed it down and sprayed the beach a few hundred feet from where we were dug in. I heard that killed 130 Navy personnel. Later, on the night shift, I had radio duty. An admiral came on and gave a report about it and while doing so he was crying. Who said admirals don't cry?"

After those first 10 days or so, the communications groups moved inland a little farther and set up tents for radio and visual communications, at a higher elevation, from which they could send blinking signals to ships and receive messages for the troops now moving inland.

They were also close enough to see and visit the many cemeteries the inland-moving troops built. "A careful walk in the area was a tragic sight. The open fields were now massive cemeteries. Watching the troops marching inland, one wondered how many would return alive and how many would fill up another cemetery."

There were many more to fill the cemeteries. By the time the struggle for the island was declared over, more than 12,000 Americans and 110,071 Japanese were dead *(p. 588, The American Heritage Picture History of W.W. II)*.

The bunker area where Gutekunst lived was still bombed regularly. "I think we averaged about three alerts in a 24-hour period and some bombings came at night. The targets were our supply dumps. When they hit ammunitions or fuel, there were a lot of flames and fireworks. At night, to mask the area, the Army used many fog machines and the whole area became fogged in, which made it difficult to find our way. However, I generally felt safe in our position because Japs were going after the supplies."

The Hero Next Door Returns

Safe was a relative term, however.

Accidental friendly fire—aimed at those incoming planes—continued to be a danger on the beach as well.

"Our forces had giant spotlights to spot enemy planes at night. When they did, our 20mm tracers and 5-inch gun shells filled the sky but I never saw any reach the planes flying high above us. The resulting shrapnel dropping to the ground was so extensive one could not walk barefoot on the beach. And, the shrapnel could be dangerous too. In one instance shrapnel hit one of our bunks where a man had been sitting moments before."

Some were not so lucky. "Besides combat, there were many tragic accidents in war. One of the Seabees tried to light a fire with gasoline and caught himself on fire. He started running until two of his shipmates ran after him and put him out. He was in severe pain when they carried him off in a stretcher. It was not a pleasant sight or sound.

"Another time, a number of men in a tent were having a party. They used ditto fluid *(alcohol used to clean ditto [copy] machines)* mixed with grape juice. The next morning, one man was dead, another dying, another temporarily blind, and a fourth had flushed face but recovered. He was from the Kentucky hills and was probably immune to the effects of 'corn liquor.'"

The fighting may not have been as fierce but the weather on Okinawa proved more troublesome than Normandy.

"There was an awful lot of rain in Okinawa and it made everything more difficult. When we first built a bomb shelter on the side of the hill, we woke the next morning to find it filled with mud and the bunks floating away in the rain. So we gave up on that endeavor in favor of our foxholes.

"Then, there were rather nasty insects. The worst were these little insets that got into your belt area and just itched at you. Finally we had to boil our clothes

and they sprayed the area with DDT to take care of it."

And, like all Pacific troops, Gutekunst had to guard against malaria and other jungle diseases. But, he must have let his guard down on Okinawa. "I'd been taking Atabrine tablets but I still may have gotten a touch of malaria. I often hitched rides to our ship where most of our gear was stored in lockers. I went aboard for some of my clothing and decided to eat in the mess hall. Before I got to the food I suddenly developed a severe case of chills and fever and headed for sick bay. While getting an examination I made a big mess of the place. The corpsman said it appeared to be malaria but the test did not confirm it. Meanwhile, I had not returned to camp and they sent someone to the ship to find me. I must have been in the head (bathroom) when the man looked for me. The next day, when I returned to camp, I discovered that they were getting ready to visit the grave registration to see if I was there."

Boredom could be almost as irritating, as the troops did what they could to make spare time pass more quickly. "We played cards or took walks well behind our friendly troops. Also, I maintained the motor generators, sometimes in the middle of the night, and did some carpenter work. Once there were no more alerts we also watched a lot of movies in Okinawa, weather permitting. Aboard ship, I read many books—as many as one a day!"

But, on the beach, there was work to do. "Signal duty was interesting but the messages we always had to our station just said 'here's a copy for you,' and didn't talk about taking any kind of action. I wondered what the purpose of our unit was.

"Daily we listened to the radio we hooked up in the signal station. We turned on the military station and heard reports regularly about how our planes and picket ships were destroyed by enemy fire. The picket ships surrounded the entire island and were very im-

The Hero Next Door Returns

portant for protection of our air power and us on the beach. However, they were very vulnerable to Kamikaze and other attacks.

"We had a system of alerts from 'all clear' to 'unidentified' to 'enemy planes in the area.' On two occasions in broad daylight, two Kamikaze planes came over the ships in the harbor. One plane was shot down before hitting a ship; the other hit a ship and killed and injured many on board. I felt safer at the signal station than aboard a ship."

Even the latrines proved explosive. "On one occasion someone decided to kill all the flies in our Navy head (latrine). He poured fuel oil into the hole and lit it. He killed all the flies to be sure, but he burned down the outhouse too! So, I looked for another latrine close by and found a nice one. But, while I was there, a black soldier came in and informed me it was for 'Negroes only.'"

The men probably spent most of their time thinking of—and trying not to think of—home, however.

Home seemed farther away than ever, and any news from America was a Godsend. Much of the correspondence took place via V-Mail, which was faster than letters and allowed more space to write than a telegram. "I always tried to keep things positive because my mother was a worrier," as he did in a letter he wrote her on April 15, 1945:

"*Dear Mom: Suppose you've worried about me by this time. I'm still OK and, as you might have guessed, I've been in another invasion. Wasn't so bad as my last, but I'd still prefer to invade Milwaukee ... I probably won't be home as soon after this one either. Life isn't bad here except for lice; they sure drained a lot of blood out of me already. ... I'm sorry I can't give any information about my location but perhaps you can guess by the newspapers. ... Don't worry about me. Prayer and faith in the Lord comforts me and I know it comforts you too.*"

Gutekunst's letters could never be too detailed because they were heavily censored. "I always tried to

get something past the censors though. It became sort of a game. I gave my buddies in Milwaukee our longitude and latitude on Okinawa by using street addresses in Milwaukee and I mentioned one woman and gave her the first name of Manila. Then, when we were in Plymouth England, I said the place reminded me of my cousin (who lived in Plymouth, Wis.)."

YET ANOTHER D-DAY?

After two months communicating ship to shore on the beach, Gutekunst and his team reboarded a ship and headed for Subic Bay in the Philippines, training to serve on yet a third invasion force—one set to invade mainland Japan.

The unit did a lot of "dry landing," wading waist deep from landing craft to shore while carrying all the visual and radio equipment high enough so it didn't get wet.

Such preparations made Gutekunst uneasy. This D-Day would be much more like Utah Beach, probably worse.

"We knew that as horrible as anything before that was, this would be worse. We knew we would be among the first going in as communications teams landing on—it was rumored—a beach in Southern Japan.

"So, when we heard that the atomic bombs were dropped, we were stunned by the power of this one bomb but were all relieved that we didn't have to partake in what probably would have been the bloodiest and most costly battle. Everyone I knew felt President Truman made the correct decision. We were all very much aware of the fierce fighting the Japanese were capable of in defense of their cause. They would rather die than surrender and I think those bombs saved our lives."

The Japanese surrendered Aug. 14. "We celebrated by calling short our dry landings. Censorship of mail ceased and suddenly I didn't know what to write be-

The Hero Next Door Returns

cause I'd always been trying to outwit and irritate the censors!"

The war may have been over but Gutekunst would not be going home. In fact, he would still land in Japan. This time, though, the invasion force marched in peacefully as a post-war presence.

"Everyone, of course, calculated their points to go home and I had more than enough. But, with my records still in Hawaii, there was nothing I could do about it. Though I could have been sent back to the U.S., I was thrilled to see Batangas, Philippines, along the way and take part in the Navy occupation force in Japan."

Gutekunst was among the troops stationed in Yokohama, Japan. "We came into Tokyo harbor the same day Japan signed the surrender, Sept. 2, 1945. We weren't close enough to see the personnel but we could see the USS MISSOURI where the Japanese signed their surrender. It was a relief to know the war was over."

Gutekunst spent two months in Japan, operating ship to shore communications. "We set up a communications center in a dock warehouse. We slept on cots along with lice-infested rats that climbed the walls and mosquitoes that were a constant bother even with mosquito netting around our cots. We also had our first experience with the squat-down toilet facilities; so there were no problems with anyone staying too long in there."

They also had their first introduction to Japanese civilians—a cool reception at first.

"The Japanese avoided contact with us and would cross the street when we approached. The Army must have taken their tallest men to march around Yokohama for a show of our strength and control. The Japanese soon warmed up when we showed no animosity toward them. They were also interested in our cigarettes for which we paid 50 cents a carton and sold for up to $40 a carton, though the price dropped

Land Seaman

as more Americans came in. One non-smoker made $700 while we were there, but I spent most of my 'fortune' on souvenirs—which were cheap by today's prices though most were very inferior quality."

The troops also took in native shows and were entertained by the likes of Leo Durocher and Danny Kaye. "Though we complained continually, we did enjoy many activities and participated in world events we did not appreciate until almost 50 years later."

Those events included a typhoon in September, 1945. *"We had a big typhoon here yesterday and today," he wrote his mother. "So far I haven't heard of much damage. The wind was so strong for a while I thought our tower was going to head for home with me in it!"*

When he wasn't holding down the signal tower, Gutekunst wandered around the devastated city. "Yokohama had a great amount of destruction; however the U.S. embassy remained intact. I told an Air Corps pilot that they must have been very accurate and he said he believed it was 'just luck.'"

"The Japanese were also destitute and hungry. For a small fee they'd do our laundry and we referred to them as 'washy-washy.' They would stand at the exit of the mess hall and grab leftovers we dumped into garbage cans. Grabbing food out of the garbage turned our stomachs but we had empathy for them. In no way did we demean them. The war was over. As far as I was concerned we did what our country said we should; they did what theirs ordered and we were now friends."

Gutekunst was happy not to stay long enough to get to know the Japanese any better though. Two months after his arrival he got word that they would be shipping out again—this time for home.

The beach invasion veteran picked up a Japanese rifle for a souvenir and boarded THE PROTEUS, a subtender that later served nuclear submarines. Gutekunst had a short layover in Guam "where we were able to visit a Jap submarine that could launch

149

The Hero Next Door Returns

planes. It looked like a huge bowling alley and the planes would catapult from the bow door."

When the ship reached Hawaii on Nov. 15, home was still further off than Gutekunst imagined.

"By the time I got there, they had finally shipped my records to the Philippines so I had to wait a few more weeks. When the papers finally came through the yeoman said 'you should have been out a long time ago.' If it weren't for the fact that I was now leaving for home, I was tempted to push his head down his shirt!"

Gutekunst boarded the USS NEVADA Nov. 25, "it was the sixth time I walked up and down gang planks, but my rifle continually slid off my shoulder because, with all the other gear, the rifle with a bayonet kept catching on the railings."

On board Gutekunst decided some of his souvenirs might prove too cumbersome back in the states "so someone found a buyer for the rifle, a quick decision I've never regretted. Some of my other military souvenirs from Okinawa also didn't survive the trip, including a U.S. grenade and a small Japanese bomb with a propeller on it designed to float down to earth (both defused). I pitched them through the port hole as I was anxious to get out without a hitch."

By Dec. 1, the ship was docking at Long Beach, Calif., complete with a welcoming band. But, Gutekunst was more exhausted than excited to be home. "I don't know if it was the fact that the war was over or if it was battle fatigue that caused me not to have the same thrill I had passing the Statue of Liberty after Normandy. It seems to me that Europe was more of a gung-ho feeling. The Pacific fighting was too spread out for that; there was no one main push to really rally around like there was in Europe."

After a debriefing and a weekend pass in Long Beach—complete with newly issued uniforms—the troops were at last on their way to their final destination.

"We had so many men on the train to the U.S. Naval

Land Seaman

Martin and Lois Gutekunst revisited Utah Beach in 1984 and are standing on the exact spot where Gutekunst went ashore.

Personnel Separation Center at Great Lakes, Ill. that we had to sleep two to a lower berth. An advantage to having been promoted to Signalman 3rd Class was I was exempted from mess hall duty on the train—not that mess hall duty lasted as long as the trip. Our food supply was two days shorter than our trip and we were anxious and hungry by the time we disembarked Dec. 13."

HOME AT LAST

A 28-year-old Gutekunst finally returned to the Badger State Dec. 16, 1945, to the welcoming cool air of a Wisconsin winter. "It was the greatest homecoming, and the cold, after the tropics, was so refreshing. I just couldn't believe I really made it!"

He spent much of his first few months just trying to catch up. "I missed four weddings, including two of my sisters' and two brothers', and some of my nieces and nephews were born while I was gone."

Gutekunst returned to work, as a draftsman, at Mil-

The Hero Next Door Returns

waukee Boiler Manufacturing Co. and took some courses on the GI Bill. He retired as chief engineer of quality control 45 years later. While the company became famous for boilers during the war years, Gutekunst worked on designing pressure vessels for tunnel construction. "I designed the compressed air locks that kept the underground water out of the tunnels. The first time I had to go down in one of those tunnels, though, I was scared. That is until I remembered who had designed the locks!"

Shortly after coming home, Gutekunst met Lois Marquardt in a young people's group at Mt. Calvary Lutheran Church. They were married in 1948 and had three children, daughters in 1952 and '56 and a son in '53. They lived in Milwaukee for eight years before moving to Brookfield, Wis. in 1956. They retired to Oconomowoc in 1990.

Together they dedicated a great deal of time to their churches, she belonging to the Lois Club, he to the Martin Club. Gutekunst is also a VFW and American Legion member. In addition to holding many church offices over the years, Gutekunst currently serves as president of the Oconomowoc AARP and belongs to several engineering societies. He is also a registered professional engineer with the State of Wisconsin. He and his wife have also dedicated a great deal of time to their passion for traveling, visiting 30 foreign countries and 49 states so far.

Above all else Gutekunst remains ever grateful to God, he stresses, for not just sparing him on the beaches of W.W.II but for blessing him with such a wonderful life afterwards. "Life in general has been great. The 50-plus years of married life, the children, a very satisfying occupation. All these blessings were by God's direction. Our family, my family, and I praise God for his generosity."

They also praise the men and women who fought with Gutekunst to save the world more than 55 years ago. "Though it was not by choice, I am proud to have

Land Seaman

served my country in combat and I'm very proud of the men I served with. We should all be proud of them."

THE WAR
IN THE PACIFIC

THE WAR IN THE PACIFIC

In this section you'll come to know a small sampling of the Wisconsinites who fought with hundreds of thousands of Allies to free the Pacific Islands and much of Asia from the stronghold of Imperial Japan. These *Heroes Next Door* include:

• **Marvin Langeteig,** a tech sergeant with Wisconsin's 32nd Red Arrow Division who fought in some of the earliest land battles against the Japanese to reclaim New Guinea and the Philippines.

• **Art Orlowski,** a Milwaukee boy who altered his birth certificate to join the Marine Corps when he was barely 16 and saw combat from Guam to Okinawa by the time he was old enough to vote.

• **Earl Baumgart,** a submariner aboard the ill-fated USS FLIER who swam enemy-held waters with seven surviving crewmates from desolate island to more desolate island before being rescued by Philippine guerilla fighters.

• **Dave Brenzel,** an Army artilleryman who "dodged" the draft by enlisting in the Army in 1939 and was taken prisoner by the Japanese in May of 1942—and survived 40 months as a prisoner of war.

• **George Watson,** a Navy corpsman aboard the USS FRANKLIN who lived to tell the amazing tale of a ship—and a crew—that refused to quit.

• **Marion Dorfmeister,** an Army nurse who tended wounds and held worried hands at the 54th General Hospital in Hollandia, New Guinea.

• **Gus Boerner,** a U.S. Marine who arrived among replacement troops in time to survive fierce fighting on Okinawa and serve his country in post-war China.

RED ARROW MAN
Marv Langeteig

For most Americans W.W. II began on Dec. 7, 1941. But, for Marvin Langeteig and a division's worth of Wisconsin fighting men, the war began much earlier—in the spring of 1941—when Langeteig was drafted into the Wisconsin National Guard's 32nd Division.

Nicknamed the Red Arrow Division, the 32nd became the first National Guard unit to be mobilized into federal service in W.W. II when, in September of 1940, the U.S. government began drafting men into the National Guard and regular military in anticipation of heated confrontations as the war in Europe escalated. However, seemingly no one envisioned the worldwide combat these early servicemen—and America—would soon encounter.

Wisconsin's 32nd Division draftees little anticipated what awaited them when they began their one year of required duty. By the time the then looming world war was over, members of the 32nd Red Arrow Division would have served more than 13,000 hours in combat in the Pacific from 1942 and 1945—the equivalent of working some eight hours a day seven days a week for five years.

According to the *32nd Division: "Les Terribles"* by

The Hero Next Door Returns

Dave Turner, the division was the first to go into action at the foot of the road back to Japan and would still be fighting when the cease fire came Aug. 15, 1945. Eleven Red Arrowmen won the Congressional Medal of Honor—all posthumously—during those days, including three Wisconsinites—First Sgt. Elmer Burr of Menasha, Sgt. Kenneth Greunnert of Jefferson and Staff Sgt. Gerald Endl of Janesville.

The Red Arrow Division faced 543 days of hard combat—which the book *13,000 Hours: Combat History of the 32nd Infantry Division—World War II* called "days of death and destruction, of disease and hunger and thirst, of pain and agony and self sacrifice."

Langeteig had little concern that he'd be called into the looming fray when he was drafted in spring of 1941. Then came Dec. 7, 1941, and the surprise Japanese attack on Pearl Harbor, Hawaii. The news reached Langeteig while he was doing K.P. duty at Camp Livingston, La., and the one-time farmhand knew his country's call would last longer than he'd envisioned.

"The night before was the one and only time I've ever gotten drunk in my life. And, the morning of Dec. 7, 1941, was the one and only time I had K.P. duty while in uniform. I recall sitting on a stool peeling potatoes when the radio blared the news. Besides the shock of it, all I could think was, 'well, I'm not going home anytime soon.'"

"Not soon," proved an understatement. The DeForest High School graduate did not see Wisconsin again for four years.

ON ALERT

Langeteig was still a newlywed when he and some 350 National Guardsmen left Madison for Milwaukee induction and joined a shipment of hundreds of Wisconsinites to Camp Grant in Rockford, Ill. "That first day in Milwaukee we stood there naked all day while they gave us shots and checked us over before shipping us on."

Red Arrow Man

At 22, other Guardsmen considered Langeteig an old draftee but he was by no means the oldest Red Arrow Division member. "Some guys were 35 or 37 years old!"

Youthful years of hard work on the farm and in a cannery before being drafted had prepared Langeteig well for the monotony and labor of Army training. But, the Dane County native found a few quirks of military training he wasn't quite sure how to handle.

"When we were called out for roll call, they never called my name. The sergeant asked me my name, which I told him. He thought a second and then said 'I called your name a long time ago but I didn't pronounce it like that.'" Pronunciation aside, Langeteig was in the Army now!

"Thirteen weeks of basic training (at Camp Livingston, La.) consisted of nothing but one order after another but we made it in spite of missing home and doing little on our so-called free time, except running, hiking, push-ups—always with a pack on our backs."

Langeteig spent October and November of 1941 on maneuvers around Louisiana, Georgia and the Carolinas. He even became familiar with the "old fashioned" Army cavalry. "The Army had not retired their cavalry yet and we liked their horses. While we were 'playing war' we would sneak in and let their horses loose during the night, but only the horses were happy about it!"

By December of 1941, after Pearl Harbor, training and military life got more serious. The 32nd Division spent a great deal of time on alert and "packing and unpacking" in anticipation of shipping out to destinations unknown.

"We were always on alert and there were no more passes. We prepared and waited many times, and preparing meant completely packing and waiting and then unpacking and waiting and then packing and waiting all over again. It was like 'get ready, we're leaving for good ... no go back to your tent.' We supposedly were

The Hero Next Door Returns

Marvin and Laverne Langeteig posed in Massachuesetts next to the car Laverne put thousands of miles on to visit her husband at training posts across the U.S.

confusing the enemy."

In between alerts, Langeteig was able to steal some lasting moments with his new wife Laverne (Mueller), when she came to visit. Langeteig met the Ong, Neb., native in 1939 on a blind date to an Eagles Club Dance, arranged through relatives Langeteig was living with in Madison while he worked for Oscar Mayer. They were married March 23, 1941, just a few weeks before Langeteig received his unexpected draft notice.

Since that brief honeymoon, the newlyweds had lived married life apart with Laverne driving down to wherever her husband may be stationed and Langeteig making the most of his leave time to be together.

After the Pearl Harbor attack, visiting time grew more complicated and, they suspected, time together was growing short.

"I was glad to see her even if getting together was

Red Arrow Man

not easy. When she and a friend drove down to see me for a few weeks one time, we went on alert a lot. Laverne and the other girls (wives) were never informed as to what was going on. One alert she and a friend came out to camp, but there was so much traffic at the gate that she was forced to take the narrow shoulder and our car came to rest against the right bank of the road just outside the main gate. Somehow the girls had enough smarts to get the car out and 'back in action' and all was well. I didn't learn about any of this until our alert for that period was over."

But, Langeteig would soon wish the alert periods had lasted longer. At least Laverne could visit. Where the alerts were preparing him to go, there would be few welcomed visitors.

The mock alerts ended in January 1942, and Langeteig received orders to pack up for good. The unit was moving out to Fort Devens, Mass.

"I received permission to drive our car to Massachusetts. I had Laverne and two other wives along. When we got there, the couples all lived in the same house in Leominster, Mass. We each had a room in the police chief's home. I went to Fort Devons for training and Laverne went to work in a novelty store for a while. By this time I'd been promoted to private first class and my Army pay had jumped to $39 a month, up from $30. It went to $42 per month when I was named corporal soon after" (and eventually reached $120 a month when he made tech sergeant).

Soon, the 32nd was on alert again. This time the whole division boarded a train for Canada, at least that's what they thought. "We headed north toward Canada, but the train went south again through Illinois, then West, then South and soon Northwest. We wound up in Ogden, Utah, where we got off the train, ran for blocks and blocks and boarded the train and headed northwest and then south again before arriving in Fort Ord, Calif.—again, all to confuse the enemy."

The Hero Next Door Returns

The division spent several weeks in California training in eight-man rafts and learning how to get on and off a ship. "We trained boarding a ship on the starboard side, crossing the deck and getting off on the other side into our rafts again and riding the surf back to shore. All the rafts upset coming in because we sure didn't know how to handle them. We never got very good at it but no one drowned."

Wet clothes were little discomfort, however, compared to the gnawing feeling the Arrowmen had that they would soon see combat, though they knew not where. With all the confusion tactics used thus far, being in California did not seem to guarantee the 32nd would be Pacific Theater-bound.

But, Pacific-bound they were.

TRAINING DOWN UNDER

By April 22, 1942, the 32nd Division was aboard a converted luxury liner, which after 25 seasick days, had little luxury left. "Wow! Were some of the guys sick! Some were getting sick before the Golden Gate Bridge was even out of sight!"

In May, 1942, the division landed in Adelaide, Australia. The Japanese were literally just island footsteps away from the Australian mainland and the troops had been sent there to prevent them from reaching it. If you had to serve somewhere in the war-torn Pacific, the Australian coast was a beautiful place to be. Still, even paradise has its trying moments.

"We were put on charcoal burning trucks for a ride north into the Mount Lofty Mountain Range. These trucks were so loaded with men that the truck would run out of fuel and the driver would have to stop and fire it up again."

Eventually, the 32nd chugged its way to Camp Cable, a row of converted sheep sheds with a pot-bellied stove on each end that would be its home for the next several months. "When the wind blew, the center didn't get any heat. We spent those weeks conditioning with marches day after day. Some excursions would last several days and we were to live off the land. There were days we ate better off the land than we did in camp. We would pool our money and find some farmer in the hills and pay him well for chicken eggs, even ham and milk. We left some happy farmers up there."

With Japanese troops landing in Hollandia and Wewak, New Guinea, the division soon had to leave its egg supply behind, however, and board trains for Brisbane, Australia. It was an intriguing ride, much different than American rail travel. "As one travels in Australia, you discover the railroad gauge (track width) changed size. At each state line, trains would pull alongside each other and shift all the equipment from one train to another and then go on to the next state line and do it all over again."

After arriving at their Brisbane "camp site," the work began. "We were in the middle of nowhere and had to clean up an area of all kinds of scrub vegetation, junk and vermin. We started setting up our pup tents in rows without a single one out of line. Then intensive jungle training began, which meant cleaning and re-cleaning all our equipment and then hiking the terrain there—as many as 30 miles in one day."

Soon, troops added packing back onto the list of chores, this time with the uneasiness of knowing *what* they were packing for, if not yet *where*.

"We still weren't sure exactly where we were going. We were all in wool uniforms when we boarded a train to Townsend, Australia, and then boarded transport planes (DC3s). We had wool uniforms so the enemy would assume we were going someplace cold; the rumor was the Aleutian Islands."

After landing at the Australian base at Port Moresby, on New Guinea's southern tip, 14,900 men of the 32nd Division knew "cold" would be as far away as heaven from the heat of hell and battle they were in now. The wool uniforms were soon discarded in favor of "jungle

The Hero Next Door Returns

jeans."

The Japanese by now were just 32 miles from Port Moresby, which—at the southwestern base of New Guinea—was a dangerously close 340 miles from Australia. The 32nd Division's 128th and 126th Regimental Combat Teams had joined Australian troops just in time.

JUNGLE HEAT

Tech Sgt. Langeteig's command of 39 men—including four corporals, a kitchen crew, a medic and a sergeant that formed part of the division's 128th Infantry antitank company—were soon taken into the New Guinea jungle. Their job was to help keep the Japanese on the other side of the Owen Stanley Mountains and eventually push them north and off of the world's second largest island for good. It was a goal that would take nearly two years to achieve.

Those two years began with a nerve-wracking plane trip into the jungle. "We flew over the mountains so low to avoid being spotted that the wingtips appeared to shake the tree tops. We landed on a grass strip with grass at least a foot or two high. When the pilot got her stopped he turned and said, 'OK everybody out!' Of course, at that time, everybody thought it was funny. We all got out as fast as possible and the plane turned around, took off and disappeared."

The 128th was now alone in a strange land and the challenge of the jungle loomed ahead. "We only had our backpack with a change of clothes, blanket, and mosquito bar, and two belts of ammo and our two days ration. When we headed into the jungle for 10 days we were supposedly pursuing Japs, who by now were headed back to Buna to set up their fronts. We received supplies from the air, dropped by the same planes that flew us in. At that point the U.S. didn't have many planes and as of then we had seen just three U.S. fighters and saw and heard Jap planes aplenty."

Moving and sleeping in the wet heat of the jungle

was hard to bear. "It was drudgery to carry so much, so we got rid of the woolen blanket and got rid of everything—even cigarettes—just so you wouldn't have to carry them. It rained a lot and you couldn't distinguish thunder from artillery shells. It was very wet but never cold. There were many times we laid down in water and just slept in the water. But, we learned not to lay down too long against our mosquito bar because if we did our buttocks or elbow—or whatever was resting on it—would swell up more than twice its size."

Langeteig at camp in New Guinea in 1944.

To get the troops off the wet ground, the Army later tried to issue hammocks to make use of the jungle's many trees. "They had a little roof and mosquito netting and were probably comfortable but not very practical. Even in the jungle, there wouldn't be enough trees to supply 400-500 guys with hammock space. Plus, when air raid sirens sounded you didn't have time to unzipper and climb out. And, hammocks hold a lot of water so they made better bathtubs than beds."

Langeteig's company was more concerned at first about their uncomfortable surroundings than the prospect of combat. "It wasn't a matter of being scared

The Hero Next Door Returns

because we didn't know what was next. After our first combat, when we learned what was next, things were different."

Though those first 10 days saw more foliage than fighting, the introduction to jungle life wasn't an easy adjustment. "The jungle was a mess to fight in, even walk in. You can't see 50 feet ahead of you, and at night it's darker than pitch dark. In fact, in the jungle we had a squad positioned out front for a listening post and would have to switch places at night. In the daytime we strung vines to follow out there but, when you ran into someone coming the other way in the dark on that vine, it was quite a fright because you couldn't see if it was a Jap or not until they identified themselves or until the fight was over. Though it didn't happen with my platoon, fighting broke out on the vines even if it was one of your own men because you couldn't tell who it was."

The division made its way through all the jungle's mud, rain, more mud, and more rain, crossing many rivers on foot.

"We crossed rivers every day and we were always wet. Some rivers were not even two feet deep but so swift we'd have to form a line of men hanging on to one another to get across. Other rivers were so deep we had to hold our equipment over our heads, and when you were in the middle, the current would start to take you and you'd just hope you didn't go too far into enemy lines. Like many guys there, I couldn't swim. It didn't matter too much though because, with all that equipment over your head, it's not like there was much chance for swimming anyway.

"When they were not passable, natives ferried us across rivers with outrigger canoes. We passed through many native villages and saw some sorry sights—at least we thought so since we'd never been exposed to this type of history. The natives we encountered wore traditional, over-sized loin cloth (rags) around their lower body and the women had skirts of many materials and were topless—yes, all of them. It wasn't long before they all looked the same though for their droops.

"The villages were native homes of bamboo and palm fronts with no doors, windows or floors nor any furniture. Whatever else they had that wasn't jungle grown was handmade. Disease among the natives was quite evident. They lived through whatever problems they had. Elephantiasis of body parts was seen in several villages; one man had one testicle so large he sat on it and carried it around like a bag. Legs on some of them looked like elephant legs. The scenes didn't always help your appetite.

"They were all friendly, though. In fact, some would run pack (supply) lines for us in the morning and for the Japanese in the afternoon."

The jungle was made tougher by the lack of decent food.

"Needless to say, there wasn't much to find dead or alive. There was no edible vegetation that we knew of. There weren't even coconuts in the jungle; those are just on the shorelines. There were no such things as stores or any other structures for food storage where we might scrounge something, though we did try supplementing rations with the big parrots on the island but they were tough and probably just too old. And, we would have tried pigs but the natives considered them sacred; we even saw some native women nursing little pigs."

After some 10 days, Langeteig's unit left the jungle and found the shoreline. But the water proved little comfort. "We were fed our first full meal since leaving Australia and then were loaded, some 50 men each, on some fishing boats and taken north. Of course, after such a meal on idle stomachs, the boat ride over rough waters quickly produced many fannies hanging over the sides, all just shining in the moonlight!"

Parts of the 32nd Division—less that last meal—gathered in Pongani, just 25 miles south of Buna by Nov.

The Hero Next Door Returns

2, 1942. While much of the division arrived via similar routes to Langeteig's company, the 2nd Battalion of the 126th Infantry paid a high price just to get to the official battle lines. The battalion marched and fought its way over the rugged, 8,000-foot high Owen Stanley Mountains in a trip that took 42 ration-poor, disease- and combat-filled days. Those that made it arrived "with weapons, ammunition, a cup and spoon and the tattered, sweat-stained, mold-stinking battle dress they had worn ever since leaving Port Moresby," reports *13,000 Hours*.

They may have arrived, but there certainly was no sanctuary waiting for them. "There were no such things as bathrooms or showers any time we were in New Guinea. There were no washcloths and we just used our slit trenches, the ocean and rivers. We just lived" under conditions Turner echoes in *Les Terribles* that were: "abysmal," and allowed malnutrition, disease and tropic heat to further deplete the ranks.

BATTLE WEARY

The division's orders were to take and hold the airstrip near Buna in an offensive that began Nov. 15—with the 128th joining the 126th to make the initial attack—and lasted into January, 1943. "This was our first big introduction to the Japs in a battle referred to as the Buna Campaign."

While U.S. Marine battles at Guadalcanal earned many of the headlines of the day, "hollow-eyed with jungle fever and hunger," the Army troops in the Buna Campaign met with combat that "was every bit as savage, and the cost in dead and wounded was even higher." (Reported C.L. Sulzberger in *The American Heritage Picture History of World War II*.) In all, 17,215 Allied soldiers were killed, wounded or felled by disease in the swampy ground around Buna between November 1942 and January 1943.

"Most of our casualties on New Guinea resulted from Mother Nature. Dysentery (severe diarrhea) was part of the program for everybody because we had to eat what we could when we could. When some had jungle sores from a scratch that got infected and would not heal or we got malaria, back to the rear they went. Some of the parasites were our own people, cranky because they were there or because they just weren't physically fit to do it and couldn't stand up under the pressure. Some got Jungle Goofy and just couldn't take it any more."

A soldier's feet were especially vulnerable and pretty much every one had jungle rot or other infections in their feet "because you couldn't really get your feet dry. Your feet would start to rot and you'd get this strange disease that would work its way in through a mosquito bite or scratch until it got to the bone and then stop. It was more terrible looking than painful but it would fester and then drain. Some men's feet were just terrible looking when they had dozens of little infections like that."

Tropical dangers eventually caught up to Langeteig when he was hospitalized for two days with malaria in December, 1942, in a native structure-turned-aid station "with a gravel floor and stretchers only."

But, if Mother Nature was a tough opponent at Buna, the Japanese were savage.

In his account of the fighting in the *32nd Infantry Division in World War II by Maj. Gen. H.W. Blakely, USA ret.*, American Army General Eichelberger—who was in charge of the Buna forces for much of the campaign—recalls how difficult it was to push the enemy out of Buna between Sept. 28, 1942 and Jan. 22, 1943:

"The Army's official history summarizes the situation. 'The Japanese line at Buna was, in its way, a masterpiece. It forced the 32nd Division to attack the enemy where he was strongest ... (Buna) was bought at a substantial price in deaths, wounds, disease, despair and human suffering. No one who fought there, however hard he tries, will ever forget it. ... Buna is still to me, in retrospect, a nightmare."

The Hero Next Door Returns

Wisconsin boys like Langeteig were among the thousands living—and dying—in that nightmare.

"The noise was incredible as the 105- and 175-millimeter shells blasted day and night! We were under heavy small arms fire as well and all of us knew better than to go to the bathroom standing up; you'd just roll over—something that was good to learn since, later in the Philippines, the terrain was even more susceptible to open fire from any direction. Fighting in New Guinea was a real step-by-step operation; you stayed real close to each other."

The Red Arrowmen learned the first hard and deadly lessons of combat with the Japanese—lessons future soldiers would benefit from. They developed tactics for penetrating the so-called impregnable Japanese defenses like interlocking pill boxes, mutually protective fields of fire, infiltration parties and enemy snipers tied high up in trees—"which provided good hiding spots for them," Langeteig recalls. "Some might say the 32nd Division 'wrote the book' on jungle fighting."

The platoon also had to all but tiptoe through the swampy terrain so as not to set off 20-pound parachute bombs—dropped by American planes—that had gotten tangled in the trees above the action.

Most of the airborne danger came from 'unfriendly planes,' however.

"Our platoon was assigned to protect an airstrip near Pogani and we'd been informed that our air corps was at last getting supplied with more planes. We didn't have many there, and I personally never saw an America plane chasing a Japanese plane until we got to the Philippines.

"So, we just watched as we saw 21 planes coming in toward the airstrip. We were so happy ... until we realized they were Jap zeros. They came in and strafed us. Somehow no one was seriously hurt, but some of my men had scratches from diving for cover and the telephone was knocked out of my hand and out of commission."

That wasn't the only run-in with Japanese planes. "Many nights we'd lay there and listen to Jap planes overhead and we could tell when they were unloading their bombs because there was a discharge blast they made. We'd hear that and all go to the trenches until we heard the first bomb drop. Then, if it wasn't near us, we knew they weren't going to hit our platoon."

Though there weren't many, Langeteig did see some American planes "land" at the airstrip. "We watched a B-25 that had to land there with no landing gear and the bomb bay doors open. He cut the engines and sailed across the dirt. The dirt filled up the bomb bay area and encased the bombs so no one was hurt. Then, there were three Air Cobras that we saw make runs over Buna. One had to land all shot to pieces on our airstrip. He coasted off to one side and the pilot had to stay the night with us. In the morning he said 'I'll never criticize you guys again.' He didn't want to stay another night."

All during the fighting at Buna—and throughout his time in combat—the Army brass left Tech Sgt. Langeteig relatively alone to command his platoon, though many times a lieutenant was assigned to lead other units. "We served in the darndest places and were kind of an isolated platoon. The four months I was up in the front of my platoon, I never had an officer leading all of us. The squad leaders ran it with me."

But, it was the whole unit working together as a team that helped the 32nd Division keep the Japanese at bay and eventually drive them out, Langeteig stresses. "Our platoon equipment included four Jeeps and three 37-mm anti-tank guns, which we used for things other than tanks because we could never navigate much of the terrain we covered, though they were used at Buna to open sighting lanes for machine guns. And, we would use canister ammo to clear out the weeds and

The Hero Next Door Returns

underbrush and lost one man in that operation."

In the end, the 32nd Division and other American and Australian troops annihilated the Japanese garrison of 5,000 troops around Buna and proved that the Japanese were not as invincible at they thought. The Red Arrow Division won its first Presidential Unit Citation for the Buna Campaign. Even the Japanese respected their enemy's determined tactics and nicknamed the division, "The Bloody Butchers of Buna" *(13,000 Hours)*.

Between combat, the troops ate what they could and slept where they were able.

"Our kitchen was a tent that stored mostly Army rations that were either sent in by our company headquarters or dropped by air depending on our location. We had lots of Oscar Mayer skinless wieners. At one time, we had 22 cases for our platoon. We sliced them for breakfast, ate them whole for lunch and cut them lengthwise for supper. There was nothing else until our next delivery."

After the vicious Buna Campaign wound down, the division was flown back to Port Moresby with little left of the shirts on their backs. "When we first left there, we only owned the clothes on our backs and extra socks. When we came back, we didn't look well dressed. Most our clothes were just rags and cutoffs and our company commander—who had vacated the front long before—told us we looked terrible. We ignored him."

BACK UNDER

From Port Moresby, the 32nd sailed back to Australia, to Coolangata, near Melbourne, in February of 1943 for some more training and a little rest, though their arrival was less than well executed.

"The departure from the ship was interesting. When we landed, we were greeted by many people including the Red Cross. They served us ice cream and such goodies, but we had no idea that this good stuff was

Red Arrow Man

This family of New Guinea natives was typical of those Langeteig encountered.

not what our stomachs wanted after months of the food we'd been given at the front. Boy! Did some of us get sick to our stomachs! But, it did not take us long to recover and dive into anything that looked good."

Coolangata was a far cry from the New Guinea front in every way. "It was right by the seashore and we lived like what we thought was kings. We were well fed and had free time. We spent a couple months there setting up on shore to practice resisting any Japanese landing, and even set up our 37-mm anti-tank guns, before heading back to New Guinea."

They arrived in the former battle ground at a place called Good Enough Island—"yes, that's the actual name—to practice landings with real equipment and not the makeshift stuff we'd had earlier.

"Our first night there proved the 'value' of the hammocks. During the night we had a lot of rain. By morning, we were just hanging over the flood area. Not only did we get our feet wet, but our hammocks were half full of water too!"

After a few days practice, in early 1944, the 128th

The Hero Next Door Returns

Infantry was on landing craft heading for Saidor, New Guinea where they would fight through April 1944. They arrived to little opposition. After units were set up to defend the area for the big guns that were coming, headquarters was able to at last distribute some backlogged mail by the second day.

"I received a letter from Laverne telling me she saw in the paper that we were at Saidor. Here she knew and we didn't even know where the hell we were! "

The division held the Saidor field for the Howitzers that "barked for days" until the area was declared safe. Once safety was "assured," it was time for the 32nd to ship out into less secure terrain.

They traveled by landing craft up the Driniumor River to Aitape and held the area for several weeks in bitter jungle fighting against a Japanese counterattack launched July 10.

It was the night before the counterattack that Langeteig and the rest of the division welcomed some replacements, fresh from training.

"One night about 2 a.m. at the Driniumor River I got replacements. Back then they just dropped these guys into battle with no battle experience and no time to get accustomed to the climate or anything. It was quite a shock for the early replacements, and later on, they tried to bring them into an island first to get a bit more acclimated before just sending them to fight in the jungle."

Among those early replacements was a soldier, "who I don't think was even 18. It was pitch dark and he hung close for a few days until he got accustomed to things. He was from California and, after the war, he came to Wisconsin to see me. All the replacements had a bad time with their introduction into combat under those conditions."

And, there were rarely worse conditions than the Japanese counterattack at Aitape.

According to *13,000 Hours*, three Jap regiments forced their way across the Driniumor River and it

Red Arrow Man

"was red with the blood of more than 200 Japanese troops the following morning." American troops fell back two miles, reorganized and counter-attacked, driving the Japanese further and further back in "three weeks of bitter jungle fighting."

"Our platoon had been placed out in front of the howitzers about 100 yards for their protection. They blasted over our heads for nearly 48 hours, but we were not totally aware of how worse our situation was until the next morning when we found out we'd been cut off by the Japs. Later that day, our forces recaptured the lost ground and drove the Japs out. Again, lucky me!"

By the fall of 1944, he was a seasoned veteran, and the division had pushed north to Hollanidia where Langeteig's platoon spent several weeks doing "mop-up" missions and preparing for their next stop—the Philippines.

PHLIPPINE FIGHTING

The 32nd Division landed on the large Philippine Island of Leyte in mid-November 1944, stepping right back in combat.

"About two weeks later we heard that Gen. MacArthur had returned to the Philippines (on Oct. 20, 1944) but, of course, we couldn't see him from our perch. We tramped through the mud there like you can't believe, for days."

Though the inland fight to secure Leyte would last from Nov. 16, 1944, to Jan. 2, 1945, Langeteig would only face the Japanese on Leyte for that first, bloodiest, month of the campaign.

Leyte island terrain was a bit easier to fight in as there "were more open fields and we had more opportunities to use the Howitzers and could maneuver a lot more than in New Guinea."

Where New Guinea had been swampy jungle; the Philippine mountains proved made of mud.

Typhoon season began as the troops arrived on

The Hero Next Door Returns

Leyte Island and everything and everyone was soaked through from the first day to the last. In *13,000 Hours* the division records: "Drenching, persistent tropical rains continued almost without break for the duration of the operation . . . Long stretches of roadbed washed out ... Combat troops and their equipment ... never completely dried out until the division was relieved, ... and infantrymen slipped and slid and crawled forward. They slept and ate and fought in a sea of mud."

The fighting proved extra-tough in the wet, cumbersome terrain because the 32nd Division was up against the Japanese Imperial First Division—some 6,700 of whom died in the fight. It was "an epic struggle," Turner writes in *Les Terribles*. "Inch by inch, using all the stamina, knowledge, guts and modern technology ... slowly (the 32nd) pushed the enemy out of his fox holes, bunkers, trenches and shelters."

Much of the fighting was done from one side of a hilltop to the other side of the hill as each side would lob artillery and even grenades onto the enemy on the other side.

"We would see the big gun—which could shoot a 500-pound shell about 20 miles—flash and then hear it and then hear it go over the hill with a whistle. In between, we were lobbying grenades 50 yards over to the Jap side so they'd roll down on them; just like they were doing to us."

Such fighting took its toll, but harder still was rousting the Japanese nearly one-by-one from small and deadly hiding places. "The foxholes they dug were deep enough for them to sit in and had camouflage covers. When we passed these, we didn't see them until they started firing at our backs. There was always one Jap in that foxhole, one Jap in that tree."

The struggles of Leyte Island fell—especially for the Americans—at an emotionally charged time of year, from Thanksgiving to Christmas. Still, Langeteig recalls that Thanksgiving with special fondness.

Red Arrow Man

The platoon was hunkered down against Japanese shelling on Thanksgiving, 1944. "The Japanese fire was bombarding us from the backside of the hill and hitting in front of us, just a bit beyond our position. In the middle of this, I looked over and saw this pick-up truck coming off to our left. Here it was the Salvation Army, going through all that to bring us turkey and dressing and everything! When the firing was over, we all crawled to that truck and gave thanks to the Salvation Army for the fine meal we had. That's why I still give to the Salvation Army to this day."

Just a few weeks after that extra-grateful Thanksgiving, Langeteig would give thanks again. This time, because he was going home.

"We had just finished most of our mission taking Leyte in late December. We were up on top of a mountain heading down the west side when I received word my rotation number was up and I could go home. It didn't take me long to do an about face and find my way back to Tacloben where the ships were that would take us out of there. I hitched a ride back on a duck—of the Wisconsin Dells type and the first one I'd seen over there—which saved me wet socks and shoes on the way back. I spent Christmas of 1944 in Tacloben waiting to ship home."

"As things happened you didn't find a strip and pray right there. It was later on that you got on your knees and were thankful. And I was so grateful to get out of there alive and get to go home. I was grateful too to have served with all the men I served with. I would have no qualms about serving with any of them again."

UNCERTAIN SEAS

Langeteig caught a ship in early January 1945, that would return him for a time to the familiar ground of Hollandia where he'd catch the final ride, he hoped, for home.

"The trip back to Hollandia was not the most pleasant because the Japs by then were up against the wall

The Hero Next Door Returns

and tried anything with their planes." Kamikaze suicidal attacks grew more and more common as the Philippine campaign wore on. By the end of the war, Japanese kamikaze corps "had sunk or damaged more than 300 U.S. ships and exacted some 15,000 casualties," Sulzberger reports.

The supply ship Langeteig was riding on was nearly one of the many casualties of Japanese fighters in those waning days of war.

"We'd been on the boat the better part of a week when we were sitting on deck eating lunch. All of a sudden the rear gun opens up. We see a Jap plane circle around and then here he is coming right at us! We didn't have time to think about anything; we just saw it happen. I was up against the railing and I could see when the bomb came. I can still picture that Jap pilot looking down at us as he dropped it. The bomb just missed the bow of the ship and exploded. If it had been another 10 feet over, it would have hit the bow. He made another circle and came around again but this time he was shot down. Our mess kits wound up full of gun powder and water, which of course spoiled the main course."

It was a final reminder of the close calls of war—how 10 feet, 10 steps or 10 seconds can be the difference between a direct hit and a near miss.

Fortunately, Langeteig would have no more near misses. After a week-long wait in Hollandia, he was San Francisco bound. "The seas were very rough sailing home but who cared."

In late January of 1945, Langeteig was eating good old American food in San Francisco, U.S.A., served to him by German prisoners of war. "They were being held there for safekeeping, I guess, and put to work. But returning GIs were not very pleased with that set up."

From California Langeteig was able to give his wife—who he had not seen for three years—a quick call to "warn her I was coming. But, we could hardly hear each other until an operator cut into the party line and informed all the rubbernecks on the line to hang up so we could hear."

Then, it was back to the cross-country train rides, though this time Langeteig knew his destination—Chicago. It was not however, the speediest of trips.

"Every once in a while we had to stop to allow other trains with war material to get to the coast for immediate shipment overseas. These stops proved well worthwhile, though, because they provided someone the time to dash to the nearest tavern and purchase as many cases of beer as the delegated man could carry. Those who went didn't care if they ended up stranded or not, 'after all,' they said 'we are home.' When we hit Chicago, the officer in charge to free us for a month said, 'you guys are the sorriest bunch of men I've ever seen' and then busted out laughing. I guess the beer must have made us look tired."

All that beer was a rarity up until then, Langeteig stresses. "We kept reading in the paper that there were shortages back home because everything was going to the GIs, but we could never figure out where they were sending it or who those GIs were that they were sending it to. The whole time we were overseas, we had been issued only two six packs of beer and ate no steaks."

When Langeteig finally arrived in Madison, Wis., he quickly called the best man from his wedding, Joe Tuschl, and asked him to take him to North Bristol, where Langeteig's father Andrew ran a tavern. (His mother Bertha died of blood poisoning in 1926.)

"Laverne was there and ... she was beautiful!"

Laverene thought her husband was the best thing she'd ever seen as well, though 'beautiful' wasn't quite the word she might have used. "He was 138 pounds when he came back and almost orange from the malaria medication."

Langeteig's father was simultaneously moved and taken back by the sight of his war veteran son. "Dad

The Hero Next Door Returns

took one look at me and cried. He thought I looked that bad."

A DIFFERENT KIND OF THEATER

Though his time in combat was over, Langeteig's time in the service was continuing to stretch long beyond that long-ago draft promise.

After three weeks at home, Langeteig followed orders to go to Miami Beach for rehabilitation the first part of February. "We stayed at the Grossinger Hotel for three weeks and Laverne was with me and the cost for her was $1 per day for food and room. Our room was on the 11th floor. What luxury we thought! We—the veterans—went to sessions each morning for three weeks. Every day, upon our return to our rooms, there was lots of fresh fruit."

Accommodations changed more than a little when he and Laverne arrived in Fort Benning, Ga., for his six weeks training for homefront duties. "We found rooms with kitchen

A friend of Langeteig's visits a dentist in the field in Australia.

privileges but high class it was not. The kitchen had an accompaniment of cockroaches that rattled the pots and pans when we snapped on the lights."

Fortunately, he didn't spend much time cooking. Instead the combat veterans were training to play in a whole different kind of theater.

"Our mission was to put on a show that would sell war bonds. The show was a mock battle put on in various cities in eastern Texas at stadiums of bigger schools. The show was infantry orientated with men on their bellies crawling forward as a trained camp."

Even this seemingly light duty proved more difficult than expected. "I had malaria hit me 13 times in 26 days.

"He'd come home just shivering and shaking. I'd cover him with a blanket and he'd just shake to pieces," Laverne recalls.

"All the men I was with knew my problem though," Langeteig explains, "so I was assigned just to handle the P.A. system. Most stadiums just turned everything over to me and that was all there was to it. Anyone can flip switches and check volume.

"Our announcer was a former radio man from Ohio who had served in England. As he narrated the action, our electrician manned a board all wired for various explosives at the proper places on the field. The men all wore camouflage suits and crawled down the football field as the announcer described what was happening. It was very effective.

"The finale was the pillbox set up with two men firing a 30-caliber machine gun with blank ammo. While the announcer described another incident the two men left their location in the pillbox. Before they left, they set off a large string of firecrackers for the audience to think the men were still there. The announcer then said the flame throwers were now in action. The pillbox was engulfed in flames and the audience went dead quiet thinking the men had been burned up. Then they emerged from the shadows and all was well.

The Hero Next Door Returns

That brought tears to everyone's eyes and really helped sell bonds. We probably played to millions, in about a dozen cities in six weeks."

While all this was going on, Laverne had returned to her family in Nebraska.

Langeteig transferred from Fort Benning to Fort McClellan, Ala., where he learned he would be among the men being discharged. "The thought of getting out of the service after the bond tour; that was probably the happiest days of my life because I knew I was heading out, going home for good."

On Aug. 14, 1945, Langeteig boarded his last military train—this one to Camp McCoy, Wis. From there, "I headed straight for Fairmont, Neb., and Laverne. At the platform in Fairmont was Laverne waiting with her parents—a welcome sight with the knowledge that I was home for good."

While in Nebraska, the reunited "newlyweds" took time to visit Langeteig's brother Merlin who was stationed in Sioux City, Iowa, and had been stateside in the service since 1939 and later visited his brother Alvin who entered the Army Air Corps before Langeteig's induction in April 1941. Both brothers were discharged a short time later.

The reunited Langeteigs were soon back in Madison, driving the 1936 Plymouth Laverne had made all those war-time visits to her husband in.

By Oct. of 1945, Langeteig was temporarily pumping gas and fixing tires in Madison at a Shell station on East Washington Ave. Then, for a time, he worked two jobs—one as a messenger boy in the First National Bank in Madison for $106 a month and another for Confidential Reports Inc., checking theaters in the area at night to be sure their take was properly submitted.

While at the bank, Langeteig took courses in bookkeeping, auditing, and investments on the GI Bill through the University of Wisconsin and vocational schools, as well as the National Association of Bank

Red Arrow Man

Auditors and Comptrollers of which he was a member. "After about a year, I was put on the program for returning servicemen for $250 a month and said 'I'll never complain again.'"

By spring of 1946, Laverne was pregnant with their first child, Marsha Ann. They had another daughter, Deanne, in 1948, followed by two sons: Alan in 1951 and Jim in 1953. "She used to get pregnant every time we went square dancing, so we stopped going square dancing and had no more children after that!" (However, the family has since grown to include eight grandchildren and four great grandchildren.)

As the family got bigger, the Langeteigs moved from their first one bedroom home—with a bedroom too small for a double bed—to a home on Hoard Street before Langeteig built a new home, with help from his friends in Lakeview Heights in 1950.

Langeteig had meanwhile moved up through the bank's ranks. In May 1953, he accepted an assistant cashier position at the First National Bank of Sterling, Ill., and the family moved there for two years. In 1955, he was hired to operate the McFarland State Bank. The family stayed with friends until they could build a new home, this one in McFarland, in 1960.

Langeteig left in 1975, but didn't stay away from banking long. On Jan. 1, 1976, he was hired to help organize the Bank of Evansville. He and Laverne moved to Evansville in 1977. "We had no building, no charter, no FDIC approval. Nothing, just go to work and get it operating. Then I had to buy a trailer to work from, obtain the charter, FDIC approval, find real estate and obtain all the equipment needed to operate with. We opened May 3, 1976, and moved into a new building in October."

Shortly thereafter he and Laverne began to wage another war, this one against the ovarian cancer Laverne was diagnosed with in 1978. She beat the odds and the cancer, and Langeteig retired again—this time for good—in March of 1984.

The Hero Next Door Returns

In between, he and Laverne spent time traveling. They took a memorable 1972 trip with his brother Merlin and his wife to Norway, to trace heritage in the land their parents had immigrated from before W.W. II. "We grew up speaking Norwegian, and I didn't speak English when I started school. When we went to Norway, we visited Dad's brothers near Balistrnd up on the fjords and his sister in Drummond near Oslo. She was 95 at the time and still on the homestead. Part of the building had a sod roof and the original floors were 12-15 inch planks at least 3-inches thick."

Langeteig's retirement years are filled with many more travel adventures including much time spent in Tuscon, Ariz., the first few years after retirement. Langeteig has also served as past president of various banking and church organizations, and was the first president of, the McFarland Lions Club in 1962. He has been a member of the McFarland American Legion for 55 years and is a member of the Evansville VFW.

In his latter role, Langeteig has supported the veterans organizations' efforts to preserve Wisconsin's war past and educate people about it. "We should have more people cognizant of the history of war, of how and why we get into them. War is not always wrong but war can become wrong like it did in Vietnam. In W.W. II, war was absolutely right. We had our country to protect and everyone became involved. I'm proud to have been an ordinary guy who did his job as part of that; and grateful to have survived it."

YOUNG MARINE
ART ORLOWSKI

Combat ages a man to be sure— turns boys into men in a hurry, it's been said. Those who fought in W.W. II were barely men when they started, many of them just 18 years old and all of them still "just boys" to their mothers.

Art Orlowski was more of a boy than most. The Milwaukee altar boy was just 15 and a half when he enlisted in the United States Marine Corps.

By the time he was old enough for a driver's license, Orlowski was in charge of ammunition supply for a gun battery based at Guadalcanal, a recently-recaptured island in the South Pacific. When this youngest of 11 children came marching home again three war years later, he was a man made by combat. But, he was still only 18, the same age most the Marines he fought with were when they enlisted.

Orlowski wanted in on the war from the moment the Japanese bombed Pearl Harbor Dec. 7, 1941. He wanted to join his sister and two brothers who'd already signed up to fight. "My brother Stanley was in the Red Arrow Division in New Guinea and my brother

The Hero Next Door Returns

Bernard was in the U.S. Navy on a destroyer while my sister Susan was in the Navy in Norfolk, Va., so I wanted to be in the Navy."

His father John Orlowski—who raised his clan on South 14th Street in South Milwaukee largely by himself after Anna Orlowski died—was proud enough of his youngest son's determination to serve America that he signed the permission slip required when a 17-year-old enlisted.

Of course, his son was not yet 16. "I altered my birth certificate to say I was 17. I used a bottle of ink iradicator I bought from Walgreens for 10 cents and took it down to the Navy recruiting office."

"The Navy put it under a light, found I'd tampered with it and told me to get out. I was very depressed, but then, I passed the Marine Corps recruit office on the way out. The Marines put me through a series of interviews and, at 5:30 p.m. on the same day, I was on a train to Marine Corps Recruit Depot, in San Diego, Calif."

After eight weeks of boot training and two weeks on the rifle range "learning how to shoot people," the 15-year-old recruit was well on his way to manhood, with no one seemingly the wiser about his real age.

"I didn't cause any trouble in boot camp, and I did everything I could not to stand out too much, so no one would find out my age. I wasn't the smallest Marine there so I wasn't too suspicious looking. About the only thing is I never needed to shave much and the others teased me some about it at first. But, there were other guys—older than me—who didn't shave too much either so I guess it wasn't that suspicious."

After graduation, the Marines were broken up into groups by alphabetical order. Orlowski was assigned to the field artillery and first sent to Terminal Island, Calif., as part of a guard company. Though he didn't see one until much later in the war, Japanese subs had been spotted along the California shore and the Terminal Island company was there to keep watch.

Young Marine

THE REINFORCER

It wasn't long before losses in the Pacific Campaign demanded more replacements. Orlowski was among the reinforcements for the 1st Division Marines and left for training in Wellington, New Zealand, in November, 1942.

By the time he reached New Zealand, the rest of the division had just arrived for some rest and relaxation from hard fighting in America's first land offense, a four-month often hand-to-hand combat struggle, for the island of Guadalcanal.

Orlowski was assigned to the 1st Marine Amphibious Force as part of a 155mm-gun battalion.

"That was an artillery piece that could shoot 18 miles. I was chosen to be in the property ammunitions section, which kept all the battalion's property in order and kept the ammunition counted for."

After training in New Zealand, Orlowski was shipped with the rest of the division back to Guadalcanal. The once bloody battleground would now be a staging area for assaults on surrounding islands as the Allies pushed the Japanese northward. "Guadalcanal was our first move in the Pacific and became a jumping off point. By the time we got there the only other people we saw were the natives."

Though he'd yet to see combat, the boy Marine was soon promoted.

"We had an inspection by our commanding officer on Guadalcanal in spring of 1943. I had to stand at attention in front of my property tent in full battle gear. He stopped and asked me why I didn't have my rank painted on. (Marines painted rank on their uniforms at this time instead of sewing on patches.) I explained I had no rank as I was a private—and boy, was I a private!

"Generally ranks were only handed out when someone was rotated or killed but, given my responsibili-

The Hero Next Door Returns

ties, he wanted me promoted immediately to corporal. So now, I was a 16-year-old corporal!"

As a corporal, Orlowski occasionally found himself in charge of men much older than he. "Everybody was older. At 16, I went out on patrols and was sort of leading a 15-man patrol because that's what corporals did. We made daily patrols of our area. Fortunately, our patrol never came across anything but other patrols did."

Patrols on Guadalcanal were mostly a jungle affair. "The island was all jungle. And, because I didn't fight there, I can say that Guadalcanal was quite a beautiful island and there were thousands of coconut trees."

But, the island had its misery. "It rained just about every day and it was humid and disease infected. You had to put an iodine pill in the water to drink it. The living conditions were tough for everyone."

Even iodine couldn't prevent most of the jungle-borne illnesses the Marines fought longer than the Japanese on Guadalcanal. In fact, while some 621 1st Division Marines were killed in the original fight for Guadalcanal, more than 5,600 suffered from malaria from August through December of 1942 alone, according to *The Old Breed: A History of the First Marine Division in World War II.*

Orlowski was among the Marines adding to the malaria statistic when the division returned to the island in early spring of 1943.

"I had malaria that re-occurred 12 different times, mostly in the U.S. after I returned, and my skin turned yellow from the Atabrine medication." Orlowski also battled dysentery and dengue fever—which "gave me a high fever and vomiting. Every bone in my body ached, even my hair hurt. I had it so bad that one day I just wanted somebody to shoot me."

After several months withstanding life on Guadalcanal, part of the amphibious corps was called to fight in the Solomon Islands, including Bougainville, and later sent out to the Marianas Islands. After it be-

Young Marine

came the 3rd Marine Amphibious Force, Orlowski's gun battalion went along with the 3rd Marine Corps under the direction of Gen. Roy Geiger.

The gun battery went in on the invasion of Guam on July 21, 1944, in the Marianas islands. "The island of Guam is also a beautiful place when there's no war there. It looks like someone sawed the top off the island because there are mountains but no peaks. It's all red soil."

The blood of some 7,800 Marine casualties—and 16,526 Japanese—turned the dirt there redder still by July 29, according to *The United States Marine Corps in W.W. II*. It was a three-week battle that Rear Admiral W.L. Ainsworth called a "tough, swirling struggle with cooks and clerks sometimes thrown into the action when Jap counterattacks pierced American lines." *(The American Heritage Picture History of World War II*, p. 540.)

Guam was the first time the 16-year-old saw the color of real combat.

"I was assigned to one of four guns in our battery. We all set the guns up and waited for orders from our forward OP (observation post). They would let us know when a good target was available. One duty was to keep enough projectiles to supply firepower. Each projectile weighed 95 pounds, so it was hard work. Also, before each shot, a powder bag was used to shoot each shell or projectile.

"Ours, as well as my own thoughts, were to stay alive and still do your duty as commanded from sergeants to officers. Our officers, though, were good men and we never had any problems with them. Their duty was stressful at times."

As stressful as anything else, was getting the equipment into combat position. It was heavy work.

"The hardest thing in combat was getting the guns ashore and digging them in and trying to stay alive while doing it. Every single day was hard work for us and every single day in combat you had just one

The Hero Next Door Returns

thought, 'stay alive, stay alive.'"

"Moving artillery is very tough. It's a 15-ton gun and a giant tractor. You make one mistake and you get crushed. We lost one gun over the side of the landing craft at Guam.

"Then, when you get the gun on shore, it sinks in the sand. You're moving slow, out in the open. Digging the guns in was the toughest because the ground was wet.

"Every piece of ammo weighed 95 pounds. My responsibility was ammunition. Two men brought each projectile in by hand as the crew was shooting and then it took two men to lift it and a third to ram it in.

"The shell is a high explosive propelled by a powder bag. The shell is rammed in and the powder inserted after. A good crew could probably fire four such rounds in a minute."

That kind of speed produced its own dangers. "The projectile had brass rings on the end and you had to ram it until you heard a 'conk.' But, you have to be careful not to create a spark in there" or the gun could blow back on the men firing it. "So, you had to swab it out in between and make sure the sparks were out. Then you put the powder in and close the breech, put the primer in and the primer was fired using a lanyard (a piece of rope that attached to the firing pin)."

Each gun battery had four guns, including the 155mm, and was commanded by one captain, three lieutenants, one first sergeant and one gun sergeant. "Our officers were great guys and treated us nicely, especially Capt. Pearson. If you treat a man as a man and not as a subordinate, you're going to get full efficiency out of him at all times and that's how Capt. Pearson treated us. He used to call us gentlemen all the time."

In general, a gun battery's job was to stand by and wait for fire missions assigned from a forward infantry observation post. "We would fire ahead of the in-

fantry, often at Japanese supply depots."

Each battery's sergeant was responsible for aiming the gun and taking care of the quadrants for each shot. But, getting those quadrants just right before firing—to avoid firing on their own troops or the wrong target—was especially tough.

"An aiming post must be let out. A few men go out in front of the gun and act like surveyors to position the gun right. The observation men would tell us if we hit the target of if we needed to move it this way or that. Generally they ask for a smoke round to get it sighted in at first. These men were way out ahead and it was very dangerous."

Fortunately, most of Orlowski's time was spent further behind the front lines. "We generally were shelling ahead of our infantry and were behind the lines but sometimes not far enough behind. Sometimes the Japanese shelled us back."

And, in case the fighting got closer yet, Orlowski had a carbine "to shoot at anyone shooting at us."

FINAL FIGHT

Rarely, for the gun battery, did the fighting get that close until things "got really tough."

And, they got really tough in the last W.W. II battle Orlwoski fought in—after the gun battery had been attached to the 3rd Marine Amphibious Force—the struggle for Okinawa.

Okinawa was the last major island on the Allies' way to mainland Japan, some 350 miles further north. Just getting there was more of a battle than they bargained for.

"The trip to Okinawa was very hairy for our troop ship because of typhoons in the area. The seas turned into torrential rain and darkness. We were barely out to sea when we were all ordered below decks and locked in our compartments so no one would wander around—standard procedure during bad storms. We did a lot of praying down in those holds and an awful

The Hero Next Door Returns

lot of people got sick as the rest of us lived in this polluted air."

The Okinawa offensive itself went much smoother when the 3rd Marine Amphibious Force hit Okinawa beaches on Easter Sunday, 1945, north of the capital of Naha. The Marines all but strolled onto the beach, unopposed by the Japanese. It was such a peaceful invasion that D-Day on Okinawa was nicknamed "Love Day," and the first elements of the artillery divisions—usually a few days behind the first waves in coming ashore—were on the beach by noon on D-Day reports George McMillan in *The Old Breed: A History of the First Marine Division in World War II*.

The easy April 1, 1945—April Fool's Day—entrance was all part of the Japanese master battle plan, however. The easy maneuvers wouldn't last.

"The Jap's tactics were to let us land and move back into the hills and then start to counterattack. That's when all hell broke loose.

"Okinawa became the roughest place I was at. They were all rough, but Okinawa was the worst because the Japanese were willing to die and it was nothing but caves and an island full of tombs where the Japanese hid. It was such a long, delayed, tiring fight to get them all out of there and most died before they'd ever surrender. You had to kill them. The Japs shelled us back the most there and they were experts with mortar shells. We did an awful lot of shooting on Okinawa."

Those nearly non-stop artillery barrages helped the infantry drive, pin down and eventually liberate the island. And, they gave many ground troops an extra sense of security.

Still, for all its close calls, Orlowski's gun battery was spared the dire statistics of the American infantry units at Okinawa. The joint Marine and Army assault force took Okinawa in a series of bloody pushes that proved the last and largest amphibious operation in the Pacific. By June 21, 1945, more than 12,000 Americans and an estimated 110,071 Japanese—nine for every American—were killed in the battle.

"We lost one guy who stepped on a land mine. A few were sent back as Section Eight's (psychological discharges). Other than that we were pretty lucky not to lose anybody because the 3rd Marine Amphibious Force as a whole lost a lot."

Still, the odds were not good when the heat of battle raged.

"I was Catholic but it didn't matter what you were. Religion has a lot to do in combat because you have no one else to talk to but God sometimes. When you're in the Higgins boat waiting to land, there's no talking going on so there's a lot of boys trying to make their prayers last and, for a lot of them, it was their last.

"In combat, you just spend your day trying to stay alive. But, that's what all the guys are trying to do—stay alive—and, in war, not everybody can do that. In war, some men have to die every day sometimes, sometimes every hour, every minute. We may have won, but in war, everyone still loses."

MAKING DO

Combat was not every day, however. For a 16-year-old kid far from home for the first time there were issues beyond mortality to contemplate—like hunger and loneliness.

"The hardest part of being overseas was being away from family and trying to exist on nothing. I got very few letters from home. My mom was dead and my dad wasn't a writer. It made me more lonely than the other guys. I didn't even have a girlfriend like most guys, but I was too young at first to really know what all that was about anyway.

"For some reason, I never got any packages from the Red Cross either. However, someone would occasionally send over miniature *Milwaukee Journals* and I used to love to get that because it was so good to read."

The Hero Next Door Returns

Although "the Marine Corps tried to feed us the best they could," the best they could was often barely enough.

"In combat the first three days you get nothing but C-rations for breakfast, lunch and dinner. But, they sure are good when you're hungry!"

"They gave us a lot of Spam and dehydrated potatoes but the cooks sure tried. They'd scrounge and steal to feed us and they kept us going. In fact on Okinawa they had a typhoon and everything on the beaches was in bad shape. But, inside of four or five hours, they had a galley going. They did a hell of a good job!"

Others would often go "above and beyond" to bring an extra smile as well.

"On Guadalcanal Capt. Pearson called us together and said 'Gentlemen, I've got two movies here but we have no generator to watch them.' At that, our first sergeant jumped in a Jeep and 'borrowed' a two-wheel generator from the Seabees. We sprayed it green and put a Marine Corps number on it and in 12-15 hours we had it all set up and the offices and galley had light. About four months later, the Shore Patrol came down and scratched it to find gray paint underneath and took it away. We acquired another one."

One time Orlowski got an extra sweet treat. "We saw guys walking by with doughnuts and heard the Red Cross was handing them out at the airfield. We hurried over and there were four girls selling them for five cents a piece, if you had it, or they were free!"

THROUGH THE GATE

After three Christmases and 34 months in the Pacific, Orlowski rotated back to the U.S. in summer of 1945.

"We were in the high seas on the way back when the atomic bombs dropped. The scuttlebutt said it was a very powerful bomb and would end the war but we had heard those kinds of rumors before. This time,

though, it turned out to be true! There was an old saying, 'the Golden Gate by '48.' Here it was just '45 and we were crossing under it and wouldn't have to go back to war!!"

Back in California, at the Treasure Island Naval Base in San Francisco, every man was inspected for contraband. "We were allowed Japanese souvenirs and most of mine—including a Japanese pistol, flag, headband and a lot of Japanese money—were stolen on the ship home by Navy guys."

As soon as they were processed, every man "wanted to eat good food, get a car and find a woman," Orlowski recalls; but first things first.

The young veteran went to the galley for his first stateside meal in nearly three years—"hot dogs and sauerkraut and all the milk you could drink. We were absolutely delighted. But, it was served by very healthy, strong looking German prisoners of war and we were all malnutrition ridden and run down with battle fatigue and weren't very happy about the sight of them."

What remained of the gun battery returned to Marine Corps Recruit Depot, San Diego, where it all started. "A first lieutenant sat me down and offered me two more chevrons (ranks) to stay in and ship back over for post-war duty but I decided that, since I'd not been home for 42 months, that's where I wanted to be. A few years later, we got into the Korean War, which really by age should have been my war. I had no business being in W.W. II."

Orlowski and his siblings all survived the war. The youngest of them was the last to return. "When I came home I went immediately to visit my dad. I found my dad in the basement, the same place I'd left him. I was only 18 and we broke open a couple bottles of beer. I had $3,800 because I never spent any money overseas and he asked me what I wanted to do with it. I wanted a car but couldn't even buy one because I wasn't 21 so he signed for me. Then, I went back to

The Hero Next Door Returns

school and got my high school education."

Seven years later, Orlowski joined the Milwaukee Fire Department.

"I loved the fire department because of the work they do saving lives and property. It was a lot like the Marine Corps, a brotherhood, but nobody was shooting at you."

Orlowski spent 35 years battling blazes to save lives, serving first with the City of Milwaukee before becoming the full-time Captain of the Greendale, Wis., fire department. He fought in some of the biggest Milwaukee area fires, including the Plankington Packing Company fire where one firemen was killed. And, Orlowski won a Milwaukee Fire Department life saving award in 1967.

He married Grace Sliga in 1951, and they had a daughter Adine and son Tim and have one grandson Matthew. After his first wife died in 1985, Orlowski married Mary Kern in 1988. They divide their residence now between Wisconsin Dells, Wis., and Leesburg, Fla., and spend much time in between volunteering with the Boggy Creek Gang, a kind of hospice for terminally ill kids in Illinois, Connecticut and Florida—a charity supported by actor Paul Newman and Gen. Norman Swartzkoff. "I work in the kitchen and cut a lot of patches for quilts the women make for the kids."

They've also worked with Toys for Tots over the years—a rewarding experience that gave Orlowski the opportunity to do one thing every young Marine hopes to do some day.

"One time, at a distribution center where a couple hundred people were lined up, a young girl fell over. I went over to her and looked up at the Marine Corps Master Gunnery Sergeant, who was there to do the collection in his full dress blues. I hollered to him to 'go get an ambulance' and he took off like a shot. Afterward, I called him over and said 'you made my day. I always wanted to give one of you guys an order and, by the way, button up that middle button!'"

Young Marine

In W.W. II, Orlowski never did have the rank to give such an order to a master gunnery sergeant. But, after all the one-time altar boy went through in the Pacific, and in 55 years of life since, he was certainly man enough to give it.

The Hero Next Door Returns

At left, Brenzel while he was stationed at Corregidor; middle, during his time in captivity; and at right, when he was editor of the *Wisconsin Tax News*.

'DRAFT DODGER'
DAVE BRENZEL

David Brenzel of Oregon, Wis., was in W.W. II even before it officially began for the United States. But, his war was not the war of beach invasions, kamikaze attacks and C-rations. In the three and a half years between the bombing of Pearl Harbor and the dropping of atomic bombs on Japan, Brenzel was fighting a war all right—battling against disease, oppression and his own mind as a prisoner of war of the Japanese.

The Milwaukee native was among the first groups of American POWs in W.W. II taken captive by the Japanese. He was captured May 6, 1942, after the fall of the last American stronghold in the Philippines—the island fortification of Corregidor, a place the men who lived among its protective tunnels call The Rock.

Fifty-five years later, it is still difficult to talk about the 40 months he bore the torture, near starvation and stench of death as a POW.

"Ex-POWs have problems that can't be solved merely by a few square meals and a clean shirt after libera-

Draft Dodger

tion," Brenzel explains. "In truth, the majority of former POWs were so overjoyed to be free and eating that all they wanted was their back pay, instant separation and to be left alone. Many survivors have endured 55-plus years in virtual solitude, telling no one of the recurring nightmares in which they relived the tortures and deprivation of their war years.

"Remembering some of my 1,200 POW days is easier than telling about most of them," he adds. "There had to be days when something different happened, something that burned itself into my memory. Most of the time, you pulled into your shell, into your memories and toughed it out, secure at least in the conviction that the war would end with the Allies victorious."

PHILIPPINES BOUND

Brenzel took the first steps down the road to being a POW on a path he thought would be an easier way to serve his country than the draft he knew would eventually catch up to him. (The following is based on author interviews and on the memoirs Brenzel wrote for his family, *Confessions of a POW: 45 Months Between the Rock and the Hard Place.*)

"I'd moved from Milwaukee to California in 1936, in search of work during The Great Depression. By 1939, I was a young bachelor—with no children and an 'unessential job' tending paper bag making machines—who spent his spare time weight-lifting and hobnobbing with the Hell's Angels motorcycle gang. I couldn't claim I was physically unfit for service, and it looked like my draft was inevitable."

So, Brenzel gave up his job, his motorcycle, books and shotgun and enlisted for a two-year tour specifically in the Philippine Islands—because volunteering for overseas duty meant a two vs. a three-year stint in the military. In all, Brenzel would spend 5 and a half years in the service, more than three of them as a POW.

"I was taking a creative writing class at UCLA and

The Hero Next Door Returns

they said it helps to have unique experiences to write about, so I wanted to go to the Philippines to get that experience." Brenzel got a unique experience to be sure, but not the kind he wanted to write—or talk—about much at all.

Brenzel's first Army physical should have served to foreshadow what was to come. "During the exams, occasionally the doctor would grab a swab and paint a large 'P' on a man's chest and gingerly ease him back a pace with the swab. The scarlet letter signified either crabs or lice. I was horrified. Two years later, every man in the lineup, including me, would have been eligible for that swab."

The doctor pushed Brenzel out of line too—for other reasons—when a quick listen detected an apparent heart murmur. "I stood paralyzed in panic contemplating the bridges burning behind me. No job, no motorcycle and now 4F!" But, the doctor listened again and Brenzel passed. "Often, I wished he had been right the first time.

"Two years later I remembered that doctor as I sat in a grass shack in the Cabanatuan prison camp enduring the whine of a GI. This moaner looked like an undernourished stork wearing spectacles with lenses about as thick as the bottom of a Coke bottle. 'The Army never should have taken a man in my condition,' he wailed."

Twenty days after enlistment, Brenzel boarded the USAT GRANT. "I think Noah built the GRANT for practice while he was planning the ark," Brenzel remembers of the accommodations for his nearly month-long trip to the Philippines. "My stateroom measured some 8 feet by 30 feet but it housed 40 men in bunks five tiers high. I grabbed a top bunk immediately. It was a long way up but peaceful looking at the ceiling without having to worry about things dropping on me (when the landlubbers got helplessly seasick just out of port)."

Once in Manila, on Nov. 1, 1940, he got his assign-

Draft Dodger

ment to the 100-man Battery C (Battery Wheeler) of the 59th Coast Artillery Corps, Fort Mills, on the little island in Manila Bay called Corregidor. The outfit had two disappearing guns with 12-inch bores that could "drop a one-ton projectile on a blanket five miles away." Brenzel was assigned to permanent duty with a five-man gun maintenance team at a post about a mile from the Topside barracks, located 600 feet above sea level at the highest point on the island.

Because he'd told the recruiter he was a machine operator, he was assigned special duty on The Rock. The assignment was a "prize" because Battery Wheeler's five-man detail all got specialist ratings and extra pay. "It was good duty. No dress uniform, no reveille, and no lights out. It was true we had to walk two miles for a meal but the cooks fed us whenever we showed up at a reasonable hour. We also had our own water cooler and snack bar at the big gun emplacement, courtesy of the mess sergeant."

The battery shared its space on the rock with jungle natives—of the less-than-friendly variety. "Rats liked the battery, especially our toilet soap, with some reservations. Ivory they ignored. They left tooth marks on Palmolive. Cashmere Bouqet they carried off. And, your first move before you put a foot on the floor in the morning was to shake the scorpions out of your boots."

While certainly not the lap of luxury, Battery Wheeler accommodations would seem like heaven just a few months later.

ON THE ROCK AT WAR

When the Japanese bombed Pearl Harbor, Hawaii, Dec. 7, 1941, the troops on Corregidor grew more wary of possible Japanese attacks there.

"Battery Wheeler was ready for the Japs, in a way. We had plenty of firepower to match anything stupid enough to get in range by land or sea, though we couldn't bring either gun to bear on suitable targets.

The Hero Next Door Returns

But, air defenses on The Rock were virtually zilch. There were 76 antiaircraft guns on the island and none could reach high enough to touch the first waves of arrogant Jap bombers who hit their targets at will.

"When Pearl Harbor was hit, we were actually on maneuvers but no one had any ammunition. Soon after, our new lieutenant read everyone the *Articles of War*—which I hadn't heard since enlistment—which, he was happy to note, gave him more power."

The men on Corregidor were little concerned, however, about the Japanese threat on Dec. 7. "In truth, there was scarcely concealed jubilation among us ... We thought there would be an oh-so-brief war to punish the upstart Japs and we'd be heroes parading down Frisco's Market street with our medals charming the girls in a couple of months."

But, "The Rock" at war was still different than it had been. "For most of us, the war took the fun out of the Army."

In fact, until May 5, 1942, few on Corregidor would have taken a bet on Japanese victory. "It was not imaginable. I had yet to lay eyes on any Nip closer than one buzzing Zero pilot and he'd been merely cap and goggles."

Not that The Rock hadn't been under fire. However, the Japanese focused most of their time below Battery Wheeler, keeping most Corregidor occupants in the supply and hospital tunnels at "Bottomside."

"The Rock, so to speak, was on the Japanese back burner. We were sort of a lost garrison at Topside. We definitely were part of it, but we were out of it. We didn't have the stimulation of the fight and pull back and regroup routine that kept the men on Bataan going despite starvation and exhaustion. For us, it was wait for the next flight of bombers and the next barrage."

As the Japanese bombers turned up the heat in the Spring of 1942, Brenzel spent many nights "on my belly on the oil-covered floor of the engine room trying to

Draft Dodger

get some sleep and babying a cranky water pump. One night a bomb hit right outside the engine room; the concussion knocked me out but not out of action."

By May 6, 1942, the fight for The Rock was over. It was relatively quiet on Corregidor that morning. Then, at 9 a.m. the Battery Wheeler phone rang. "There was only a skeleton garrison with a noncommissioned finance officer in command because many, including the cooks, had been converted to infantrymen and sent down to Manila Bay the night before for beach defense."

When the finance man hung up, he ordered Brenzel to destroy the Battery's guns. "The island belongs to the Japs at noon and nothing can be destroyed after that," he explained. "The next voice we heard was the mess sergeant. 'No more seconds,' he said loud and sad."

With the help of six Filipino mess boys, Brenzel disabled gun No. 2 by ramming a practice projectile into the breech, followed by a full charge of powder and detonating it with a one-minute fuse. "The No. 1 gun was disabled with a little less pizzazz. Draining the oil out of the recoil cylinders, we tripped the gun up into firing position. With no oil in the recoil cylinders, the gun kept right on going forward and threw itself off the platform. Then I made sure all my powerhouse engines were running wide open and drained the crank cases."

By noon, there was nobody except Brenzel and five casualties—as Battery Wheeler had been serving as a first aid station.

"Thus ended my career as a gun mechanic, powerhouse engineer and artillery man. The unexplored world of the POW lay before me and already I was regretting a decision I'd made a month earlier while scrounging in the bombed-out post library. Still on the shelves I found several books about how to speak

The Hero Next Door Returns

Japanese but tossed them aside certain they'd never be of any use to me!"

BIRTH OF A POW

Brenzel's first introduction to the enemy that would hold him captive for the next 40 months left him with little hope for tolerable treatment.

As Battery C remnants made their way down from Topside, Brenzel—to avoid looking like a "skulker" as men scrambled not to be first—took the lead himself. "Soon we came upon our conquerors, about two dozen of them, half standing, half squatting, one with his shoes off picking at his toes, but all with fixed bayonets and all grinning, displaying a dazzling array of metal dental work."

Then one of those squatting stood and gave Brenzel a motion that looked like he was shooing him away. "I backed away from him sharply, like a good soldier. Just as sharply, I was staggered by a rifle butt in the middle of my back. As I lurched forward another guy raised his rifle and let me have it with the tip of the bayonet in my left forearm.

"Immediately, every Jap was on his feet without grin and with rifle pointed at us. That was our first lesson in Japanese communication. The common American gesture for shooing someone away is the same one the Japs use for 'come here.'"

A short time later another Japanese soldier directed Brenzel to wait, at which time he removed Brenzel's eyeglasses. "He placed them on his own nose and looked around with obvious pleasure. 'Arigato,' he said as he waved me on. The same bastard had relieved me of my watch as well when he gave me my shirt [from my musette bag] for a bandage.

"That was the last time I ever tried to act anything like a leader if I thought there might be a Jap within miles."

Hundreds of men soon joined thousands, all march-

Draft Dodger

ing their way eastward toward the 92nd Garage—at least the slab left of the garage after a bomb had blown the rest away—located at the east end of the island, 20 miles west of Manila. As night fell, the troops crowded onto a hillside abutting San Jose.

"This was one waiting period where we really sweated, looking down at an assortment of manned Japanese machine guns and one tiny Jap tank. As we waited for we knew not what, we saw General Wainwright [who took charge of The Rock after Gen. Douglas MacArthur escaped to Australia] and several other officers paraded through under guard. That was the only time I ever saw 'Skinny,' and before nightfall the officers were separated from the enlisted men and marched off to their own fate."

By nightfall the next day, Brenzel was in his new home at the 92nd Garage, which a few quickly nicknamed "MacArthur Park" and "Shit City."

The POWs jammed into the area may have been a potpourri of the Army, Navy, Marines and Air Force but they were all assigned to the same horrible living.

There were no cooking facilities and no running water. The latrine—used often as the POWs nearly all suffered dysentery by now—"was a ditch 10 feet wide and six feet deep running along one side of the compound." All this pitted against the stench from the bloated corpses lining shallow foxholes on the beach near the garage.

But, Brenzel and the other fresh POWs were not yet overly concerned about their situation. "We figured no humans would force, or even permit, other humans to live under such conditions for very long. Our belief that our discomforts would be only temporary was fortified by the presence of Japanese newsreel cameramen at the gate as we walked into the garage area."

By day three the Japanese had grown exasperated at the state of things themselves and permitted some POWs to forage outside the compound for what food or supplies they could use. Brenzel did not join the

The Hero Next Door Returns

first of these foraging details.

"My first contact with the Japs had chilled permanently any desire to be prominent among the POWs. This reluctance cut me out of the delicacies of trying to believe potatoes fried in furniture wax can be palatable.

"However, it did encourage me to look more closely at what earlier scroungers had ignored. One long-term treasure was a can of lighter fluid, which I transferred to a bottle labeled 'Vaseline Hair Tonic.' What I am convinced was a lifesaver was a supply of a chemical used to chlorinate swimming pools. I put a couple tablespoons of that in a pill bottle. Through some critical water shortages and questionable sources, I never failed to put a few grains in my canteen and let it work before I drank. Some guys thought I was nuts but I'm here today and they wound up in little boxes."

By coincidence, Brenzel's buddy Sgt. William W. (Bill) Hutchinson III from San Francisco—a finance noncom from Manila who'd been stationed with Battery C-59 when The Rock fell—was at the 92nd Garage with him.

The two nearly died together as well on their 10th day. "We decided to forage in some ravines that had escaped direct gunfire from the mainland. We were like twin Red Riding Hoods wandering the woods when we met a Jap officer apparently on the same mission, except he had a little pistol. He began popping away with his sidearm and Bill and I took off down the ravine like quail scurrying under brush before a hunter."

Since the POWs were fairly sure the Japs were preparing to move them elsewhere, not kill them outright, much of the foraging became a scramble for whatever portable tools for survival might come in handy.

After 16 days, Brenzel left for Manila in a landing barge with an extra canteen, deck of cards and a dictionary. "They were all perishable but proved to be worth their weight in gold as time went by. That deck of cards was a treasure both in terms of the number

Draft Dodger

of hours I was able to spend with it playing bridge and cribbage and for the bits of food and cigarettes I got as rental from POWs who wanted to use it."

Such small bits and pieces were key to survival over the next 40 months, Brenzel is convinced. "To me, survival as a POW was a question of early recognition of the practicalities of existence. When we were to march to the dock for the trip to Manila, I noticed one man who'd bedded down near us wasn't going to be making the trip. He died in the night wearing a brand new pair of boots my size.

"I was wearing those boots when I hopped off the landing barge into Manila Bay for the long march through the city to Bilibid prison. The boots fit beautifully and served me well until the following November when I managed to liberate a better pair from a British officer's luggage—which the Japanese had assigned us to carry after British POWs from Singapore joined the ranks."

'ON PARADE'

The forced march to their new accommodations was a bizarre, but largely silent parade past Filipinos lining Dewey Boulevard. "We didn't know how to accept the mostly silent populace. There were occasional shouts and waves from a Filipino who would recognize a POW. If there was no Jap guard, someone might dart from the crowd with a cigarette or bit of food. The Samaritans were taking a risk and some paid for it with blows from the Japs. The acts of bravery and kindness were many all the way to Bilibid."

While he recognized none of the Filipino Samaritans along the boulevard, Brenzel spotted one familiar face. "I saw Col. Paul Bunker squatting red-faced, mopping his face as a frozen-faced Jap stood behind him with a ready rifle. That was the last time I saw the colonel with whom I had had several run-ins earlier. He died the following year in prison in Taiwan."

Their march through town—and all they'd so far

The Hero Next Door Returns

endured—was tough. But, Brenzel stresses, it was nothing compared to what other POWs had survived—if they survived—on the Bataan Death March six weeks prior.

"Still, most of us remained convinced our captivity would be only a matter of weeks, or maybe months at the most. If it wouldn't be a fast war, at least there would soon be an exchange of prisoners." Either way, the POWs believed, this uncomfortable existence was only temporary.

Even the walled prison accommodations at Bilibid seemed all right, at first, Brenzel recalls. "We were given a bounteous meal of well-cooked rice and as much hot tea as we wanted."

But, the peace of a full stomach wasn't to last. "About 500 of us were soon prodded into marching order again and off we went to the railroad. We were literally rammed into freight cars without room to sit. In the rattling, scorching darkness and stench came full realization of our impotence. When the doors were opened—at Cabanatuan six hours later—a few exploded out onto the railbed, others staggered out, some crawled, and some were dragged out unconscious or dead. How many of the latter we never knew. We were nameless, numberless, rankless members of no organization. We were just carloads of POWs the Japs were moving."

Once in Cabanatuan the strange parade of POWs began again. As soon as they reached their destination—a former Filipino army training camp about 60 miles north of Manila—the rainy season began in earnest.

"After a couple of bold souls shed the few clothes they were wearing and showered under the pouring eaves with obvious enjoyment, the rest of us joined in. The Japs and Filipinos enjoyed the show, and we the shower—an hour after rubbing shoulders with corpses in the boxcars."

Some sense of order returned among the POWs as

Draft Dodger

Navy and Army prisoners were separated and broken into 10-men squads. "Each squad was in one stall in a long line of stalls that were open to the elements on one side with the "living quarters" raised about chair-height from the ground.

"There were no officers among us and no recognized rank or seniority among enlisted men. Any grouping that happened to match pre-surrender organization was merely coincidental. It was as though you were reborn when you became a POW."

LIFE OF A POW

With the order came more rules. In addition to the "nit-picking bowing and saluting we had to render every Jap yardbird ... every man was a guard over the other nine men in his squad. If one man escaped the other nine would be shot. We POWs had to set up a roster and mount guard 24 hours a day at positions inside the fence on the entire camp perimeter.

"No one ever asked what would happen if an entire squad went under the fence at once. Fresh in our memory was the unconscious man tied to a post at the guard house entrance to the camp when we arrived. Early the following day, a truck pulled up with three trussed POWs who'd been on the train with us. They were stripped and tied to stakes and beaten for three days before they were hanged—as they'd been caught walking down the road to Cabanatuan.

"Every day or so some POW was to be found tied to a post near the guardhouse, stripped and beaten for God knows what real or fancied infraction. A favorite punishment was to make a man squat with a stick behind his knees and his wrists tied to his ankles."

It was just a few days into their stay at Cabanatuan that POWs began to suffer from the worst—and in some ways most deadly—ailment possible, depression.

"Until then things were happening every day to almost everybody. True, they weren't generally pleas-

The Hero Next Door Returns

ant things but they tended to get your attention. Now, we could sit around and contemplate our navels, which were approaching our backbones. We were able to devote more attention to our dysentery, malaria, beriberi and ulcers. The morning burial detail had more work every day. The meals were an almost unvarying diet of overcooked sloppy rice and onion soup.

"Cabanatuan clearly was a dead end, and POW morale got steadily lower, which doubtless boosted the death rate. So, I worked every angle I could to get out—without trying to escape. Sick as I was, I hung around the doctors and said I never felt better and volunteered for any and every work detail outside camp. I reasoned that if they wanted to work me, they'd have to feed me."

Of course, what they fed the working POW was less-than-sufficient. For weeks on end the prisoners ate a rice gruel called "lugau" that softened their teeth and gums too much to enjoy the tougher, occasional coconut.

"But, one time, the cook miraculously softened dried ears of corn enough so it could be eaten off the cob. One glorious meal, each of us got a hot roll and the chief cook—also a POW—strutted about that accomplishment.

"About once a week a live carabao materialized, though this was one carabao for several thousand men and it had to stretch a long way in the soup. The butchering was always witnessed by hundreds of critical troops and even the blood was saved."

Getting food and talking about food broke the monotony and provided the few light moments of POW life.

"Service bull sessions were traditionally heavily laced with sex. But, with POWs, such sessions focused on food as our libido diminished greatly as we lost weight. GI bull sessions—which formerly would have made Don Juan look like a monk—became swap meets

Draft Dodger

Brenzel drew this map of Corregidor and picture of a POW looking for "zampan" (garbage) while a POW at the Yokohama shipyard. A break to use to the "benjo" (bathroom) was always a chance for a POW to perhaps check out the zampan boxes around the shipyard for any food cooks on Japanese ships may have tossed. "A stomach-stretching find of edible garbage was rare but the hope of one was enough to keep you trying, though if caught by a guard you wound up with some cuts and bruises to go along with your aching gut. Supposedly the Japs Army was feeding us and lost face if we were seen hunting garbage."

The Hero Next Door Returns

for gourmet recipes.

"To measure the strength of this conversion to celibacy, I would test the recipe hounds. I'd ask them to imagine a table groaning with their favorite foods on one side of the room while in bed on the other side would be a gorgeous woman begging for their attention. When asked which they'd choose, they invariably took the food, refusing to accept the concept that the food might wait while they attended to the lady."

The POWs took some storytelling to the next level, however, putting on occasional vaudeville-style shows. "Heat and tedium made story tellers interesting and a good yarn spinner soon had an audience. The camp show emerged. The Japs gave us a few musical instruments for the musicians among us to use. Then comedians stepped out of the ranks, including a former vaudevillian named Melody who made a good master of ceremonies. The Japs always had front row seats and usually laughed as loud as the POWs at the jokes," often made at the Japanese's expense.

After three months, Brenzel volunteered to join a 350-man labor detail rumored to be headed to Japan. "I hit the medical screening crew at once and asked for the assignment, maintaining I was ready, willing and able. Actually the doctors didn't care what condition I was in as I was ambulatory and the glass rod they eased into my rectum wasn't red when they withdrew it."

The work crew was soon loaded onto trucks and then into rail cars bound for a special work detail.

"We were pretty sure we were leaving hell behind us. At least we were leaving a lot of friends behind us, buried under beer bottles. We used Pale Pilsen bottles for grave markers, neck down and stuffed with curled records of the man's name, rank and serial number. Later victims were stripped and dumped in mass graves and burial details then hoped they did not float when the rain flooded the trenches."

Draft Dodger

Those first three months would soon be thought of as "the good old days," however, compared to what conditions awaited the work detail and those they left behind. "Monotonous as the diet was there was food enough to sustain life. Jap morale was high because they still had momentum and hadn't suffered the losses that marked the turn of the tide later in 1942." As the Japanese gave back territory, they gave less and less to the POWs. Food became scarce and acts of viciousness increased.

DEATH AT SEA

Brenzel soon would know that hell on earth could live on water.

A few hours after leaving Cabanatuan, Brenzel was back at Bilibid prison. From there they walked to the docks and boarded the Lima Maru, a ship with "a rusting hulk of flaking paint, of leaking, hissing steam pipes and dripping oil lines. With a shuddering speed of six knots, she displaced about 4,000 tons." Yet the POWs were anxious to board her. "Her decks suggested shade and we smelled food."

The ship was filled with drunken Japanese, eager to return to their home island for a bit or rest and recreation. POWs were packed into a 60-by-80-foot compartment that was eight-feet high and located on the bottom deck, just above the bilge.

"Dimly we could make out platforms extending from the sides dividing the eight feet into four-foot levels. Before our eyes became accustomed to the reduced light, our noses told us of new degrees of corruption. As we packed into the two levels, our sweat-lubricated bodies slid like worms in a bait can as we squirmed to make space where there was none. Hunger we forgot until the next day; thirst was with us soon."

For a month, the POWs that could survived in this dark, rank pit. Only the dead—and a few men assigned to haul food and latrine buckets—went to an upper deck.

215

The Hero Next Door Returns

"Boiled rice and water were lowered to us in buckets; slop was hauled up and often the buckets were dropped. When their task was finished, the bucket men were herded below immediately. Each man drank his twice-daily water ration as soon as he got it; otherwise, it disappeared while he slept."

After three days, it was more than food and slop being hauled topside. For days men had been screaming, crying for their mothers, "howling like dogs."

"On the third day, a man died screaming. On each succeeding day, one, two or three corpses had a line tied around their middle and were hauled to the top deck and probably tossed over the side. Toward the end of the month, heat, malaria, dysentery and thirst weakened them so they died quietly. Death was no enemy, no stranger. 'Pass the line over this way. There's one over here.' No prayers, just a bowline, a heave and another man's troubles were over."

The Lima Maru continued on its course, zigzagging to avoid Allied submarines. "It took a month and 50 lives to sail what roughly is 500 miles in a straight line" to Taikow, the southernmost port of Formosa.

Thirteen days before that ultimate destination—after the ship had reached Japanese waters—the hatch covers were rolled off the POW quarters completely and groups of 10 were brought topside to be washed with cold, but refreshing, sea water.

WORKING THE RAILROAD

Upon their arrival in Taikow the POWs were "marched and marched and marched" through the city, flanked by thousands of children lining the street to see the parade. After two hot hours, they reached a modern railroad depot and, to their amazement, boarded actual coach cars.

"The station was only 400 yards away from the dock! The proud guards had taken us on a tour of the city to exhibit us! We rode all night and finally stopped at another station, this one with a diminutive engine and

Draft Dodger

tiny flatcars."

The POWs boarded the small train on a two-hour ride past ample fields of bananas, rice, sugar, sweet potatoes and peanuts. "It finally looked as though the feeding part of working us would be easy." However, food was nowhere to be found when the train finally stopped on a desolate patch of rocks. "This was to be the scene of our labor for almost two months. Our camp was about a mile from the tracks with high barbed wire surrounding long, low grass huts."

Eventually, a small camp commander came to inspect his new workers. As he watched, "we stripped and walked to the side of the compound. While the soldiers pawed over our belongings, a perspiring doctor examined us briefly. He was fat but, as he grunted, he poked with surprisingly long white fingers. His skin looked like the belly of a catfish."

Once dressed, each POW got "a small loaf of bread with some strange tasting soup to which was added a banana. With this menu our hopes rose, but it happened to be the best meal we were to have for months."

After leaving their shoes in a pile—not realizing they would not see them again for many weeks—the work detail filed, by groups of 60, into their grass huts.

While smoking would be allowed in camp, and special boxes had been placed in the center of each hut as ashtrays, the accommodations were little better than the Lima Maru. "Along either side of the hut was a platform of bamboo slats about 18 inches from the ground. For each man there were three food bowls and a pair of chopsticks. There was a mosquito net for each 15 men. If most of us hadn't brought blankets, we'd have been bled to exhaustion. The nights were warm enough so we could sleep uncovered and use the blankets to seal the cracks between the bamboo slats beneath us."

'DILIGENT AND CLEAN'

These quarters would be Brenzel's home as the

217

The Hero Next Door Returns
POWs worked to build a railroad. The prisoners soon met their taskmaster, a low-rank Japanese schoolmaster-turned-interpreter—nicknamed both Tanglefoot, for his lanky, 6-foot-tall awkwardness, and Boris, for his resemblance to movie star Boris Karloff.

He addressed the prisoners at dawn their first day in camp. "With a faintly German accent, he spoke the ridiculous brand of English used to caricature the Japanese. He stood on a platform two feet high and held a small English-Japanese dictionary, which he carried around like a priest's breviary.

"'You will get shoes. Every man will get shoes,' Tanglefoot said, waving his arm dramatically to summon 10 Jap recruits dragging straw sacks which spilled pairs of canvas sneakers in the dust. 'We have three sizes: large, larger and largest. Do you 'onnerstsan? Answer in a loud voice.' 'HAI' we roared, though perhaps a third had feet small enough to get into size 'largest.'

"'You will have clothing also,' he said as recruits brought forth green bundles. Each man got a shirt and pair of shorts of rough cloth like cheesecloth. By swapping around later, we found the clothes came in three sizes as well: small, smaller and smallest but we managed to get into them."

Then Tanglefoot took to explaining how POWs were to conduct themselves.

"'We must be diligent. We must be clean. We must drink only water boiled in the kitchen. We must salute every soldier we approach, if we are wearing a hat (and we were permitted to wear whatever headgear we had, most often a tropical sun helmet). If we are bareheaded, we must bow from the waist.'"

"'We go to the labor. You must be diligent,'" Tanglefoot continued, adding—after prodding from the commander's shout—that POWs further must goosestep past the main gate guardhouse, keeping eyes right, each time they passed. "He evidently was not familiar with the phrase 'goosestep' so he demon-

Draft Dodger

strated ... and fell off the platform. We were careful not to react to this slapstick as the 12 to 16-year-old militia that guarded us looked eager to use their bayonets."

The prisoners were herded from camp to the railroad tracks where they were to reinforce the trestle using short handled, pointed hoes, shallow baskets and about 40 four-wheeled gondolas. Using line and five-foot poles civilian overseers showed the prisoners how to tie two full baskets to a pole, shoulder load them and hurry them to the destination.

"The IQ of the POWs en masse became zero. We understood nothing. We were clumsy. Every time Jap backs were turned the rushing current of the river below the trestle was likely to swallow lines and poles."

Though the prisoners didn't know how long they'd be working at this new camp, they were sure it wouldn't be overly long. "We felt we were in a probationary period before being shipped to Japan because none of us was ever beaten so badly he was unable to work. The viciousness of the teenage guards seldom went beyond a kick in the shins or playful bayonet jab."

Still, the probationary camp was no POW holiday.

"After several days of rice, we were served a new dish, which at first we thought was oatmeal. Actually, it was rough barley, which soon supplanted the more costly rice. Scurvy and beriberi—among other things—became more obvious. Cracked, bleeding lips and sore tongues and throats made the act of eating painful. Many men could not work at all. An increase in the vegetable ration helped as did fruit. Twice we were issued grapefruit in such quantities that we had to divide one fruit among 11 men. The sick shared with the well, though we had orders not to give the sick any because 'it is not good for them.'"

While POWs helped each other and did what they could to undermine Japanese efforts, displays of true patriotism were rare. At least Brenzel thought so until one day, two weeks after they reached the camp.

The Hero Next Door Returns

"We were roused from our mats earlier than usual and herded roughly to our 'parade' ground in the mist that the dawn wipes away. Thinly clad, we shivered unfed until the sun was above the horizon as the teenage guards circled us grimly, now and then poking a POW not rigidly at attention.

"Standing at attention for extended periods was a condition we had many chances to get used to in coming weeks and years. It was a form of mass punishment and torture that did not incapacitate workers. After a while, you learn to lock the joints and muscles and turn off the brain and almost go to sleep."

About noon two trucks pulled up loaded with armed Japanese servicemen. In English, one explained there were good jobs with plenty of food for anyone who could operate cryptographs or knew radio codes.

"Not a muscle moved in the POW ranks. Virtually every one of us knew who the communications men among us were.

'Come out,' the Jap roared! About 15 minutes later he stalked through the ranks tugging at whatever he could see in the way of dogtags, finally seizing one man and shoving him out front and marching the POW out of the compound. A half-hour later, they returned without him. Again the interrogator demanded experts step out; again he was ignored. This time, four POWs were marched out never to be seen again. At sunset, the rest of us still stood at attention, many sadly in need of clean underwear. We heard the two trucks roar off. We got no food that day."

It was back to work the next day, and the next, and the next .... A routine seldom broken except for a command inspection or, in one case, a visit by the press.

"Well-dressed civilians appeared at our work site carrying a camera and Tanglefoot asked if any of us had parents who had been born in Italy or Germany. Buscaglio, a New York boy, raised his hands. Sure, and the O'Rourkes and McDaniels among my forebears were spinning in their graves when I raised my

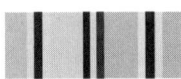

Draft Dodger

hand as well. It was my turn to help push the gondola and I was game for anything to break the routine.

"We two POWs were returned to camp with the civilians. One reporter who spoke enough English to serve as spokesman, was strictly Hollywood newshack, with pencil, pad and snap brim hat."

Brenzel gave his name when asked, though POW protocol was to give answers as far from the truth as possible. "But, he could have found out my name easily enough. Then he asked 'where is your home?'

"'Ohio,' I replied, knowing the Japanese word for 'good morning' is 'ohayo.'

"'Good morning. Where is your home?'

"'Ohio,' I reiterated.

"'Good morning. Where do you live?' He snapped.

"I figured the joke had gone far enough and didn't want him to lose face. 'My home is in Columbus, Ohio. Columbus is a city in the state of Ohio,'" I lied.

Tanglefoot himself provided some break in the routine as well as he wandered among the POWs trying to improve his English.

"His arrival never caused silence or change of subject. We merely switched to slang and he was lost. One day he squatted beside Bal, a GI from the Bronx. 'Why did you enter the Army?' Tanglefoot asked. 'I had to beat a rap for swiping 17 jalopies,' Bal said. After consulting his dictionary, Tanglefoot returned to the group and selected me for a confidential interview. Nodding toward Bal he asked, 'what did he say? He speaks broken English.'"

One day, Brenzel found his own break from the routine in the pharmacy. "There was a Japanese doctor but he didn't have much for what ailed us. Aspirin seemed to be the same cure-all it is in America but a POW had to put on a pretty good act to get that. A common Japanese remedy for diarrhea is powdered opium. I managed to filch a good-sized pinch while alone in the pharmacy on sick call. For medicinal purposes you swallow it; I smoked it and slept well that

221

The Hero Next Door Returns

night."

One routine from which there seemed no break was death.

"Malaria and dysentery took their toll. A GI named Wilbur Huntsinger went first. His body was placed in a pine box on the parade ground. There was a bouquet of flowers on top. With bowed heads we stood silent in formation as a Marine read a passage from the Bible. We were moved when Tanglefoot read a message he probably found in some catalog of English for appropriate occasions. All the Japs formed and presented arms as the bugler sounded a mournful call. Even the camp commander stood by and saluted with his saber. Then, we returned to our huts for the remainder of the day. The Japs took him away in a long box and brought his ashes back two days later in a small pine cube painted blue.

"Tanglefoot's memorial was moving at the time. Just how canned it was became obvious in a few days. He gave the same message for the next three funerals with Huntsinger's name in it instead of the man we were sending off!"

BACK TO SEA

In the middle of November, the POWs knew they'd soon be shipping out. "We found our shoes piled on the parade ground when we assembled. 'Wash your clothing. You must be diligent,' Tanglefoot ordered."

By the end of the next day, they were back in Taikow and aboard a rusty freighter, the Daichi Maru. Though not a pleasant ride, this voyage would be better than their last journey by sea.

"It took little urging to get us down into the hold quickly because we knew from past experience it was important to establish territorial rights in any new quarters."

But, they soon found they'd be sharing their quarters with other English-speaking POWs. "Limeys actually, though it took months to sort out all the accents,

Draft Dodger

as they were from all parts of the British Empire. In addition, there were a few Dutch from Sumatra, whose lack of language could be spotted at once. But, Limey or Dutch, these new POWs represented a brand new civilization for us to explore."

However, it was obvious this new civilization knew too well the life of a POW. "The Limeys were in worse shape than the Yanks for fever and dysentery."

Regardless of where they were from, POWs shared the same agony. "Much of everyone's time above deck was spent in line waiting to use the benjo [Japanese for latrine]. Some carried their pants instead of wearing them, some stood straddle-legged hoping against hope that it wasn't their lives draining away."

The prisoners' confinement was "more relaxed" as homebound Nipponese soldiers had "almost a festive attitude. Food and water supplies were ample. POWs were fed twice a day but plenty. There was fish in the soup."

After a 1,000-mile voyage northeast of Taikow, the ship arrived in Moji on the southern Japanese island of Kyushu.

"We encountered the complete Japanese bureaucrat on the dock as we had to go through customs! We had to display our pitiful belongings to prove we were not bringing in any contraband. The cards I'd been guarding so jealously since Corregidor came to light. The customs agent picked up the box, took out the deck, riffled through it, fingered his rubber stamp, put the deck back in the box and then stamped the official red-ink Japanese OK on the box. I had been afraid he was either going to confiscate the deck or stamp every card!"

After a ferry boat ride to Honshu, Japan's biggest island, they boarded a passenger train. The POWs got their first look at Mt. Fuji and noted it was Thanksgiving Day. They rode through Hiroshima, Kobe, Osaka, Nagoya and Kyoto before arriving at Yokohama. "It

The Hero Next Door Returns

was a land untouched by war, but shabby—like a Midwest dairy farm with a trim herd of cattle and a lot of buildings in need of paint."

SHIP BUILDING 101

In the usual column of four, the prisoners marched a few miles to the dock area and warehouse that would be their home—from Nov. 28, 1942, to May 12, 1945—the Mitsubishi Heavy Industries Ltd. Warehouse at Yokohama. By mid-point there were some 484 prisoners working for Mitsubishi of which 272 were American.

"Our Yokohama crew included two from our artillery outfit from the top of Corregidor, a P40 pilot who was at Clark Field in Luzon (attacked while Pearl Harbor was still smoking)—who was attached to us because there were no P40s for him to pilot at Corregidor—and some 4th Marines from Shanghai that arrived via the Bataan Death March or Corregidor. The British among us included survivors of the PRINCE OF WHALES and the REPULSE. There were Dutch submariners from Batavia, men who'd been in the short siege of Singapore, and a civilian engineer from San Francisco who'd been captured on Wake Island.

"Our compound was a warehouse where Yokohama touched Tokyo Bay. Bread awaited us as did an assortment of shoes and Japanese army uniforms and overcoats as well as one blanket per man. On the sixth day we each got a work uniform: black, baggy pants and a coat."

God may have rested on the seventh day but POWs at Mitsubishi started work. That first day "eight Japanese soldiers herded us along. Over the months, this guard-type operation dwindled to two soldiers with rifles and six company guards with vitamin sticks, which vaguely resembled pick handles and made a POW apply himself with renewed vigor when applied to his back."

And, if they wanted to eat, they had to apply them-

Draft Dodger

selves to their work.

"The day began with a shrill 'Sho,' from a sleepy Jap sentry ambling through the warehouse who rousted us from the low wooden platform we lived on when we didn't have our feet on concrete floors. We slept on straw mats, which were tossed out in the spring along with their tiny tenants.

"Five minutes later came 'Tenko' and we went outside to form squads. The Jap officer of the day, a noncom, made the rounds with two bowlegged sentries, listened to reports and checked the count. When the O.D. called 'Bango' we gave an eyes-right and counted off in Japanese, each man turning his head forward as he shouted his number."

A few minutes of calisthenics was followed by a rushed breakfast. "On a table or bunk each man in the 40-man squad placed two containers for his food—soup in one spot, 'entree' in the other. Round Dutch messkits, rectangular British dixies, oval American messkits, tin cans, china and wooden bowls, these mealtime assemblies looked like orderly rummage sales. All containers and utensils were scrupulously clean. Though we had no dish soap, we knew the penalty for contamination.

"The Limeys called 'mess orderlies,' the Yanks yelled, 'chow down,' and the buckets arrived. The thin soup usually contained greens of some kind and was faintly salty. Solid food, frequently boiled barley, was first packed into a measuring bowl by the dipper and then transferred to a waiting container. Sometimes it was boiled potatoes.

"After the bowls were licked clean, those with tobacco may have had time for a quick smoke before the order 'Shigoto (work)' was heard."

Brenzel went to work on a welding detail, coached by a stately old gentleman nicknamed Old Gent, who taught the prisoners—through effective pantomiming as he knew no English—the intricacies of the Japanese bowing ceremonies. "Old Gent was the only Jap

The Hero Next Door Returns

I ever heard saying 'sukaji' to a POW. It is the top-drawer way of saying it is time to eat. As a race, the Japanese do as much bowing as breathing and the more superior the person, the deeper the bow or 'keirei.' The really deep bow for a few high pooh-bahs is 'saikeirei,' which is a bow of at least 90 degrees. Without English, Old Gent did as good a job at explaining the bow as Emily Post could have."

But, few of those in charge were so courteous. "The few minutes between chow and bedtime were not always to be enjoyed if the Bull was on duty. Bull was a tall and burly private first class who knew a few words of English and delighted in conducting final roll call. He also gloried in using a POW for a judo dummy when he felt the urge, which was frequently."

GRAY GHOSTS

The first winter at Yokohama took its toll. Of the original 500, 450 POWs remained and some 50 of those were too sick to work, though the POWs had to maintain a work quota of 400.

Since the Japanese gave the "too-sick-to-work" only half or two-thirds rations to 'bring them back to a diligent state of mind,' cooks—who were also POWs—managed to massage the statistics so the sick always got full rations. We were working, and wasting away, on 1,000 calories a day and agreed that cutting a sick man to 500 was a death sentence.

"Decisions on feeding the sick were reached by consensus among the POWs. Matters of internal discipline were handled the same way, with the Japs in total ignorance of what we were doing. For example, a POW caught stealing from another POW was encircled by a half dozen men and thoroughly punched out with other POWs standing by to be sure no Japs saw."

Brenzel had been assigned with 32 other POWs to the welding squad. By the spring of 1945, his squad alone lost nine to pneumonia and dysentery.

Brenzel himself had survived a bad bout with pneu-

Draft Dodger

monia. Even his bunkmates Larry and Jake told him later they didn't think he'd pull through. "Out of earshot they referred to me as the 'gray ghost.'"

"During that period we got one of our rare Red Cross parcels. I ate the contents with dispatch except for the chocolate bar. I couldn't smell it, so I hoarded it until I was certain I'd be able to taste it. Every day for three weeks I took that bar out and sniffed it. Nothing. Finally the day came when I detected the chocolate aroma and ate the bar in front of my comrades, entirely unconcerned about their drooling."

Disease took its toll on all of them in one form or another. "But, to dwell out loud or to yourself on your infirmities, discomforts, hunger or cold was fatal. It was a good way to ask for isolation from your fellow victims or a ticket to Squad 13. Putting it simply, if you moped, you were dead meat."

Squad 13 was what the POWs had taken to naming the blue boxes—which contained the ashes of those who had died—that lined up in growing number in the corner of the warehouse. "Death in Yokohama was denied the ceremony it received on Formosa. Everyone was walking sick or 'byoki' most the time and sick-in-bed or 'shushin' some of the time."

A desire to get the food that helped keep such illness at bay was so overpowering many POWs sacrificed "a meal tomorrow for a bone tonight." A bone in the soup was a prize, Brenzel recalled because "there was always the possibility of marrow. You could swap the bone for tobacco or perhaps someone's future breakfast if you didn't want to suck on it or grate it into your own dinner.

"Willingness to sacrifice a meal tomorrow resulted in the creation of a level of plutocrats and ultimately Squad 14. Dealers accumulating hoards of smokes and meal futures had fellow POWs doing their laundry or making their beds. The sharpies got sharper; the weak got weaker. The pernicious system got out of hand and dangerous to the extent that it was boost-

The Hero Next Door Returns

ing the death rate.

"No man could have been considered mentally normal. The average weight was 50 pounds below prewar level. Some staggering skeletons would approach a dealer and offer him a Sunday meal for one today. Keeping up that from day to day they could reach a condition where they had promised one or several men three meals a day for weeks ahead. The next step would be violence.

"Lt. Van Buskirk, apparent senior among the five American officers at our Yokohama camp—and actually a grand guy—finally had all the dog-eat-dog he could take. He had no following, no precedent and, for all practical purposes, no authority. But, he drew up an order that all trading in food was to stop immediately. He swore that after the 'lashup' was over, he'd move heaven and earth to court martial any man caught trading food. All debts were canceled and each man had to sign a certificate that he'd heard the order.

"That stopped a large part of the trading. To safeguard the weak, Squad 14 was formed. All notorious traders were assigned to a definite area of camp for meals. No man assigned to that area could leave it until he left to wash emptied bowls."

AN ORDERLY BUNCH

The Mitsubishi POW workforce was nothing if not orderly. "On underwear, shirt and coat we wore breast tags bearing our name in 'katakana'—phonetic Japanese—and a number in Arabic numerals, mine was 762. The back of our coats bore large numbers. Even our small-peaked caps had tiny white tags, like pigtails, flapping our numbers, this time in Japanese numerals."

At first the group marched the two miles from the bay, through the city and to the shipyard in an orderly fashion. But, "after a couple of months the parade degenerated into a ragged ramble, with the guards

Draft Dodger

bunched and gossiping and the POWs freely breaking ranks to salvage cigarette butts from gutters or to empty bladders, regardless of spectators.

"We had some civilian precedent for the latter. Beside our march through the city was a low bluff atop which was a small home in which lived, we decided, an unfriendly Japanese 'Gold Star' mother. Sometimes she would come to the lip of the hill, lift her skirts and urinate a long stream in our direction."

The march was educational in other ways. The POWs could gauge, over time, that Japan was slowly losing the war. "At first there were candy shops, food shops and restaurants open for business along the line. Eventually we were to see all these shops entirely close and air raid shelters appear like mushrooms over night. We occasionally would find a discarded newspaper and maps inside would prove useful in updating us on our progress.

"But, if we had no other means of getting information we would have known how the Japs were faring just by watching the air raid shelters. At first, shallow trenches appeared here and there and then multiplied. Trenches got deeper and eventually became long mounds with entrances at either end. In time, we'd see entire blocks of flimsy houses pulled down to make fire lanes through the city."

Occasionally civilians or German sailors would fill in some of the war news gaps. The POWs worked alongside civilian Japanese at the shipyards every day, and "they were little better dressed than the POWs. We found the civilian Jap to be altogether human, simple, kind and credulous, while if you put a uniform on him there could be a diabolical transformation."

Brenzel found his time working with small crews of Japanese civilians a bit of respite. "Occasionally, one would be an aspiring welder and I'd spend the day observing, coaching, mooching smokes and trying to keep warm. Most Jap welders were kids about 12 to16

229

The Hero Next Door Returns

who knew their stuff but were cocky and convinced the war would end in a stalemate. Nevertheless, they were eager to hear about things American. Thus, a lone Yank working with a handful of Japs was more frequently a mine of exotic information than a target for abuse. Every chance I got, I was a member-at-large of the Chamber of Commerce, extolling the glories of America and its inevitable invincibility."

Of course, even with civilians, a POW could only get away with so much. "I worked alone with one crew for four days, feuding with the youngest member all the time. He was mean. I kept smiling despite his continuous stream of abuse. I did, however, give him my choicest cuss words, in English of course. About noon on the fourth day I was alone with the old man who bossed the crew and, in Japanese, I asked him the time.

"'Eleven o'clock, kid. We don't eat for an hour yet,' he said in English. Well, if I had any loose teeth they'd have dropped out! 'You have to be more careful what you say around here. More people speak English than you think.' Fortunately, he had not revealed to the rest of the crew what I'd been saying about the kid's ancestry and personal habits."

SMALL ACTS OF DISOBEDIENCE

POWs did what they could to hasten the Japanese defeat. While small acts of sabotage were not a daily occurrence, "a couple hundred POWs wandering around a Japanese shipyard for 30 months can get into a lot of mischief.

"In any of our wanderings, it was understood that we picked up anything left unguarded—whether a tool or ship part. As the POWs had many legitimate errands in the yard, once one acquired a tool he didn't have to conceal it. Where he carried it is what counted. It usually wound up in the drink or close to the bottom of the scrap pile."

In fact, the Japanese even thanked Brenzel for his

sabotage efforts. "I was commended for my diligence in returning to the supply room so often for electrodes. It was customary to get more than you needed by saying the surplus was for another welder. On the way back to the job, the extra bundles could be dropped into the bay or any convenient puddle. Once soaked, the rods were no good unless recoated."

During his time working in coating the rods, Brenzel and other POWs would often add disruptive materials to the dipping mix. "I was welder enough by that time to know the importance of having good material to work with."

There were other small acts of sabotage as well. "If the coast was clear, an alert POW passing a stockpile selected a piece and moved it as far as he safely could. You always took the steel with the greatest number of drilled holes or evident importance.

"The POW sent to sharpen punches, chisels or drills knew how to burn them by holding them to the wheel too long or too tightly. A pinch of carborundum dust sneaked from the grinding wheels could be slipped into the piston chambers of the pneumatic tools.

"Rivets in the heating pot tended to be heated into uselessness or were not quite hot enough when needed. Air hoses and welding cables worked their way to positions where walking cranes or shifting metal plates would cut them.

"Also, you could hold up welding by tampering with the clamp that holds the welding electrode threaded to the end of the cable. If the clamp is loose, heat is generated sometimes to the extent the connection melts off and welding cannot continue until the connection is reattached.

"Or, a POW welder going to adjust the power at his box may have opportunity to adjust others. In this case, the adjustment is followed by muttering Japanese welders looking for leaks in their lines."

When they could, POWs produced weak welds to help weaken the Japanese fleet. "When a ship was

The Hero Next Door Returns

launched the first things to go aboard were welding cables to repair all the welds that ruptured with the strain of hitting the water. POWs weren't the only ones making defective welds. I welded a gun platform on the side of a tanker and I'd bet that gun fell into the ocean the first time it was fired!"

Even unintentional defects could be kept on the ship skeleton line with a little POW ingenuity. When inspectors tested a rivet—by tapping on it—they'd circle defective rivets with white paint. "The self-assumed duty of any POW in the area was to remove the circle, if he got a chance."

Even the POWs didn't want rivets circled, however, because it meant a demerit for the riveter, be he prisoner or civilian. "A Jap riveter showed me how to rectify this when he was concerned about one he'd put in. It didn't ring right so the Jap borrowed my welding equipment and put a little bead on the edge of the rivet, tying it to the sheet of steel it was binding. He tapped it with my hammer and it sounded OK. This meant, while it was still defective, it would sound OK to the old inspector. From that time on, whenever I found a circled rivet, I gave it a tap with my electrode. The heat of the arc generally was enough to burn off the tell-tale circle left by the inspector!"

One POW an old Dutchman named Barkey was especially adept at fooling the Japanese and getting away with hardly working. "Barkey is pronounced much like 'baka,' the Japanese word for fool, and that's the way Barkey played it. His contribution to the Japanese war effort was virtually nil.

"After much effort, they taught him to weld. He pretended to grasp just enough to prevent being transferred to some iron-toting job that would have killed him in a week. As soon as he graduated to welder's status, he wandered more than his eyes did. He'd be assigned to a job and then blend into nothingness, only to appear at lunch. He'd find a corner and sit— always managing to keep out of sight. He actually had

Draft Dodger

a working knowledge of Japanese but chose not to work it. He got by with only two words, 'wakaru nai,' 'I don't understand.'

"Rather than get angry with the old bird, the rest of the POWs admired him for his ability to get away with his deception and did all they could to preserve the loony legend." Occasionally, though, a Jap would get fed up and pull Barkey out of ranks. A physical beating would have disabled him so his dressing down was verbal. But Barkey would put on his best Harpo Marx expression and the tirade would end like a sputtering outboard motor. Without changing expression Barkey shuffled back into his spot and always said, softly so only POWs would hear, 'Yes, ve haff no bananas.'"

MIXED EMOTIONS

Not all dangers of POW life at Yokohama were Japanese inflicted. By 1945, Allied bombers were perilously close to significantly raising the weekly death rate.

"If there ever was a cause of mixed emotions, the B-29 raids were it. We were near the waterfront and never knew whether we were on target when those B-29s with their firebombs cruised over in insolent fleets. At times, we were in the center of a semicircle of fire when the all-clear sounded."

When fire bombing raids came, the POWs and civilians sought shelter in something solid at ground level as there were no air raid shelters for POWs. But, one day, Brenzel's own exhaustion overcame safety.

"I nodded off below decks in an aircraft-carrier-to-be when I was awakened by the quiet. Thinking everyone had gone home and I'd be shot, I rushed up on deck to find full sunshine but not a human in sight. Then I looked at the sky. Directly overhead in all its arrogance—to me it appeared to be floating as slowly as a Goodyear Blimp—was one of our B-29 bombers. I hadn't heard the air raid siren. The Mitsubishi shipyard was not part of the B29's mission that day. But,

The Hero Next Door Returns

many came close and one fire raid in Tokyo resulted in more Japanese deaths than the atom bomb at Nagasaki."

Japan certainly had its feet to the fire. "In early May 1945, the POWs lined up as usual for the march to Mitsubishi but were herded in a new direction. An hour later we found ourselves at a golf course. This was a surprise. Japan had been at war for many years with civilians living under severe restrictions long before Pearl Harbor. The golf course made it obvious not everyone was tightening the belt.

"We were handed hoes and shovels and ordered to peel the sod off the fairways to prepare the land for planting vegetables—more evidence that the end was near. Japan finally was sacrificing golf courses and considered it more important that we till soil than build ships!

"The next day began the same but our labors were interrupted and shortened by an air raid. We lay in the bunkers watching two of our Navy fighters down three Jap planes. When the all clear sounded, we were marched back to our compound instead of back to digging. That was one of the better days in Yokohama."

It was also one of their last. Without warning, on May 12, 1945, the POWs joined the general exodus from the Tokyo metropolitan area and were transported by train more than 400-miles north, high into the mountains and snow, to the copper mine at Kosaka.

KOSAKA AND COUNTING

While they knew the Japanese couldn't hold out much longer, the POWs weren't sure how much longer they could hold out in this colder hell either.

"Kosaka was a new ball game for us, but not for the Japs. They had been working POWs for years, including two men from my battery who I'd not seen since two days before the surrender at Corregidor.

"The change in scenery was good—if anything was

Draft Dodger

good. The mountains were beautiful if we took time to appreciate them when we assembled every morning for calisthenics, roll call and the daily bow toward the emperor. But, Kosaka was a colder, hungrier and buggier place. No bedbug or louse eradication program ever had been undertaken there.

"We POWs had not been stuck with the deep 'saikeirei' bow until we reached Kosaka in May of 1945, when we were saddled with a camp commander who was martinet for imperial protocol. Every morning before calisthenics we had to face south in the direction of Hirohito's palace. At the barked command 'saikeirei,' all had to do the deep bow as, under our breath, we muttered 'kiss my ass the long way around.'"

In May 1942, Japan had requisitioned all gongs, bells and metal altarpieces of every temple and shrine. "The veritable mountain of the stuff was accumulated in the smelter area along with loot from China, including tons of brass coins with square holes in their centers.

"The good fortune that assigned me to the welding crew at the shipyard was repeated. Evidently some record of our skills accompanied us and I was assigned to the repair shop, the only POW there, thus escaping any chain gang job in the mine or smelter.

"Satosan was my boss, 'Sato' being the Japanese word for sugar, he was always Mr. Sugar to me. In this land where most young men were in uniform, Sato had somehow escaped induction. A husky 5-foot-2, with a Chico Marx hat and toothbrush mustache, Sato spent much of his day bent over a blinding welding arc bonding metal to worn down railroad car wheels.

"Sato was also a bachelor. There was a surplus of women in the village and he had many girls visit, one at a time, almost daily. They were tiny, shapeless masses, yet feminine, showing many metal teeth, wearing scarves, long skirts, long pants gathered around the ankles, and bearing gifts of food. They waited

The Hero Next Door Returns

humbly at the back door of the high-ceilinged shop until Sato would deign to notice them and accept their offerings.

"Sato and I were generally alone except for rare visits from Moonface, an Army guard carrying a vitamin stick instead of a rifle. This relative privacy gave me ample opportunity to campaign for a cut of the goodies the girls brought.

"I pulled out all the stops with my tales of my exalted station in America and what I could do for Sato when the war was over. 'Deb'—as he called me because he couldn't pronounce Dave—gave Sato an education in the American way of life. Every American had two or three wives and an equal number of automobiles. Every Yank owned his own home and ate five times a day, meat each time. To the little mountain man I was Marco Polo.

"Some lessons were in home economics and the great variety of foods in the U.S. When I switched to cooking methods, I met a temporary setback. I told Sato of cooking with gas, kerosene, coal, wood and electricity. With that he stalked away wagging his decrepit hat. I was a liar. He refused to stretch credulity beyond wood or charcoal cooking.

"I moved into my personal life, my wonderful education, personal fortune, four wives, welding shop in San Francisco ... The welding shop was the payoff.

"'Could I work for you after the war?' he asked.

"'Sure, Sato, you're my friend. You're a good welder. You could be my partner. As soon as I get home I'll send you money for a ticket.'"

That promise meant less work for Brenzel and more bits of the food the girls brought. And the shop's production slowed as Sato insisted Brenzel watch as he demonstrated every welding technique he knew.

Most of the time, Sato and "Deb" were alone, but somtimes they had the unpleasant company of a guard nicknamed Moonface.

"Squat, bowlegged Moonface did not toil and did

Draft Dodger

not spin, however, his job was to see guys like me did not loaf on the job." His visits to the welding shop were infrequent and, one day, especially ill timed.

Sato had asked Deb if he could fix his radio. "I said 'sure I can fix any radio ever made' and examined it expertly. It appeared the obvious sickness was caused by a loose wire. Actually, I knew little about radios but every professional worth his salt is going to go beyond a mere loose wire when you bring him in on a job.

"Mouthing 'the leg bone's connected to the hip bone,' I diagrammed the radio and began to tear down the set. When pieces were scattered all over, Moonface showed up! He had caught the enemy with radio parts and technical diagrams!

"Head, back and shoulder, I got hit with the vitamin stick. As he flailed away deciding what to do next, he threw in a few swings at Sato. Then he strip-searched me for radio parts and, for all I knew, blueprints.

"'Baka! Kanero' (fool, stupid little fellow). You let a furyo get his hand on a radio in this most important defense plant? 'Shigoto, razio nai! (to work, no more radios),' he yelled.

"Many a POW had died for less than the crime of which Moonface thought I was guilty, but nothing ever happened after the session with the vitamin stick. Evidently Moonface would have had a problem explaining his own lapse. Nevertheless, for the rest of the day I trembled so much I couldn't weld. Sato had tears in his eyes. Not only was his radio sicker than ever, but he had got me into trouble."

Sato did not abuse Brenzel and "the occasional tidbit he gave me on the sly no doubt played a part in my survival because at the compound rations got skimpier."

"When we had arrived at the established camp at Kosaka there was literally a skeleton crew of surviving Yanks and Dutch there. One Dutch man was 6-feet two and weighed only 78 pounds. Of course, few of

The Hero Next Door Returns

us were much better off. If a guy had a shirt off you could tell at a glance if he had any cracked or missing ribs."

The news blackout was total at Kosaka and somehow the living conditions were worse than ever, as POWs were housed in a tight dark grubby tunnel-like building where they lived like cave dwellers.

Brenzel was determined to keep going, however. "Grimly I told myself 'use it or lose it' and tried to do a few pushups every night. Outside the shop was a chinning bar the Japs had used in better days. Without an ounce of lard on me I managed daily to perform the gymnastic tactic called a kip where you wind up stiff-armed supporting your torso above the bar.

With food rations dwindling and the war nearing completion, the Japanese sent POWs out on details to find something to eat, well, almost something.

"We were supposed to have Sundays 'off' but instead 100 of us walking wounded (actually none of us walked; all of us shambled when we weren't limping) were drafted for this special detail and given baskets. Then, we marched into the mountains instead of to the mine.

"We spent the day picking fuki (wild rhubarb). It was edible but leaves and grass are also edible when you have been a POW a few years. In fact, when we left Yokohama there wasn't a blade of grass anywhere inside the compound fence.

"Leafless fuki stems are about a foot long with the diameter of a pencil, green, and covered with ribs like a licorice twist. The stringy ribs must be stripped before fuki is cooked. Cooking does not tenderize what is left but softens it enough so you can get it in your stomach. Your stomach tells your brain you have been fed; your brain soon tells your stomach it is a liar."

Aug. 17, 1945, was the last day POWs worked at the smelter. On Aug. 18 all their uniformed tormentors had disappeared and only hunger and disease remained.

Still, some 400 miles north of Tokyo and well be-

Draft Dodger

hind the "front," the POWs did not receive official word the war was over until Aug. 20, 1945. Five days later a Navy torpedo plane from the USS BENNINGTON dropped a note saying food was on the way. The note read:

"Greetings fellows. We are getting a few odds and ends to drop you tomorrow. By the looks on your faces today you can use everything we have and more too." Two ensigns signed the scribbled note. Bruce Boucher of Luper, Mo., and C.G. Wickham of Long Beach, Calif.'

"With the end of the war in my mind's eye, the living quarters changed into neat, well-kept barracks. Nor was there a cloud in the bright blue sky.

"The following day, the Navy dropped a few hundred pounds of canned goods, cigarettes for all and a few old magazines. We had access to what little remained of Japanese food in the kitchen but the American food made it a banquet. On Aug. 27, drops began in quantity as B29s came over and parachuted pallets loaded with clothing, food, medicine and every consumable good a serviceman could desire.

"We were instructed to stay clear of the drop area until all the colored chutes were down but one damned fool—who shall forever remain nameless—was afraid he wouldn't get his share. He moved in too fast and was killed by a swiftly dropping load of canned tomatoes. As far as I know he was the only POW who was a casualty where *having* food was concerned. All of us advised each other to be careful about overeating or injudicious mixing of goodies. Of course, we all ignored the advice."

Though Japan had surrendered nearly a month earlier, the POWs would not leave Kosaka until Sept. 14, 1945.

Brenzel took little with him but memories of the horrible places he'd endured. But he did salvage four socks worth of those square-centered, brass Chinese coins from the smelter. "I thought they'd make good poker chips."

The Hero Next Door Returns

The souvenir never made it past Kosaka. "Sato was among the villagers seeing us off. He gave me a big grin and wild wave. As we were loading on the cars, I called Sato over and gave him a pack of cigarettes. Then, before he could escape, I handed him the four socks I'd loaded with Chinese coins. I was filled with a sense of accomplishment.

"Finally, I was getting the message some POWs had been trying to send me. You don't have to scrounge for butts and pieces of string any more. You're going to the land of plenty. Travel light."

THE LAND OF PLENTY

It would seem an eternity before they reached that homeland of plenty, however.

First, the narrow-gauge railroad took them down the mountains from Kosaka to the port of Sendai where a British destroyer was waiting to rush them to Yokohama. There, they boarded the hospital ship, the SS RESCUE that took them to Okinawa in preparation for a return trip to where it had all begun—Manila.

"At Okinawa I got fed up with peacetime red tape and abandoned my over-solicitous rescuers and hitchhiked a ride on a DC-3 cargo plane headed for Manila. There, I blended with POWs from other camps and went through the regular debriefing and rehabilitation program. By the time we got to Manila, they were ready for POWs and had been treating them for weeks. Kosaka was among the last Eastern theater camps liberated. At Manila, there was no limit where food was concerned and cooks had orders to bring us anything we wanted day or night."

After a long 21-day boat ride to North America, "the POWs were greeted at Victoria, Canada by a jazz band on a little tug before we sailed down Puget Sound to dock at Tacoma. The jazz band accompanied a redhead wearing a mink stole and little else singing "It's Been a Long, Long Time."

Indeed, it had been a long time. "The two years of

Draft Dodger

foreign service I figured I could do standing on my head had stretched into five years!"

After a few days at Madigan General Hospital for perfunctory physicals and new uniforms, Brenzel boarded a troop train to Ft. Sheridan, Ill. and went home on an extended rehabilitation, "having been judged harmless for mingling with civilians."

The trading instincts he had sharpened in prison "were not dulled by liberation, however. Liquor was rationed in the state of Washington, except rum. I got on the troop train at Tacoma with a suitcase full of rum and quadrupled my money before we hit Chicago.

"For months, one of the greatest thrills was to get out on the streets of Milwaukee and walk and walk and walk without a fence or gate or someone wagging a vitamin stick at me."

Before discharge, Brenzel registered at Marquette University and later received a degree in journalism and philosophy. In between, he finally met the real girl next door, Mary Booth.

"Her family lived next door but we met at a welcome home party for a couple of other guys. There had been an awful snowstorm and I got a ride home in the same car with her and she had to ride on my lap, so it was easy to get acquainted."

Mary was a nurse living at the county hospital through December. One week after she returned home, Brenzel called. They were married at St. John's Cathedral on Jackson Street in 1948. And Brenzel finally wed the unknown girl he'd written a poem about back in the Yokohama shipyards in 1943. It read:

A Wish and a Prayer
I'm wishing you this letter, dear, wanting you to know
  Whenever I need comfort, straight to you I go.
You're here through all my slumbers,
  But with coming of the morn
My spirit screams in anguish as from you I am torn.

The Hero Next Door Returns

Just as the minutes drag on while from you I'm away
My weary feet are lagging through each eternal day.
   My constant hopes are victim
   Of fate's cruel twisted whims
   Though we be miles and years apart
   Your picture never dims.

   Every gnawing hour is an agonizing pain,
   My only strength is in the thought of seeing you
     again.

   All this will be forgotten—
     As the darkness after dawn—
   Pray God on high that it be soon,
     Together we'll go on.

Though Brenzel was warned in post-POW exams that he was probably sterile, he and Mary had nine children, one boy and eight girls.

Though his life was good, Brenzel was sometimes haunted by the memories and physical ailments of what he survived to get the life he was now enjoying.

"Former prisoners of war were a source of embarrassment to the Veterans Administration for a long time. Our problems were esoteric. For months all my teeth were loose, a condition analogous to pyorrhea that was the result of malnutrition. The VA medics sprayed my mouth with penicillin as a fruitless trial remedy. I was at least three years into civilian life before X-rays by non-service doctors revealed at some time I'd had tuberculosis.

"There were no victory parades or bonuses for POWs, but like a bank handing out vice presidencies instead of pay increases, all Army POWs were promoted one grade. Years after the war, it was decided we'd been on short rations while POWs and we were given a dollar a day as compensation. That was $1,200 worth of hungry money that tipped the scales in favor of a down payment for our house."

Draft Dodger

Over the years, Mary worked part-time as an obstetrics nurse while Brenzel was editor of the *Wisconsin Tax News*, working closely with legislators and governors from 1949 through the tumultuous 1960s and '70s.

In 1983, he and Mary returned to the Philippines and Corregidor to walk through the past where his recurring post-war nightmares began. One of his last memories of the island was the bodies of American and Filipino soldiers floating near the shore. When he returned, he was struck by how much the same everything still was, though in need of some repair (a condition that's reportedly only deteriorated). While his memories remain hard to shake, his visit to the past did help soften them a bit. "He never talked about his experience until we went there," Mary notes. "Every night he used to have nightmares and when I'd ask he'd just say 'Oh, I fought in the war last night.' Going back helped a little bit; the nightmares decreased."

Keeping busy also helped. And, even after retirement in 1985, Brenzel didn't slow down. He audited classes at the University of Wisconsin-Madison, including spoken Japanese to get "past the shipyard Japanese I knew."

And, the GI who'd spent five years in some of the worst war had to offer took some W.W. II history classes as well "because I wanted to know what happened, what I missed."

The Hero Next Door Returns

UNSINKABLE SEAMAN
George Watson

As the war in the Pacific neared its conclusion, Navy ships continued to fight fierce battles against Japanese destroyers, bombers, submarines, and especially kamikaze (suicide) attacks.

Among them was an aircraft carrier named the USS FRANKLIN.

The 27,000-ton ship launched from Newport News, Va., in October of 1943. Wisconsin native George Watson, a pharmacist's mate, soon joined its crew.

By June of 1944, the FRANKLIN and its 3,400-man crew was steaming into the war in the Pacific. Between that summer and the next spring the carrier had seen its share of combat—27 different actions in all—from the waters off Iwo Jima, Guam, and Peleliu to Okinawa, Formosa and the Philipines.

In its first four months of service the FRANKLIN is reported to have sunk or damaged 34 enemy warships and 126 merchant ships and downed 338 planes with few incidents—save for an Oct. 29, 1944 kamikaze attack that killed 56 men and wounded 60.

For a Navy ship at war, such damage and casualties were remarkably slight.

Combat—and the history books—caught up with FRANKLIN, however, shortly after the carrier launched its own bombers toward Japan from some 60 nautical miles away as part of Task Force 58 on March 19, 1945. According to the *History of the 2nd World War: The War at Sea*, the line of ships sailing that day included more

Unsinkable Seaman

George and Cecilia Watson, at left, when the war started and, at right, on their 50th wedding anniversary.

than one-half million men aboard 300-plus warships and 1,139 auxiliary vessels.

UNSINKABLE

A little after 7 a.m., two Japanese bombers came out of the clouds and dropped their deadly load square on the carrier's deck. Since the carrier's own bombers had just been launched, the attack caught many of the men in mess halls and stations below deck.

The initial explosions rained down six decks of the carrier and set off the ship's own explosives and some 40,000 gallons of high-octane gasoline stored on board. The carrier was quickly engulfed in smoke and flames as explosions below decks continued.

In a made-for-TV documentary about the FRANKLIN, called "The Ship That Wouldn't Die," Capt. Leslie Garries recalled watching his ship explode in all directions—with blasts so powerful they blew men and planes from one end of the carrier to the other and far into the water.

"A sheet of flames seemed to come out from under

The Hero Next Door Returns

the flight deck and sweep along the starboard side of the ship. There was a heavy explosion and the forward elevator came up in the air and fell back ... and a tremendous column of smoke came up out of it and enveloped the bridge."

Soon, the massive ship began to list and all looked lost. In fact the rear admiral, who'd been stationed aboard, suggested—as he prepared to move his admiral post to a nearby destroyer—that Capt. Garries give the order to abandon ship.

It was a suggestion the captain refused to follow. "I had no intention of abandoning ... I was brought up to believe the captain's job was to save the ship and there were men below deck dying from heat and smoke. I knew, if we abandoned ship, the destroyers would be ordered to sink her. I also knew I had a great number of men below and I just wasn't going to let them all go down with the ship."

At the time the decision may have seemed a ludicrous one to an unknowing observer.

The ship was under constant attack from its own bombs and stored fuel. The entire carrier was engulfed in flame and smoke and listing (leaning) badly toward the ocean bottom. There were some 300 men trapped in the crew's mess hall alone—jammed shoulder to shoulder in the dark smoke-filled chamber as hundreds more struggled further below for breath and life against water, flames, electrocution and smoke.

The gravely wounded carrier had also drifted to within 52 miles of the coast of Japan and was in danger of becoming a further target of Jap bombers and submarines looking to pick her off.

The fate of the FRANKLIN and the men aboard her looked bleak indeed. But some ships—like many of the men who sailed them—simply refused to die.

HOLDING ON

Before he graduated from Beloit High School in the class of 1943, George Watson knew he'd be drafted

Unsinkable Seaman

after graduation and decided he'd rather not have to "walk through the war. So, I enlisted in the Navy because, I thought, at least I'd have a ride."

Little did he know how tough a ride it would be!

After hospital corps training at Great Lakes Naval Station near Chicago, Watson was stationed at the Naval Training Center in Sampson, N.Y., and took the advice of a doctor he was working with to apply for aviation medicine school in Pensacola, Fla. There, Watson learned to serve pilot and air crews aboard ship and at land bases.

He had just the kind of expertise the FRANKLIN would need in the Pacific, and Watson was soon called aboard.

Never one to get seasick, Watson enjoyed life on the carrier and at sea. "We always got pork chops when we put to sea and the carrier is a big enough ship that we'd even have ice cream in the canteen if we wanted it. And, there were movies—at least when we weren't in the middle of something.

"My battle station aboard the FRANKLIN was just outside the captain's cabin forward near the superstructure. Just below it was the ready room for pilots. I was forward of that and lined up somewhere forward of the elevator. It was usually a good place to be because the captain had a refrigerator full of food.

"Life on the carrier was a bit different than on other, smaller, ships because it was so huge. Certainly I knew a lot of people on the carrier but it was really like living in a small city. You could be on a ship for five or six years and never even meet a whole bunch of people. I knew a lot of pilots, of course. And, we lost a lot of pilots in the war, which was hard."

Helping pilots who did make it back, but wounded, was none too easy either as Watson "mostly treated burns, lacerations, cuts and fractures."

"Sometimes, though, I'd assist with surgeries since we could do some more minor surgeries, like appendectomies, on board a carrier. Generally, my day was

The Hero Next Door Returns

spent on the flight deck for launching and then in sick bay to take care of any injured when they came back.

"Though my duties revolved around the pilots' and air crews' needs, I treated lots of guys on the ship for lots of different things. Especially when you worked in sick bay, it didn't matter where you were assigned; you worked on whomever came in for whatever reason. The flight surgeon, the ship's company and the air group, everybody worked together to help with the sick and wounded when we had them."

Day to day, sick bay duty and pilot readiness physicals were part of the routine. It was the breaks in that routine that still haunt Watson.

"I was assigned in a forward battle station and whatever injuries came to me I had them. If I couldn't treat them—and big cuts and burns were hard to fix at the battle station—they were sent to the main sick bay.

"One of the tougher things I had to do was go from general quarters to battle stations. It was the preparing, the waiting, that was the hardest. Once whatever happened happened, then you could deal with it; then you were busy. But, the waiting; that was tough."

In the midst of action, the stream of patients was steady. But, on March 19, 1945, the gravest of situations Watson had ever anticipated at his battle station was unfolding. Watson's work became a continuous nightmare of burns and body parts and gashing wounds and shock—a nightmare he struggles to even recall with clarity more than 55 years later.

Of the nearly 3,000 men on board the FRANKLIN at dawn that morning, one-quarter of the crew would not see another dawn.

In the first transport after the explosion, hundreds of wounded and unnecessary personnel were moved via a makeshift bridge over to a sister ship that pulled precariously alongside. Many more transports followed throughout the day.

248

Unsinkable Seaman

IN THE FACE OF FEAR

But, Watson stayed on board to continue to help out where, and who, he could. He wasn't brave, he insists. He was "just doing my job."

It was a job that required Watson to keep moving, keep doing ... and "kept me from thinking too much about it at the time."

"Sure. I was afraid. Who isn't afraid? But, I was probably more afraid after everything when I had time to think about how close we were to dying. At the time, you're too busy to think about things. You think about things afterwards, for a long time."

So many of the carrier's crew put their thoughts and fears aside to help others and their ship survive, that they became the most decorated ship and crew in W.W. II.

There were handfuls of brave souls who felt their way to trapped men below decks and led them out to fresh air. Seventy determined sailors heaved and hauled the massive cable by hand when the carrier needed a tow away from Japan and the power winches wouldn't work. And, there were the five men stuck in the steering quarters, who steered the massive ship by hand as it was the only way left to control their carrier.

But no sailor, who served aboard the FRANKLIN on March 19, 1945, will ever forget the acts of self-sacrifice by one brave warrior that day. The ship's chaplain, Father Joseph O'Callahan, became the first military chaplain ever awarded the country's highest medal for valor, the Congressional Medal of Honor.

As he walked the listing and flaming deck, giving last rites and words of comfort to hundreds of men, the popular chaplain—a teaching priest who made the FRANKLIN his first parish—was easily recognizable by the large white cross on his helmet.

The chaplain did more than just comfort the wounded and dying, however. He saved many men

The Hero Next Door Returns

from that fate when, as Capt. Garries recalls in the documentary, "heat and flames exploded from a Navy gun turret and threatened the bridge and command. Father O'Callahan gathered up a work party to take a hose into that turret and then climbed right in with them and helped bring out (live) shells and drop them over the side. I remember saying to somebody 'that's the bravest man I've ever seen.' It was so clearly above and beyond the call of duty at risk of his life without detriment to his duty and in the face of the enemy."

Against all odds—and with the determination and hard work of men like Father O'Callahan—the FRANKLIN did not sink that day or any day.

"They said the order of the day became 'a ship that won't be sunk, can't be sunk' and we believed that," Watson recalls of the long trip he and some 700 remaining crew made from the dangerous Pacific waters, through Hawaiian ports and the Panama Canal, and all the way back to the Brooklyn Naval Yard in New York.

With all they'd survived and seen and heard—and a long trip to contemplate it—one would imagine the crew would be zombie-like shadows of men by the time the 40-day voyage was over.

But Capt. Garries deliberately left the men little time for contemplation.

"The captain kept most everybody busy most of the time. Although I was assigned as a medical person, I did a lot of things. I used to help rig stuff and be down in the engine room and in the galley. It was a matter of staying busy and the captain knew we needed to stay busy."

"I wanted to keep them so busy they'd just collapse asleep or I'd have had a crew of mental cases," the captain recalled in the documentary. "Instead, 40 days after lying dead in the water, I probably had the proudest crew any ship in any Navy ever had" when the USS FRANKLIN finally pulled into port.

That's not to say the long ride home from war was

Unsinkable Seaman

easy. Many men were kept busy all the way to Honolulu recovering bodies—and what was left of bodies—from below decks. The men were buried at sea. "Burial details was one detail you didn't want," Watson stresses.

And, the remaining crew gathered on the torn hanger deck for a prayer service to honor the one-quarter of the crew the carrier had left behind in the Pacific. To add to the solemn mood, the remaining crew got word enroute that their nation's leader, President Roosevelt, too had died.

"I really can't remember too much about the trip home except we were proud to bring the ship that should have sunk back home again. And, I'm proud to have survived it and served on the USS FRANKLIN."

But in the bittersweet ironies that only reality can write, the crew that fought so hard to save and return the carrier to America, would never see her sail again. "The war ended before she could return to service and they put her in moth balls. Eventually, the ship was torn down for scrap."

BACK TO SERVICE

The FRANKLIN may have been retired from service but Watson's duties in the U.S. Navy were far from over. Though the war was near an end, Watson was soon transferred to the USS PHILIPINE SEA to serve as part of a post-war air station. Serving on a new carrier took some adjusting.

"The PHILIPINE SEA was a new class of ship and I couldn't find my way around at first. On the FRANKLIN, you just go through the hatches, but the PHILIPINE SEA was all these watertight compartments and it was very confusing. I remember being lost a lot at first."

While serving with the air group on board Watson's duties largely consisted of "taking care of the pilots and their crews, checking them out for flying and handling all their medical records and physicals."

Watson's most memorable time aboard was when

The Hero Next Door Returns

the ship transported Admiral Bird on his exhibition to the South Pole after the war. "It was great to have a small part in something like that."

But, probably his best day in the Navy came when he received a telegram from his wife Cecilia, a high school sweetheart who he married in 1943.

Though she moved with him through his training during those first years of Navy life, the two had been separated for most of the war—except during some leave time after he came home on the FRANKLIN.

"I was on the PHILIPINE SEA when I got a telegram that I was a father for the first time. My wife had had a baby girl, Pam! That was such great news and I couldn't wait to see them!"

But his wife and new daughter would have to wait and worry a bit longer. After the PHILIPINE SEA, Watson was assigned to Fighting Squadron Ninety Two and based out of the east coast, an assignment that did little to calm his wife's concerns for her husband's safety.

"In all those years, of course my wife worried about me—and I thought about her a lot. But, what was kind of funny was that she most worried about me when I was flying and I did fly a lot onto and off carriers and air stations. So, I had to write to her every time I was flying. That way, she'd say, if I got killed she'd know there would be one final letter for her."

In 1948, the Watsons didn't have to wait or worry anymore. After six years of mostly war-time service that took him from the Pacific to the South Pole to the Mediterranean Sea, Watson was discharged.

Even after his discharge Watson continued to serve—this time, his community by joining the Beloit police force. However, his time away from service did not last long.

BACK TO WAR, AND HOME AGAIN

In 1950, Watson was recalled for duty again in the Pacific. This time he would serve in a new war—the

Unsinkable Seaman

Korean Conflict, where he served as hospital corpsman first class.

Watson was assigned to the 1st Marine Division and "got to Korea in time for the Chosin Reservoir where our position was overrun, and that was it for me."

After serving some eight months in the Korean War, Watson was discharged in August, 1951, and returned home to an apprenticeship in carpentry. When work got slow, he went to work full time at the post office for a while to pay bills for his growing family of five girls.

For a time his wife worked as a bookkeeper and later sold Avon and worked as an emergency medical technician. But, she mostly excelled at communicating. "That was always her thing. She'd sit down on a park bench and, in five minutes, the whole bench would be talking to her!"

Watson spent much of his working life as a firefighter in the Town of Beloit and in DePere, Wis., and lastly Monona, Wis., where he worked as full-time administrative chief of the largely volunteer fire department. There, he helped coordinate Monona's first EMS services. He also became one of the first fire service instructors in Wisconsin in 1957. In 1980, Watson taught fire service training at MATC-Madison for one year before becoming the fire service training coordinator for all district fire departments (about 12 counties) while continuing to teach through 1988, "when I really retired!"

Today, Watson still lives in Monona and enjoys six grandchildren and three great grandchildren while he cares for his ailing wife, who suffers from Alzheimers.

Though he's forever proud of his service to his communities and his country, Watson doesn't like to remember his war time experiences too much. "I never had a very good memory and usually have to write things down to remember them very well. But, then, some things I'd just rather not remember."

But, he hopes, the next generation of Americans will

The Hero Next Door Returns

learn something from his service. "People have no knowledge of what conflict is; they just don't have any basis in it. They don't understand what can happen to people. And, it's important that the next generation not only understand why W.W. II happened and how we got involved, but what it is—what it costs—to be in combat."

SUB SURVIVOR
EARL BAUMGART

Childhood swimming lessons and submariner survival training may have kept Earl Baumgart afloat in the dangerous waters of the Philippines in 1944, but it was the thought of home that kept the Milwaukee native going as he and seven other survivors of the USS FLIER battled the waves for their lives.

The home Baumgart was swimming for was the Milwaukee neighborhood he left after graduation from North Division High School in 1941.

Baumgart had moved to and was working in Milwaukee after war broke out. Knowing he'd likely be drafted, Earl followed his brother Elmer's lead and enlisted in the U.S. Navy, volunteering to serve aboard submarines. His brother was already at war in the Pacific submarine service aboard the USS SKATE, when Baumgart started training in New London, Conn.

The idea of serving on a ship—above or below the water—sounded a bit safer to Baumgart than the thought of fighting in hand-to-hand combat on land. "I wanted to come home in one piece and thought that would be safer than being on the ground."

Despite his brother's experience, Baumgart had no

The Hero Next Door Returns

way of knowing if the Navy life would agree with a Wisconsin boy. "I'd never been on a ship before so that was new, and I certainly was never in a sub. But, I didn't get seasick. That was lucky."

Still, there were some adjustments. Baumgart was tall as submariners go and "had to swing through the hatch to fit," and just the idea of living under water took getting used to. "The first time I went down in a sub, it scared me to know I was under the water."

It didn't take Baumgart long, though, to grow accustomed to underwater life. The motor machinist's mate second class especially enjoyed the strong bond of comradeship enjoyed aboard a submarine. "Officers and enlisted men were all friendly with each other because we lived and worked so close together. There was plenty of room on board, but there was no where to go and no one else to talk to but the other men on the sub. You were a family."

By October 1943, Baumgart was working as an engine room oiler surrounded by his FLIER family when the sub put to sea from New London.

The FLIER traveled through the Panama Canal and was en route to a stop in Hawaii when the crew got its first indication that the sub would see tough times. Somewhere near Hawaii, the sub reportedly had to dodge shells from a friendly merchant ship, which confused the FLIER for a Japanese sub.

The incident was quickly forgotten, however, as the crew enjoyed a respite in Hawaii before heading for the combat waters of the Pacific Ocean.

For Baumgart, the Hawaii stop was especially memorable. "I ran into my brother—also in port on leave—and we hadn't seen each other in about a year. He'd been at war; I was on my way there." The brothers wouldn't see each other again until Earl was discharged Jan. 13, 1946.

The FLIER left Hawaii on Jan. 12, 1944, but ran aground off Midway Island and had to be towed in for repairs. By spring of 1944, the sub was ready for com-

Sub Survivor

bat and quickly moved from a base in Australia out to patrol around Iwo Jima and the Philippines *(noted David McGee, a SCUBA Diver from Bridgewater, N.J., who reported his research on the FLIER in a 1996 letter to Baumgart).*

The sub entered combat with flying colors, according to the 1949 *Book on U.S. Sumbarine Losses* (p.110-111). On her first patrol west of Luzon in June, 1944, the FLIER sank four freighters and damaged a fifth along with a tanker, sinking some 19,500 tons and damaging 13,500 tons. The sub's commander Capt. John Crowley was awarded the Navy Cross for his stellar efforts.

Riding high from their first war patrol, and eager to get back into action, the FLIER left Fremantle, Australia, Aug. 2, 1944, to patrol the area between Borneo and the Philippines. She'd reached the Balabac Straight near the Sulu Sea—with Comerin Island some three miles to port and Balabac Island several miles ahead—when the sub's luck ran out.

GOING DOWN FAST

"At 2200, disaster struck. Suddenly a terrific explosion—estimated to have been (a mine) forward on the starboard side—shook the ship. ... Oil, water and debris deluged the bridge. There was a strong smell of fuel, a terrific venting of air through the conning tower hatch, and the sounds of flooding and of screaming men below. Lt. Liddell, the executive officer, had stepped below the hatch to speak to Cdr. Crowley; he was blown through it and men poured out behind him," *The Book of Submarine Losses* reports

The FLIER sank within 30 seconds, still maintaining its course at 15 knots as it took more than 70 men to a watery grave. They joined over 3,500 men from 48 U.S. submarines killed or taken prisoner in W.W. II combat actions. The book further reports that "of those lost due to enemy action, only the eight men aboard the FLIER and four men from the USS SEALION were

The Hero Next Door Returns

Baumgart, at left, and his brother Earl, also in the submarine corps, ran into each other twice in the service. They are shown in here in a Bridgeport, Conn. bar.

saved (not killed or taken prisoner).

Often, in a submarine explosion, no one reaches the surface alive. However, the FLIER had been traveling at the surface and several men were on the bridge to keep watch. A few more, like Lt. Liddell and Cdr. Crowley were close enough to the hatch to escape. In all, 14 men were believed to have made it alive into the water; eight saw home again.

Baumgart was on watch that night. "I was on lookout above the water and there was a big explosion. I got thrown off but I didn't see the sub go down. It was so fast. It didn't take too long to realize what had happened. We probably hit a mine.

"I was in the water, kind of dazed, but there was no fire. There was nothing to hold on to. I didn't know if anyone else had survived and that was a pretty lonely feeling.

"I was kicking and flailing my arms constantly. It was awfully scary. I was afraid of Japs finding me and I was afraid of drowning. I didn't really think about

Sub Survivor

sharks at the beginning; I didn't have time to think about things like that."

Fortunately, Baumgart knew how to swim before he went in the service. "But, we were in the water hours before I hooked up with some others and we started out together. None of us final eight survivors were really wounded from the explosion, but we thought we were probably the only ones that could be alive—that all our friends were gone."

In his *Submarine Journal,* survivor Alvin E. Jacobson also recalled the powerful blast. "Jim Liddel, who at the time was standing in the conning tower hatch talking to the captain, had his shirt taken off by the gush of air and it lifted him up to the bridge. He weighed over 200 pounds!"

Though it was dark and men could not see even a few feet in front of themselves, they managed to call to and gather 14 survivors. As they bobbed in the waves and tried to reserve energy, they discussed their plan to swim to an island once the moon rose and they could—hopefully—see land.

As a navigator, Liddell knew the islands well but, without light, they had little way of knowing which direction to swim in. The group quickly decided, however, they would have to swim farther than the closest island—Comerin, some three miles away—as they knew a Japanese garrison was stationed there. *(Editor's Note: some of the details of their story are based on "Men Against The Sea," and article written by Peter Amunrud, the Central Region director of the U.S. Submarine Veterans.)*

SWIMMING FOR HOME

Liddell suggested swimming to a small coral reef island they thought to be 9 miles away (actually closer to 12 miles).

"We all agreed to go and try to get to that island. Two guys with us had studied the maps on board and had a good idea. We were lucky to have them in our

The Hero Next Door Returns

group. We started swimming once the moon came up."

As luck would have it, however, the night was cloudy and the overcast moonbeams provided little real light. Then, Mother Nature provided some guidance of her own.

"It was lightning and so we could see the land. It was like a guiding light, but it seemed like a long time to get there. I worried I wasn't going to make it and worried we wouldn't all stay together."

Some men did drift away. When dawn finally came, only eight of the FLIER crew were still swimming—Baumgart, Capt. John Crowley, Arthur Gibson Howell, Al Jacobson Jr., Jim Liddell Jr., Wesley Miller, James Russo and Don Tremaine.

The eight men were losing energy fast as they stroked against the waves trying to reach the tiny island now appearing on the horizon. The swimming only got tougher as the island got closer, Jacobson recalled. "The strange thing I found about the swim was that I had to fight to keep from going to sleep. I also found I could not use one stroke very long because I would tire too much that way."

Fortunately for Baumgart and four of the others, there were floating palm tree logs not far from shore and they were able grab hold and float and kick to the beach. The men had been swimming some 16-18 hours by the time they reached the sand.

The bulk of the survivors came ashore on the three-mile long Mantangule Island at about 1530 (3:30 p.m.) They were met on the beach "by Russo, who had swum the entire distance," the *Book of Submarine Losses* notes, adding that the group hooked back up with Tremaine at 1700 and Miller the next morning as both men had come ashore in separate areas.

By the time the exhausted men reached Mantangule Island, they were already sunburned—a condition that would only worsen as the hours ticked by. To make matters worse, their feet were being shredded by coral since they had shed their shoes and everything heavy when they first hit the water.

The island provided a place to rest out of the water but offered little else. "That first island mostly had nothing. There was one good coconut for all of us. That was it."

The idea was to sleep that night and try to reach the next small island and then the next in the coral reef chain on the way to Bugsuk Island (a bigger island some eight miles away with the best chance of friendly natives).

However, between shivering sunburns and unwelcome guests, sleep did not come easy for Baumgart, if at all.

"We dug holes in the sand to cover ourselves at night with the warm sand. That proved to be futile because the sand crabs would burrow themselves in and nibble on your skin which made sleeping and resting almost impossible."

At first light, the weary group set about building a 3-foot-by-5-foot driftwood raft to help carry them the mile or so to Byan Island. It was big enough for two or three men to straddle and paddle using palm fronds while the rest hung on and kicked.

Baumgart credits his commander Capt. Crowley with providing the leadership needed to get them home. "He kept us going. He assigned us different duties so we didn't just sit and think. The first day, some looked for food while some built a lean-to for protection. The next day we all had jobs to build the raft."

Tasks were easier because the survivors worked together well. "We got along all right because we knew each other well before this happened. We were lucky to have some guys we did—ones that knew the area, Crowley—but we all worked together."

They all worked together well enough to keep everyone moving toward salvation. "Water and food were important to get to, but the main reason we survived was we worked together and all kept thinking of one thing—home and how we had to get there. We

The Hero Next Door Returns

were swimming 'for home.'"

But, wanting to get home and actually getting there seemed to drift farther away as physical exhaustion, thirst and hunger wore on the survivors. Building that small raft took eight men nearly all day to complete.

"The raft took quite a while and it was very difficult. We were so weak; everything was hard to do."

The group rested one more night in the sand and waited until slack tide the next afternoon, when the weary sailors at last cast off and started paddling and kicking against the tidal current that flowed between the islands.

Though they'd been hoping a plane would fly over and save them, they were as frightened as ever when one finally did. "It was a Jap plane and we all went under the water when it came over hoping he wouldn't see us."

In fact, not even the Americans were looking for the sub or its crew. "There wasn't even time to send a message. It went down that fast. They didn't know what happened or where."

As frightening as the Jap plane was, the constant tug of thirst and hunger was worse. "It rained while we were on the raft but we only got drops of water and it was not thirst quenching."

Three hours after leaving Mantangule, the survivors crawled ashore on the barren strip of coral rock called Byan Island and collapsed in exhaustion.

The next day—the fourth since the explosion—the group again set out, this time kicking their way 1.5 miles to Gabung Island, another coral rock outpost with little food, shelter or hopes of survival. It took them over four hours to reach.

They arrived more exhausted than ever and by the next morning—the fifth day—the survivors were literally starving. While in the previous days the group had come across many coconuts, all but two were too rotten to eat. Water consumption had been negligible at best.

262

Sub Survivor

"We couldn't find food. I went to look for some but had to come back without any. I couldn't find any. I didn't feel good about coming back with nothing; we were so hungry."

On one such sojourn, Baumgart came across a lagoon that, at first looked promising, he recalled in a letter to Jacobson in August, 1996. "I thought it would solve our drinking problems as we were very, very thirsty. You could see the bottom nearly 10 or 15 feet down but no fish or any other creatures. It proved to be very salty and unfit to drink."

Walking around any of the islands was excruciating, Jacobson recalled. "Our feet were pretty well cut up by the coral. Walking was getting harder all the time. We walked in the shallow water because the coral was grown over with weeds and was easier on our feet. Walking in the shallow water, however, put our bodies directly and unsparingly into the sun. It pushed hard and hot on us on every part of our skin, already blackened and sunburned by its fiery heat."

Desperate for food, Jacobson and Baumgart traveled together down various trails on a hunt for anything edible. "Baumgart and I became inquisitive about one trail leading into the center of the island. We started into it. Our barefoot pilgrim feet again found the surface under them layered with the hard, cookie-cutter coral ... We persisted the distance of about three city blocks. We then permitted our curiosity to be satisfied by concluding that the only inhabitants of the island must be monkeys."

For all their searching, they found just one more good coconut, which they again opened by hand and shared with the group.

To stay on Gabung any longer would have meant certain death so the desperate survivors clung one more time to their raft and pushed off that afternoon toward Bugsuk Island, three miles away—uncertain if they would encounter Japanese, natives or more nothingness.

263

The Hero Next Door Returns

"We didn't know if it was friendly or not but we had to take a chance. We would die if we didn't try."

ISLAND OASIS

The men and their shaky raft made the final leg of their watery journey, arriving on Bugsuk around sunset of the fifth day, Aug. 18. From the water, they were elated to spot several buildings along the shore but came in carefully in case there were Japanese in them.

The first building appeared empty and, when the men entered, Baumgart spotted a cistern full of water.

"The water tasted so good. We found out later the cistern was poisoned by the natives for the Japanese, but we didn't get too sick."

With some more good coconuts they found—and water to quench their thirst—the survivors slept better than they had in many days.

The next morning their nerves were tested yet again when teenage native boys came to investigate the visitors.

"We didn't know if he was friendly or not until he spoke some English and gave us food. Then, we knew he would help us. He led us away. It was pretty painful to walk because our feet were all cut up but we were not going to stop now."

The boys were part of the Bugsuk Battalion, a group of native guerrilla fighters battling against the Japanese invaders. They led the men through a sugar cane field—and cut down stalks for them to chew—on their way to a deserted school where they fixed them rice on banana leaf plates and some dried fish, Jacobson reported.

There, the survivors were quickly—and a bit apprehensively at first—introduced to the band of guerrillas.

One guerrilla—Pedro Sarmiento, leader of the Bolo Battalion and a former schoolteacher—spoke English particularly well. Jacobson recalled that "he explained

Sub Survivor

the guerrillas had seen the men come ashore but didn't know if they were Japanese or American and sent the boys in to check."

The fighters needed to take the men to the main guerrilla headquarters on Palawan Island. That meant their battered feet would have to walk five miles across the coral rock of Bugsuk to a waiting boat that would take them up the river for a ride to Palawan Island, some 20 miles away.

"Until now, we had not realized the extent of our fatigue, or the condition of our feet," Jacobson recalled. "There is no doubt that there had seldom been a more sour-looking bunch of hikers."

In eight hours, the group managed just over two miles. The next afternoon, the men reached the Bugsuk River and took off in a native boat just before sunset. They arrived at the end of the island in the dark. As it was safest to travel to Palawan at night, the group headed out in more boats.

They arrived on the southern tip of the island at 0530 (5:30 a.m.) and were greeted by Capt. Nazario B. Mayor, a native Filipino who graduated from the University of Nebraska where he received a commission in the U.S. Army through the ROTC. They walked to his home and met Mr. Edwards, an American citizen, who had a business there before the war, as well as Sgt. Amado S. Corpus, an American-born Filipino in charge of the U.S. Army Signal Corps "Coast Watcher" Unit recently stationed on the island.

Still tired, and in need of medical care, the eight men traveled by caribou-pulled carts to Mr. Edwards' home where they met the rest of the Signal Corps Group in addition to three U.S. soldiers who'd escaped Japanese prisoner camps and were awaiting rescue.

The Coast Watchers opened their medical kits and emergency rations, providing the survivors with sulfa to treat their wounds as well as cigarettes, soap, clothes, cheese and crackers, and even coffee.

The Hero Next Door Returns

RESCUE 'UNDER THE SEA'

They were also able to radio Australia and report that the FLIER had survivors. A plan was quickly devised to rescue the men from the island aboard the USS REDFIN submarine. A series of lights were to be placed in an abandoned lighthouse as the submarine's signal that the men would be at a designated rendezvous point off shore.

To celebrate the pending rescue, the natives threw the survivors and other guests a small party. However, just before the party was to begin, a gunshot rang out. "Sgt. Corpus shot himself because he felt it was his fault we were sunk," Jacobson reported. "He felt that he should have known that Balabac Strait was mined and reported the fact to Australia."

There was no party that night.

On Aug. 30, 1944, the time had come for the FLIER survivors to ride their last leg home. Borrowed livestock carried the party—which now included the former POWs, a Scottish Missionary, his wife and two children, and two American civilians who'd been caught on the island when war broke out. They boarded two boats, one equipped with a hand-cranked radio, and started out.

Hearts sank and then pounded louder as they slunk pass an unexpected Japanese merchant ship anchored just off shore. The signal lights could not be used and, for several breath-shortening hours, the REDFIN could not be reached by radio.

Finally, just as hope was nearly lost, the refugees and the REDFIN found each other. It was a bittersweet moment for Baumgart. "I was scared to get back on a sub. I knew what could happen and was afraid it would happen again while I was underwater. There would be no way out."

Still, Baumgart was elated—"and how!"—to be rescued!

Sub Survivor

Official U.S. Navy photo

The original crew of the USS FLIER pictured in New London, Conn. Some of these men were transferred off before the sub met her deadly fate in the Pacific.

By Sept. 6, 1944, the survivors had come nearly full circle and could see the Australian coast. They arrived in Perth, Australia, Sept. 7, where they were interrogated about their experience. "That's when we knew we were the only ones that survived; that's very difficult to realize."

It would be another week before anyone else—especially their families—knew why their letters had stopped coming.

"My parents received this and that's the first they knew anything:

The Hero Next Door Returns

"My dear Mr. Baumgart: Your son, Earl Raymond Baumgart, Motor Machinist's Mate third class, United States Naval Reserve, who was aboard a ship the loss of which will be announced in the near future, is safe and well. The circumstances of his rescue are such that information concerning it should not reach the enemy, and it is requested that you do not divulge any reports that may come to you concerning his experiences, or disclose the name of the ship in which he served. The Navy Department shares your pleasure over the safety of your son. It is hoped that he will communicate with you in the near future. Sincerely yours, L.E. Denfeld, The Assistant Chief of Naval Personnel."

Baumgart was not allowed to write a censored letter to his family until Oct. 10, but by early November, he was on his way back to the U.S. on a 30-day survivor leave. "I was elated; I had made it home, and I didn't want to go back!"

But, with a war still on, back he would go. Baumgart returned assigned to another service craft, the U.S.S. FALCON. However, this time, his duties could be performed on land. "I was assigned to a sub but stayed in New London, above the water."

HOME AT LAST

He was finally discharged in January 1946, "a long time, and how"—some 38 months—after he first enlisted.

Baumgart was at last reunited with his girlfriend Arlene, whom he soon married. They had one son Alan before she died of a brain tumor five years after their wedding. Baumgart later married Eunice Bassel in Milwaukee. They've been married 47 years and had a son Ronald and now have five grandchildren and one great grandchild. In between, Baumgart served as a machinist apprentice at the Kearney-Trecker plant in West Allis and then became a City of Milwaukee police patrolman for 28 years before he became a police-fire dispatcher with the city of Wauwatosa for

Sub Survivor

11 years. Police work was a job he loved because "I liked helping other people out of tight spots."

He retired in 1977, and was active in the Wauwatosa Senior Citizens Center. He belongs to American Legion Post 415 and the Police Relief Association. And, Baumgart occasionally gets together with other veterans who survived their underwater service as a member of the Southeast Wisconsin Chapter of the U.S. Submarine Veterans Association. Most recently, in November 1999, Baumgart began another battle, this one against Parkinson's Disease, but he's never forgotten—though seldom likes to talk about—the battle he and seven other men waged against the sea and their own will in 1944.

While his is an amazing story, Baumgart sees himself much more as a lucky survivor of a terribly tragedy. "I'm proud to have served and of the guys I served with, but I'm no hero. I was just doing my job, and then I was just trying to make it home. I'm glad I made it."

The Hero Next Door Returns

NEW GUINEA NIGHTINGALE
MARION DOFMEISTER

The Thorkildsens were not all that surprised when their daughter Marion (now Dorfmeister) grew up to be a nurse. After all, she spent much of her Milwaukee and Nashotah, Wis., childhood taking care of cats and kin. But, they were surely taken back a bit when their 22-year-old daughter announced, shortly after graduating Marquette University nursing school in Milwaukee in 1943, that she had not only joined the Army Nurse Corps but had volunteered for overseas duty.

Their daughter, like 75,000 other American nurses was going overseas to war. She joined well over 350,000 American women serving overseas and stateside in women divisions of the armed forces—including the WACs (Army), WAVES (Navy), WASPs (Army Air Corps), SPARS (Coast Guard), Women Marines, and other services like the American Red Cross and Salvation Army, according to *Voices of the Wisconsin Past: Women Remember the War.*

"I often wondered what my parents thought about that decision. I gave them no warning at all. I just decided one day to join the nurse corps. There was a war on and you wanted to serve, to be patriotic. I vol-

New Guinea Nightingale

unteered to go overseas I suppose because I was a new nurse in good health and I had no ties really, so I figured I should go. And, I was a small town girl from Nashotah, Wis., with youthful excitement."

That small town girl—inducted into the Army Air Corps at Camp McCoy, Wis., in December 1943—soon found herself battling the heat of the Pacific islands to help save the lives, and comfort the scars, of thousands of wounded soldiers and Marines.

Dorfmeister—or Thorky as she was nicknamed in the service—served as a first lieutenant attached to the 54th General Hospital first in Hollandia, New Guinea, a 3,500-bed camp served by a contingent of doctors, enlisted men and some 100 nurses.

"We left training in California in March, 1944, aboard the troop ship LURLINE and were well out into the Pacific on a 17-day zig-zag trip before we received a pamphlet, 'A Pocket Guide to New Guinea.' That let us know where we were going by telling us things we needed to know about New Guinea ... like malaria. We got a lot of shots before we went over and took Atabrine for malaria once we got there, which turned your skin a yellow hue by the time you got to be an 'old timer' over there."

The nurses were at first assigned temporary duty at Milne Bay, where they landed, for about four and half months, until the 54th General Hospital could be completed. By this time, there were well over 2,000 Army nurses stationed in New Guinea and the Pacific, according to *GI Nightingales*.

"I remember our first viewing of the island before we landed. It was gorgeous to look at but then it started to get cloudy. When we loaded onto ducks, we were all wearing our helmets and raincoats. It was pouring and it never stopped. All of a sudden we were someplace, lining up to get a bucket and candle and go off to find a tent.

"It just poured and poured that night. But I remember that first morning so clearly; it was a beautiful

The Hero Next Door Returns

morning. We almost whooped when we saw these fuzzy wuzzies—which is what we called the natives—outside in the sunshine building our barracks."

At that first sight of the strange scene of the natives, Dorfmeister knew she was truly far from home. But, she was not as far as a half-a-world-away might seem. "I was walking along that first morning and looked up at two GIs coming toward me. I looked at one of them twice and realized it was my Oconomowoc High School classmate Fabian Fleming from North Lake! What a great surprise! He came to see me a few times while I was there but he was an enlisted man and nurses weren't allowed to see enlisted men too easily."

When completed, the hospital—the largest U.S. general hospital overseas—consisted of Australian prefab buildings with metal roofs, each building specialized in its own injuries, such as the surgical, ambulatory, psycho and burn wards. As a general duty nurse, Dorfmeister rotated through the various wards.

WARD DUTY

Patients would be transported to the 2,000-bed hospital—stretched to house up to 3,500 patients—by ambulance from battlefield treatment at field hospitals and on hospital ships, ready for further care.

As the pace of battles increased, so too did the flow of wounded into the general hospital.

"When fighting was going on, we'd receive shiploads. The most we ever admitted was 708 at one time, at the pace of one patient every 30 seconds. When loads like that came in you were just working, eating and sleeping and coming back and doing it all again and again."

The hospital's own memory book, *The 54th in Review*, written shortly after the war, shows how busy those hot months in New Guinea were, beginning almost on the hospital's official first day of operations, Oct. 13, 1944.

"On the 25th of October, with the coming of the first

New Guinea Nightingale

Dorfmeister sits atop a gun at a cave in Corregidor, where she visited as the war was drawing to a close.

casualties from the invasion of Leyte, all departments began to work at top speed in an effort which had no appreciative let down for many months," reported Col. John M. Caldwell Jr., Medical Corps Commanding, in the memory book. In its busiest *one* month, the hospital's 100 nurses, with help from some Red Cross volunteers, treated 4,926 patients.

By the time the hospital moved to the Philippines nine months later, it had treated 18,000 patients, including 442 women, Col. Caldwell noted. In that time, the 54th General Hospital performed 4,482 operations,

The Hero Next Door Returns

used $161,872 worth of penicillin, filled 100,000 prescriptions, applied seven tons of plaster to broken bones and used 419 miles of bandages.

There were so many men that needed nursing that the sheer volume could be overwhelming. The wounds were horrific and burns were especially bad, Dorfmeister recalls. "I remember one burn patient who was so badly burned you couldn't even see the man and we couldn't keep the flies off of him."

The tropical heat only made such wounds more difficult to heal and tropical diseases took further tolls on wounded men. "Wounds heal more slowly in the tropics and there are a lot of tropical diseases but the men seemed to get a lot of jungle rot, especially their feet, and a lot of dysentery, dengue fever, fungus infections, jaundice and malaria." According to *GI Nightingale* (page 51) the worst was "scrub typhus which came from tiny insects that lived in the jungle and was similar to Rocky Mountain Spotted Fever."

"A lot of them died from their wounds, and diseases, of course. But, in a way, arriving at the general hospital gave many of them a new lease on life because they were safe there and once they were healed they'd be going home."

But, it was the mental anguish many of those combat veterans suffered that proved hardest for Dorfmeister.

"I spent time working in each ward, including the psycho ward and saw that some of them had seen such mutilation that they could never get past it."

Yet, parts of the work were rewarding.

"All of us worked very hard but we loved taking care of our men. It was very worthwhile. The adulation the men had for you because you were an American woman—and they were so happy to see an American woman—was wonderful. We reminded them of their wives and girlfriends and moms ... reminded them of home I suppose ... and that felt good to bring some happiness."

New Guinea Nightingale

How important the nurses were to the men was revealed to Dorfmeister in 1985 when she got a phone call. "Is this Thorky?" the man on the other end of the line asked, adding "I've been looking for you for 40 years."

The man, Lavern Short, was one of the hundreds of servicemen Dorfmeister had nursed in New Guinea. Though she didn't remember that one name among the hundreds; that one 6th Division 1st Infantry Marine sure remembered the nurse who'd taken such good care of him so many years before.

He invited Dorfmeister to attend an infantry reunion so he could thank her in person for "saving my leg." Dorfmeister and her husband traveled to Missouri for the occasion.

The Ozarks newspaper of Aug. 12, 1985, told the story not just of the reunion but of the gratitude servicemen like Short had for nurses like Dorfmeister. "I had gotten my leg nearly shot off and I was afraid I'd lose it. She promised me I wouldn't. She kept her promise," Short exclaimed.

Dorfmeister was flattered, though she remembered neither the promise nor the patient. "There were so many men and I was just doing my job. But when you're scared and in pain, people think an awful lot of the care they get from one person."

Back in 1944, Dorfmeister wrote a letter to her cousin Sara in the wee hours of Dec. 8, about the care she gave to Short and hundreds of others like him. The small town girl described the night shift duties as follows:

"Haven't done much letter writing lately—except for home—as we've been busy. Have plenty to do now as the casualties roll in. Working on a surgical ward and have all the shrapnel and bullet wound cases. It seems like all we've been doing lately is working, eating, sleeping, washing clothes. The time is going so fast here, which is a good thing.

"Right now it's 3:30 a.m. and I am sitting at the desk in

The Hero Next Door Returns

my ward—on 7 p.m. to 7 a.m. night duty. This is a very quiet time of the night. Has been raining a little and the coolness feels good. Made some fudge and so I have the ward men and nurses from other wards dropping in for a sample, talk a bit, find out the news, etc. It's a pleasure to be on nights for a while. It's cool and don't perspire; no one to bother us.

"You'll be getting this letter around Christmas—seems so un-Christmas-like here. Hot—every day is the same; same as though there's nothing to look forward to except another day of the usual routine. Can't last forever.

"One of our girls was married this week! Wedding was in our open chapel. She made her dress from a white parachute and it was very pretty. The couple had a reception at the Red Cross Hall later in the evening. The Seabees made a lovely cake and the affair went off fine and dandy. Was a treat to see something like that.

"Imagine the cold has settled down your way. Sorry I can't say the same. Have the same heat every day. Cools off at night but never enough to have to wear a jacket of any kind.

"I was in the hospital for a short stay a while back. Guess I had a mild case of dengue fever, etc. Most of the kids

Dorfmeister with some native children and their families in New Guinea.

New Guinea Nightingale

have had something or other by this time. The less time you have to spend in these islands, the better.

"Was in the Army one year Dec. 6, overseas 9 months. Sure didn't waste much time in the States. Seems like we're here such a long time, and yet the time has gone fast. Now that we're set up in our own hospital, time goes quickly too.

"Suppose you're busy baking cookies, etc., getting things ready for the kids' Christmas. Must be fun 'cause they believe in Santa Claus. I'll be thinking of you folks anyway. This is my first Christmas from home but can't say that I miss it. We're busy and other things.

"It's 5:30 and time to start waking my boys. They're such a swell bunch of kids too. Merry Xmas, Sara.

Love, Marion."

JUNGLE ACCLIMATION

Dorfmeister lived in one of the 20-bed barracks set up in the sectioned-off nurses' area. Each barracks had just a roof with open sides and a screen in front for privacy, but no door.

"They kept the nurses separate mostly because we women had to be very careful. We had to sign in and sign out and couldn't go out unless we had an armed escort because there were snakes in the jungle and still some Japs hiding on the island. We lost a few people that way. And, a few of our nurses became mental cases and there were a few nurses who were attacked—by our men or by the Japanese—who were sent home. The rules were strict and we lived a well-ordered life but you learned to go by the rules for your own safety.

Though Dorfmeister escaped injury there was one time—while swimming with other nurses and their armed guards at a nearby lake—that she learned why the women were so closely guarded. "I always liked to explore a bit and walked along shore awhile by myself. All of a sudden, I saw two GIs coming at me through the grass. I got scared and started to run and

The Hero Next Door Returns

they were running after me. I made it home out of breath but all right."

Some nurses were raped or fell into romantic relationships with GIs. "Two of my buddies went home pregnant and there were some nurses sent back psycho because they just couldn't take it. Sometimes it's a wonder anyone got back in one piece."

Still, while such concerns could be pushed to the back of your mind from time to time, the heat of the jungle was a daily constant.

"We all had to acclimate to the heat. It was so hot and humid every day all year that by afternoon you were swamped in your own clothes. It exhausted you, and you'd get so tired that by midday you thought you were anemic. If you worked the day shift, you worked from 7 a.m. to 1 p.m. and 4 to 7 p.m. because of the heat. You needed three hours off in the heat of the day. On the night shift you could work longer hours straight because it was a little bit cooler.

"I never saw anything as green as New Guinea in all my life. It is a beautiful place but I wouldn't take it for a gift. Besides the unending heat, it rained every day in the rainy season and we had to wear raincoats and helmets. It was unbelievable."

While rats and bats were daily companions, the wet heat was the hardest to live with. "Our clothes always smelled moldy and we washed them in our helmets. We didn't have any irons to press our trousers so we dried them and then slept on top of them to press them. But, I was an outdoors person and I never minded the conditions too much. In many ways it was a great adventure.

"You'd get used to it and, fortunately, we were young and excited and could deal with it. When you're that young you just take it in stride. It was work to be done and you just did it. You slept and you'd come back and you were ready to come back, you wanted to come back."

Dorfmeister acclimated to the jungle's challenges but

New Guinea Nightingale

its dangers were always present. She, like everyone on New Guinea, had to be wary of the diseases that flourish in tropical heat. Malaria was the main concern but there was dysentery and jungle rot and parasites.

"Our area was sprayed for malaria and we all took Atabrine. We all slept under mosquito netting and tucked ourselves into it ... or you could get scorpions and what not crawling in bed with you. Some nurses did get sick but I was generally healthy the whole time I was over there. So, there's little for me to complain about. It was the men in the field that had it a lot worse. The ground crews really took it. I mean, if they were in battery for days at a time and couldn't take their shoes off, their feet would get moldy and start to rot. We nurses never had anything like that."

COOLING OFF

There were some distractions from the work and heat of the New Guinea hospital too, Dorfmeister recalls. Certainly, there were plenty of men to date and the few women "were so in demand no matter what you looked like you could get a date." But, dating was difficult. Nurses weren't supposed to socialize with, let alone date enlisted men, "though some found ways around that too." And, there was little time for such serious pursuits, anyway.

But, there was time for occasional distractions.

"We had nightly entertainment and had an outdoor theater with all the latest movies. Often I'd take some patients with me to watch them. And, we had church every Sunday. I was a member of our church's choir back in the states so that drew me there. It gave me a feeling of home."

Dorfmeister especially liked the softball games nurses and officers played. "Growing up, it was never dolls for me. I liked baseball. I was the only girl given permission to play baseball with the boys in elementary school."

The Hero Next Door Returns

For good reason. Dorfmeister was a top-notch pitcher on one of 16 teams (consisting of nurses, officers and even patient teams), as one Red Cross volunteer, Charlotte Self, recalled in the *54th In Review* memory book. Self said she fondly remembered "manager 'Burley' Burleson falling off the bench when the nurses 'almost' beat the officers; and pitcher 'Thorky' Thorkildsen striking out Captain Lubert three times..."

Swimming was another, especially refreshing, option.

"The Bay of Hollandia beaches were out of this world. We went swimming a lot in our free time, but always with an armed escort. There were volleyball courts set up and we'd swim in the ocean.

"We also went swimming at Lake Sentani, not too far away from the hospital. It was almost like a little summer cottage that had been built for a general and we nurses changed there. I discovered something else there too, as I was always one to explore a bit. Off to one side of the lake was a little inlet and there were native women in two or three canoes made out of tree trunks. There were flat stones in the middle of the canoe with leaves on it and they would be roasting a taro root (similar to a yam). The women were in the water and positioning themselves in circle around each boat. They said something in unison that sounded like an incantation and all went under at once. They all came up with a fish in their mouth. That's how they caught fish. That was the women's job to fish and chop down small brush to use as firewood."

Dorfmeister and the other medical staff also spent rewarding time helping the New Guinea natives, accompanying the hospital chaplain on a couple of trips to Dutch missionaries serving native villages.

"We called them fuzzy wuzzies because they had mounds of fuzzy hair but they were very friendly. We went with doctors from a nearby Dutch hospital to treat some of the natives for malaria and other para-

New Guinea Nightingale

In June of 1945, Dorfmeister and her friend Jack encountered some natives returning from a wild boar hunt.

sites. They chewed beatlenut, which turns their teeth black. They lived a hard life and were much smaller than us because of the diseases and such. Their life expectancy was in the high 20s, and I remember seeing women who were our age, 20-30, who looked aged. But, they were friendly and knew sort of what we were doing. I wore my hair up in rolls at the time and gave them some of my bobby pins and they were thrilled to get them."

Most important in pastimes and hard times was the camaraderie of the other nurses. "I made many good friends there and even though we didn't see each other [until a reunion] 40 years later, what we went through bonded us together for life."

CONTINUED SERVICE

As the war in the Pacific began to wind down, the general hospital moved to Manila, capital of the Philippines in the late spring of 1945.

"The Philippines was the same humid heat only we weren't in the jungle and had a few more liberties to

The Hero Next Door Returns

move around; we didn't have to have an armed guard.

"The city itself was really bombed out and nearly destroyed. We were quartered in a couple of groups and I was in a private girls' school next to a racetrack. The racetrack building is what we used for a hospital, its rooms reserved for those who needed the most care. The bleachers were filled with cots for the more ambulatory patients."

With personal safety growing less of a concern, Dorfmeister and some friends were able to do some sight seeing, using horse-drawn taxis to visit a local Chinese cemetery for example.

Dorfmeister was also able to attend some of the war crime trials after the war ended.

"We stood in line to get in and were frisked for weapons. I saw one of the Japanese generals Tomoyuki Yamashita in November 1945 and that part stayed with me for such a long time afterward because of what I heard of the testimony, of the horrible things they did to babies and people. It made me sick."

She also used that post-war time to see some other sites in between treating the remaining wounded. She and some Army nurses visited Corregidor where more than 100 Army and Navy nurses were confined to a cave with the surrounded American defenders of the tiny island fortress in the spring of 1942. The Japanese proved victorious and the nurses became their prisoners for the duration of the war *(GI Nightingales)*. Only about half were alive at war's end.

Dorfmeister remained in Manila on temporary duty for a time before being transferred by trucks to Batangas for another short stint before finally returning to Manila to await orders to leave for home.

Once back home in Wisconsin, the small town girl met one more W.W. II survivor who she couldn't ship out, at least not without her. While in a church group, she met and married Navy veteran George Dorfmeister—a survivor of South Pacific combat and the Dec. 7, 1941, Japanese bombing of Pearl Harbor.

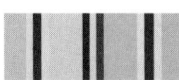

New Guinea Nightingale

Though he didn't talk much about the war, Dorfmeister says her husband was originally aboard the USS ARIZONA at Pearl Harbor but was transferred to the USS DELAWARE shortly before Dec. 7—escaping the deadly fate of most of the crew of the ship-turned-monument that still lies all but submerged in the harbor.

They were married in 1946 and had two daughters. George died in 1987.

Once her daughters were school age, Dorfmeister began volunteering through her church as a nurse at the Lutheran Home for The Aged in Oconomowoc, a volunteering service she's continued for 40 years and counting. "I continue to volunteer, to work as a nurse, out of love of my Lord and people," she explains. "My daughters, Lynne and Heidi and their families complete my joy with their caring for my well being. I am truly blessed."

In 1998 the Wisconsin Association of Homes and Services for the Aging recognized that love and dedication, awarding Dorfmeister the Wisconsin Volunteer of the Year Award.

Throughout her life, she admits, Dorfmeister has been driven by a desire for—and a love of—serving others.

"Faith has always been a part of my life. I think I took that with me from our church to New Guinea and it helped me see that no matter where you are, that your family and God is with you. I don't just start and end the day with prayer; I am conscious all the time of my Lord. And every day I wake up grateful to have another new day to serve the Lord."

Dorfmeister remains proud of her service to her country in W.W. II—and of the tireless work she and all the war's nurses did to care for the men who fought and died for their country. And she is thankful for the eye-opening opportunities her war service gave a small town girl.

"When I look over my life, my time in the service was the one and only time I really saw the world. It

The Hero Next Door Returns

Dorfmeister still likes to explore today and biking remains a summer passion.

was my first time on a train, on a luxury ship. I was young and made so many friends. In many ways it was a good experience."

And, in many ways, that experience still haunts her too.

"It was such a short period in my life, but I remember every detail about it, though I've never even talked much to my girls about it. And, to this day, I can't watch a parade without crying when I see the veterans go by because I saw what they lived through, and would have to live with."

Replacement Marine

REPLACEMENT MARINE
GUS BOERNER

Meeting Gus Boerner at the Marine Corps League hall in Beloit, Wis., no one could doubt how proud he is to be a Marine and to have served in the Marines' 1st Division in W.W. II.

Born in Wausau, Wis., in 1924, Boerner was 19 years old when he was drafted and then joined the Marine Corps May 23, 1944.

The ride from Milwaukee to California was Boerner's second on a train—his first being the train ride to Milwaukee. His train trip to the Marine Corps Recruit Depot in San Diego, Calif., was longer and hotter than he expected. He was dressed in his best clothes, complete with silk socks and dress shoes.

"We were in these old cattle cars on a coal burning train heading toward San Diego. Geez, it was hot! My feet were itching and sweating like a son of a gun. I had the stinkiest feet when I was young so I kept my shoes on. But, by the second day, they were driving me nuts. I tolerated it until night and then took off one shoe. I got one whiff and couldn't even stand it myself. I put the shoe back on and just suffered. But, boy, when we got to San Diego those feet were ripe!"

The rigors of basic training made the foot odor em-

The Hero Next Door Returns

barrassment disappear in a hurry, however, and, Boerner and some 5,000 other Marines were soon off on another long journey, this one aboard the USS HARRY TAYLOR.

While Boerner was in route to the Pacific, his fellow 1st Division Marines were already years into the fighting in the Pacific and were hunkered down on the small island of Peleliu. 1,121 1st Division Marines would die there as Boerner and other replacements made their way. It proved a longer trip than he'd expected as well.

"It was a tortuous ride, nothing to do but look at the water. It was worse because we hadn't been paid before we left San Diego so we couldn't buy nothing on the ship. Then, I found a nickel on deck one day and bought a pack of gum and split it with the guys."

The ship arrived at Pavuvuu, in the Russel Islands in September 1944, 100 miles north of Guadalcanal, and stayed there until the replacements boarded ships for Okinawa at the end of February, 1945.

Combat there was over, but fear is a constant companion in war.

"One of the two times I was really scared happened at Pavuvuu, and we weren't even in combat. The first week we got there I had guard duty. It was a beautiful night with the moon shining and cool ocean breezes. There was not a sound on the island and the other Marines were not yet back from Peleliu. You could have heard a pin drop a mile away.

"I thought, 'I'm not going to stand out in the open,' so I went and stood against a coconut tree. I was standing there a few hours when, Geez! Something crashed the ground behind me, hard! My hair stood straight up! Cripes! I was scared! I didn't move a muscle. Finally, nothing happened, and then I figured it out. It was a coconut falling. But that really scared me. It was nearly pitch dark and you know you're the target and that somebody, out there, is out to get you and then you think you hear them!"

Most of the time on Pavuvuu was spent training and

waiting and working in the kind of close quarters civilian life doesn't prepare you for. "While we were at Pavuvuu, we went to Guadalcanal on maneuvers on a LCI (landing craft, infantry). The head (bathroom) on the boat was out on the fantail of the ship—a big long line of guys sitting there out in the open. But, you couldn't sit and doodle because there was a line of guys waiting to go."

Some work was sweeter than others, though. "One day we took a Higgins boat to a refrigerator ship that had been captured from the Germans. It was loaded with oranges and lemons. They lowered the cargo net down and we threw fruit on the net. We were wearing only shorts and caps so I had more lemons stuck under my hat, in my socks, in my shorts and my pockets."

A BEAUTIFUL MORNING

Shortly after that sweet treat, Boerner boarded a transport into his first combat—and the last American beach invasion of W.W. II.

"It took a long time to get up to Okinawa. We were on the ship over 30 days, and there were ships from horizon to horizon."

Never having faced combat before Boerner wasn't as apprehensive, perhaps, as many aboard the LCIs on Easter morning April 1, 1945, as the first troops went ashore anticipating great resistance. "Geez it was a beautiful morning but we didn't know what to expect." It turned out to be a beautiful morning in every way because there was no resistance and the troops landed mostly untouched.

"I was in the 37mm anti-tank weapons company, so we didn't go ashore the first day not that there was any fighting going on. The second day we got ashore and still there was no resistance. So we unloaded our weapons and pulled those devils around by hand across the island until we finally caught up with the trucks and hooked them on.

The Hero Next Door Returns

Marion Calhoun and Gus Boerner sit on top of a tank used in patrols around Tientsin, China.

The anti-tank gun had armor piercing, incendiary and close-range, buckshot-like (antipersonnel) shells to fire. "They were accurate because we could see the tracers and see where it went. We'd use them to shoot into caves at Japanese. The infantry would call us into duty and say, 'there's a Jap in that cave.' I was a gunner and the guy loading shells. We had to hand pull it a lot. Cripes! But the mud was up to the axle, half the time!"

Not long after they began moving their gun across the island, Boerner got his first taste of combat. "Pretty soon we saw some fighters come over and could see what he was going to do, he was going to strafe us. We ducked under a truck and watched machine gun bullets go by.

"After we came across Kadena airfield and saw the first American fighter planes land on it, we were bunked behind a little hill there not 100 feet high. One night, they started shelling us. Me and two other guys were sleeping under a truck, and one came pretty close. We could hear shrapnel hit the truck and thought 'this truck's full of ammo!' There was a burial tomb in the hill and we made tracks for that. It was out with the bones and in with us! I was the last joker in and my feet were sticking out."

Those were close calls but they were far from the combat Boerner and the 1st Division Marines were about to experience as they headed into the south end of the island. Though the first month on Okinawa was relatively quiet, all hell was about to break loose in early May when the 1st Division really started to push south toward and through Naha, Okinawa. It was there that the Japanese had gathered their strongest defenses and lay in wait for the enemy, in an area that became known as the Shuri Line.

RUGGED HILLS

As Boerner and the anti-tank company followed the infantry troops south, they ran into heavy Japanese resistance and then an outright Japanese offensive. On May 11, the Japanese counterattacked viciously.

"We weren't in the initial fighting but we were there and the infantry would go ahead and when they would get held up with shooting from a cave we'd move into position and fire. When we were on the airfield one night we got shot at as Japs came down in boats along the edge of the island to infiltrate us. One outfit was between us and the ocean.

"We always figured we'd get our heads cut off if we got captured so we just kept fighting. I think the Japanese thought the same thing because a lot of them committed suicide later rather than being taken prisoner."

The Marines could take no chances when Japanese were spotted. "One day, we caught up with the infantry and here came an old scraggly Jap with no clothes on. He was so shell-shocked he didn't know what he was doing but he was going towards our ammo dump. It didn't take us long to stop him.

"Then, another time, we were in fox holes up in a bank. Down in the flats below there was a house. About

The Hero Next Door Returns

suppertime we saw someone go in. So, I asked the lieutenant what we should do about that. Another guy tells the lieutenant 'we don't take prisoners.' So, we threw a bunch of hand grenades in there."

When their company wasn't in on the fighting, it was often stopped high enough to see action elsewhere. "We could see six miles to Naha and all the antiaircraft looked so thick. We had a real ringside seat on Sunday afternoon when they had a real battle at Naha. We sometimes were watching the Jap attacks—especially kamikaze attacks—on the ships around Okinawa from our vantage point on one of the hills. Our ships were really taking a beating, and I remember we were saying how there was no place for those sailors to go when those devils started shooting at them. There were so many ships getting hit that we began to wonder if we were going to get stranded on the island!"

And the Navy ships were taking a deadly beating. More Navy men (4,907) died off shore in the fight for Okinawa than died in either the Army (4,379) or Marines (3,440), according to *The United States Marine Corps in World War II* (p. 911).

Boerner watched other battle tactics as well. "There were war dogs, actual dogs, and I saw them working one day. We were up above and the whole valley below were sugarcane patches that grew as thick as the hair on your head. At night the Japs would end up trying to sneak through the sugar cane. So, they brought them dogs down and sent them in to rout the Japs out. It reminded me of when I used to hunt brush piles back home and kick a rabbit out."

Most of the Japanese that Boerner saw close up were dead, however.

"The Japs had brown uniforms, and I'll never forget one dead Jap I saw. Everything was perfect about him except his legs had been blown clean off. There was no blood or anything. I got a Jap flag off him.

"The worst that way, I guess, was one time when we came back off the lines. We stopped and filled the

Replacement Marine

canteen up with water from the creek and thought 'geez, this water stinks and tastes bad.' Well, the next morning, we found out why. The whole creek just upstream was full of dead Japanese, and we'd been drinking the water they'd been laying in."

The island was filled with dead Marines as well, though the Marines still alive to fight were told not to touch them.

"We knew never to touch one of our dead bodies that had been there a while because they were often booby-trapped. On one ridge we moved up, I took a foxhole that was directly across from one this body was laying in. There were maggots coming out of his eyes, mouth and ears. He was lying flat on his back and, for a couple of days, every time I went into or out of my hole I had to look at him. I thought I should get his name, but I knew better than to touch him."

There were plenty of close calls in the foxholes Boerner sought refuge in, though such combat tales are the stories he prefers not to tell. "Usually, when someone asks me about the war, I remember all the

Tientsin Taxis took Al Kamcheff, Olin Woodley and Gus Boerner around China when they weren't on guard.

The Hero Next Door Returns

humorous stories because, to me, those are the most interesting to tell. For me there's no interest or enthusiasm in talking about all that bad stuff. I'd rather talk about that than the shooting and all that."

The problem is that stories that are hard to talk about are often the hardest to forget.

"The most scared I was in combat was not actually during the shooting. The worst is always the waiting for something to happen. At night, in a foxhole, most of the time you'd have two guys in it sitting back to back because the one thing I always dreaded was someone sneaking up behind me and slitting my throat."

The caves the Japanese hid in were especially eerie, even after the troops had cleared and secured a cave. The caves could be booby-trapped or, worse, a Japanese may have escaped the flame-throwers and be waiting for curious Marines or souvenir hunters to venture in.

One time, Boerner's own curiosity got the best of him and he got "the scare of my life!"

"We'd been up on a ridge fighting and right down below us was a big cave. After the fighting was over, we had to go back for some barrels of oil the Japs had buried. These guys talked me into going into the cave on the way back. It was a big cave and you could walk upright once you were in the door. It was about four- to five- feet wide and had a shelf built up with blankets on it like someone had been sleeping in there.

"The three of us went in and I was keeping my eye always on the door. I got up on the platform inside and it was almost pitch dark. Then, between me and the door, I could see just a shadow rising up ... I was just ready to shoot because I was sure it was a Jap that had been hiding and was rising up to shoot us. Then, the guy with me turned and I could see what it was. He'd stepped on a plank and raised up the other end of it. I never went into another cave after that!"

The cave area was also where Boerner saw one of

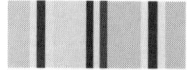

Replacement Marine

the worst sights of combat. "That was the same place we got shelled one morning. The mortar platoon below us was shooting over the ridge and the Jap mortar platoon on the other side of the hill was shooting back. Pretty soon there was a loud explosion and the shelling stopped. Our mortar platoon got hit.

"Then, here came the corpsmen leading three guys from the platoon. It looked like the scene from a Frankenstein movie only, the scary thing was, this was real. The three guys were bare-naked and had been burnt by white phosphorous when it exploded. Their skin was hanging down off of them in long strings of white from their nose, chin, ears, eyelids, fingers, chest and their genitals. I don't know how they could even walk and I felt sorry for them. You see something like that and you can't forget it."

Boerner can't forget the often non-stop sounds of bullets cracking by and mortar shells whistling overhead, either.

"One night we were in a foxhole and could hear the bullets start flying faster and faster and could hear the shells whistling, but they were well over our heads so we figured the fighting was about a mile away. Then, a bullet cracked just like a firecracker right by my face. It was so close to my face, I could feel the wind."

Boerner came close to bigger danger not long after. "We were going to move out one morning from where we were hunkered down behind this hill. Well, nature called and I took my backpack off, grabbed my shovel and walked out—walking a little further than I usually would. Anyway, I dug my hole and just squatted down when the Navy guys—who'd been shelling from way off in the distance to someplace over our heads—fired a dud or something. I was sitting there listening to a shell whistle when, out of the corner of my eye, I saw this big shell going end over end. The minute I saw it, I hit the ground and I could see the ground around me flying as high as I could see. If I would have stopped sooner and not walked quite so far to dig my hole

The Hero Next Door Returns

that shell would have got me!

"My buddy Floyd Bryson from Forks, Wash., was real lucky one time too. We were just like brothers—still are—and he and another guy, a replacement, were sitting in foxholes. He bent over to pick something up and the bullet meant for him hit the kid in the knee. We sure had a lot of close calls but we were lucky."

Some close calls were self-inflicted, however. "Shortly before it was over, as we were pulling back to the North End, we had to hold up for the night. A big bunch of us were way up the hill and somebody got a hold of some alcohol and mixed it with grapefruit juice because the water was always warm and stinky. There was this kid from Texas, a big overgrown kid, who made a hog of himself. Then, some shooting started in and Old Blazer got up, grabbed his carbine and, bare-naked, ran out of the foxhole. We were all hollering at him to get back before he got shot but he was so looped up. Somehow we talked him back in, but that's the kind of thing that happened sometimes that nobody talks much about. He was lucky he wasn't killed."

In general, the gun company was lucky. "We had some wounded but none killed. We just patched each other up and kept going," praying all the while that they would keep going.

"The chaplain was very important to me. I never forgot my Catholic faith and there was a whole lot of praying over there, believe me!"

And, Boerner is especially grateful to others who rose to help Marines in the face of the gravest of combat dangers. "I've got to give a lot of praise and honor to the Navy corpsmen who got up and went to the aid of the wounded whenever they heard that pitiful cry 'corpsman!' admist all the shooting going on."

WET & HUNGRY

Fighting at Okinawa was bad enough but the weather

and terrain didn't make the going any easier. The troops were often wet and always dirty and exhausted. "We came back off the lines one time after it had been raining a week or so and took a shower and got a pair of clean socks. You've always got to try to get clean socks. We found a pig kettle and the next morning set fire underneath it and the clothes came out OK."

But, cleanliness of any kind was hard to come by and the Marines paid an unhealthy price for it, including Boerner. "I got blood poisoning in my arm once and got dysentery in the middle of a rainstorm with three guys all in a pup tent together next to these little railroad tracks. The minute I stepped out of the tent I was up to my knees in mud. But I had to go and often. So, I'd slosh out, dig a hole, do my job, crawl back to the tent and kept that up all night.

"In the night I got so thirsty for water that I got my canteen cup out and took a swig of what turned out to be gasoline because the gas and the water cans were all mixed up. If you don't think that's a pukey taste in your mouth when you're all dry! Geez! I spit that junk out. I was lucky I didn't swallow it!

"The next day I went to sick bay, but the corpsman said 'we can't take you.' Instead he brought me a whole bunch of cans of cheese and said 'that'll plug you up,' and it did!"

Even cans of cheese were not always at hand however as ration supplies were touchy. "We were always trying to find food. One day we were on this hill when two old women came with a little boy. We stood there watching and he had a little grub hoe. That little guy swung that all day long and was always picking up something. He must have had a 10-quart pail of white potatoes when he took a break. He was no more up the road than we had his potatoes. Pretty soon it was getting toward dusk and he came back. The way that poor kid worked, I still feel bad about taking those potatoes, but they sure did taste good. So good that we looked that island over for more white potatoes

The Hero Next Door Returns

any chance we got, but we never did find any more."

Another time the Marines made a quick, tasty dinner out of some piglets they ran across. "We saw an old brood sow and a mess of youngins and got a bright idea to kill some of the young ones. Geez that was good!"

But the supplemental food was few and far between and most of the time the Marines lived off their rations and tried to scrape by until the next day and the next and the next. Then on June 21 the Japanese General Ushijima committed suicide rather than surrender. The fight for Okinawa was over.

But, there were still hardships to bear.

"After the fighting was over, we went to the North end of the island to a rest camp. We had a company street at the rest area with tents on both sides, and we were there when a typhoon hit. It took every tent down except ours because we were behind a little bank. Geez! That was a wind storm, and we were all out there tying them tents down."

It reminded Boerner of a typhoon he'd weathered aboard ship one time. "That was the first time I ever fell up the steps. I was on mess duty and was walking up the steps and the ship was rocking so that you could see straight up. Then, the boat fell out from underneath me, so I fell up the steps."

The division was still on Okinawa when the folks back home were celebrating their Independence, on July 4, 1945.

"I'll never forget that day. I had mess duty that day and I probably volunteered because we had fresh food come in and I was always a big eater. I went there at 10 or so and they had fresh eggs! Geez, they were good. Each man got one fried egg and somehow I copped an egg still in the shell and all I had was a pair of shorts to hide it in because that's all we wore in the heat. Anyway, I worked the whole dinner hour with that egg in hiding and I never broke it. I brought it in our tent, got my small can of gas out and had myself one more

Replacement Marine

fried egg. Geez, that was good!"

CHINA MEN

It proved one of Boerner's last combat meals. Though there'd been rumors they'd would soon be Hawaii-bound, the division instead went to China to help secure the Japanese surrender there.

On Sept. 26 the 1st Division arrived in Tanku, China. "They told us we went there to take care of the Japanese (and assure their surrender in China as well as the release of Allied internees), but I think the real reason was for the communist movement building there. We landed at Tanku and went to Tientsin by truck the next day. It was dark, cold, windy and wet. There was nothing. It was barren country. We found one park where we saw a couple of trees but that was it.

"When we first landed there, you couldn't stop on the streets, they'd just gather around you and stare. At first, the Chinese were excited we were there and the first thing they learned was 'one dollar.' Everything was one dollar. They had lots of beggars. The old parents would hide and send a kid in saying 'come sho, no mamma, no papa' and we old Marines would give them some phrases to add on—mostly four-letter ones."

The tall, white Marines were a curiosity. "There was a gate we came in and out of, but there were so many people around you could have used a snowplow to get them away from the gate. We were just that much of a curiosity."

Chinese culture had its own curiosities for the Americans. "First we stayed at this big school. We were up on the second floor and the bathroom had a hole in the floor with a small bowl in the hole. That was their toilet bowl."

For all the cultural differences, though, Boerner did get to know a few Chinese. "Right behind the barracks was a laundry that had a Chinaman who could talk

The Hero Next Door Returns

James Brown, Gus Boerner and Gregg Sherwood display a Japanese flag they found on Okinawa.

English and we'd even bring him into the compound. I remember watching them do laundry when they would iron and starch our khakis. They would have a bottle of water nearby. To dampen the clothes, they would fill their mouths and cheeks with water and then blow out the perfect spray of water as needed. When their mouth was empty they'd fill it up again.

"One day we got the English-speaking laundryman

Replacement Marine

talking about the war and explained that if 'I were a captain in the Army and captured a village, I'd kill every person in it' ... I always thought of Gangus Kahn because that's what he did, and that's what their culture was. He got the job as an interpreter for the Marines, but I bet all those people that associated with us didn't live very long when the communists took over. It's like that laundry guy said; I bet they killed every one of the ones that were friendly with us."

The city was divided into different controlling sections—English, French, Russian and American. "We went to the French cathedral on Sundays and I never did get to the American section as we were housed in the English barracks. All the big buildings were built with an open center. They used to bring fresh fruit into the city, and I especially remember they had these really good pears there."

But, most people who lived there were barely getting by. "Nothing went to waste in that country. They turned our tin cans into funnels, cups and plates. One day we had a detail at a machine shop where we hauled iron metal turnings to the dump all day. We'd drop off a load and, by the time we got back with the next, all the metal 'dust' was gone.

"One day we had a garbage truck and the Chinamen started crawling up and we had to knock them away to get the tailgate down. The garbage was in big 55-gallon barrels and, as the people were tipping the barrels, one fell on top of all these kids. When the crowd removed the barrel, one kid was rubbing his head with a red potato and digging into the slop with his other hand! When we came back with the second load, all that was left was a wet spot on the ground."

Without combat, some of the more "mickey-mouse" parts of military life returned. There was protocol and details in triplicate that war-veteran Marines—a few of whom had been at war since the first American offensive against the Japanese on Guadalcanal in 1942—had little patience for.

The Hero Next Door Returns

"For example, General Peck, was coming for inspection. Well it was so cold out on the parade ground and we were waiting so long in the cold that some guys passed out before the general finally showed up. Then, he just drove by quick in his Jeep."

China wasn't always just stand-at-the-ready peacetime duty. The Marines there encountered some hot spots. *The Old Breed: A History of the 1st Marine Division in World War II,* reports China duty was "full of incidents that sometimes became international in effect—of encounters, skirmishes with forces that were often apparently guerrillas on the fringe of the Chinese Communist Army, of others that were apparently only bandits and yet others that were hungry civilians raiding the division's stores."

For example, in October 1945, as one company tried to clear roadblocks from the Tientsin-Peiping Highway, it "received sporadic and irregular rifle fire from an estimated 40-50 troops ... the encounter inflicted three casualties and at least one enemy was believed hit by return fire."

Boerner's company again proved lucky. "We had to go out a couple of times for some uproar, we never did find anything but could hear machine gun fire from time to time. There were a few little skirmishes but they didn't last too long. You never knew where the communists guerrillas were. There was one part of Tientsin that was off limits because there were a lot of communists there."

Most of his time in China was spent waiting to go home, however. "We war veterans sort of wondered what we were doing there, why we couldn't go home. It was just like 'your job is done,' and to go there was all right but then, after a year, there was nothing to do there. Nothing to do except get drunk on Vodka—heavily diluted Vodka that you'd buy in the market."

Boerner's China duty ended in the spring of 1946 when fresher replacements arrived—and stayed in China until October, 1949. He caught a ride to Tanku

Replacement Marine

Gus and Ruth Boerner in 1997.

and then a troop ship for home. "On the LST (landing ship, tank) we were packed in on the bottom like a bunch of old rats but at least we were going home!"

Boerner returned through San Diego and went to Chicago where he was discharged May 15, 1946. "I was actually at Great Lakes a few weeks while they processed me so I went up to South Milwaukee where my brother and sister lived and we went out that night and 'didn't spare no bones.' About 1 o'clock I said, 'geez, I gotta catch the Northshore back to Waukegan.' I hurried but when I got there, the train was closed. So, I stayed there all night and caught the first train. Then, I got off at the wrong station in Waukegan, so I walked and walked and walked and got back literally as they were calling names for roll call—and my name starts with B!"

ALWAYS FAITHFUL

Though he loved the Marines, Boerner waited until 1956 to truly fall head over heels for Ruth Pugh, a girl from Portage, Wis., at her neighbor's daughter's wedding. "She was just a kid in W.W. II, born in 1933. But she fell in love with this old Marine anyway and we

The Hero Next Door Returns

went together one year before we were married Sept. 21, 1957. I still can't believe how lucky I was to get a wonderful wife to share life with."

Boerner had, for a short time, nearly re-enlisted in the Marines. "I considered signing up for the reserves after the war and even talked to a recruiter about it, but then he said I had to go all the way to Adams to do it and I just didn't want to go that far. I kept saying, 'if I run into him again, I'll do it.' But, I never did, which is good because when the Korean War started I'd have been there."

The Boerners had no children and dedicated themselves to the Marine Corps League in Beloit, of which Gus is a life member, and other groups including at St. Stephens Catholic Church. He is also a life member of the American Legion, Veterans of Foreign Wars, and Marine Order of Devil Dogs and is a member of the local Lions Club, Knights of Columbus and senior citizens groups. In addition, he has delivered Meals on Wheels for 14 years and spends what free time he has gardening, woodworking, wine making, reading and helping Ruth with the Beloit Marine Corps League newsletter.

Of all the jobs he's done, however, Boerner remains ever proud of his service to his country in the Marine Corps. "That Marine Corps' motto 'Semper Fidelis'—ever faithful—means a lot to me. I'm proud to be a Marine, but I didn't join the Marines to win medals. I answered our country's call and did my job.

"When we served during W.W. II, we did it with the intent to protect and preserve this country and its citizens for future generations—to share in its gifts from God. And this old Marine hopes that the future generations we fought for will never turn their backs on the veterans that sacrificed for them then and now. That, above all, they would honor the flag as we did. Because, when you've seen that flag flying on a bombed out hill where a bunch of guys died and you're tired and hungry, you can only think of how

Replacement Marine

important it is to protect that flag and what it stands for. You only think that you will be always faithful to it and the country it flies for. Semper Fi!"

Editor's Note: *See more photos of the veterans featured in this book at* The Hero Next Door™ *web site at* www.heronextdoor.org.

The Hero Next Door Returns

SOURCES LIST

Allyn's Irish Orphans: 775th Bomb Squadron of the 463rd Bomb Group, compiled by Carl B. Cassidy, U.S. Army Air Force, 1946.

American Badges & Insignia, Evans E. Kerrigan, Viking Press, 1967.

American Heritage Picture Dictionary of World War II, C.L. Sulzberger, American Heritage Publishing Inc., 1966

Anzio. Wynford Vaughan-Thomas. Popular Library, N.Y. 1962.

D-Day, June 6, 1944, Stephen Ambrose, Simon & Schuster, 1994.

Devils in Baggy Pants: The Combat Record of the 504th Parachute Infantry Regiment, April 1943-July 1945. Compiled by Lt. William d. Mandle, PR officer and PFC David H. Whittier, regimental correspondent. Draeger Freres (publisher), Paris.

The 54th In Review, official publication of the 54th General Hospital, U.S. Army publication.

GI Nightingales. Barbara Brooks Tomblin. The University Press of Kentucky, Lexington. 1996

Heroes in Dungarees: The Story of the American Merchant Marine in World War II. John Bunker. Naval Institute Press, Annapolis, Md. 1995.

History of the Second World War: The War at Sea. Vol. III, Part II. Capt. S.W. Roskill. Her Majesty's Stationery Office, London. 1961.

International Maritime Dictionary. Rene deKerchove. D. Van Norstrand Co., Princeton, N.J. 1948

Sources

Military & Naval Recognition Book, J.W. Bunkley, Rear Admiral, U.S. Navy (Ret.). D. Van Norstrand Co., Princeton, N.J. 1943.

The Military History of World War II: Volumes 11-14, Trevor N. Dupuy, Col. U.S. Army, (Ret.). Franklin Watts, Inc., 1964.

The Random House College Dictionary, Random House, 1975.

13,000 Hours: Combat History of the 32nd Infantry Division—World War II. Prepared by the Public Relations Office, 32nd Infantry Division

32nd Division: "Les Terribles," Dave Turner. Turner Publishing, 1992.

32nd Infantry Division in World War II. Maj. Gen. H.W. Blakely, USA ret. U.S. Army publication.

The Old Breed: A History of the First Marine Division in World War II. George McMillan. Infantry Journal Press. 1949.

U.S. Army in W.W. II: The Technical Services: The Medical Department, Medical Service in the Eastern Theater of Operations. Graham, Cosmas & Albert Cowdrey, Center of Military History, U.S. Army. 1992.

U.S. Army in W.W. II: The Technical Services: The Medical Department, Medical Service in the Mediterranean and Minor Theaters. Graham, Cosmas & Albert Cowdrey. Center of Military History. U.S. Army. 1992.

U.S. Army in W.W. II: The Technical Services: The Signal Corps, The Test. George R. Thompson, Dixie Harris, Pauline Oaks, Dulany Terelt. Center of Military History. U.S. Army. 1957.

U.S. Army in W.W. II: The Technical Services: The Signal Corps, The Outcome. George R. Thompson, Dixie Harris, Pauline Oaks, Dulany Terelt. Center of Military History. U.S. Army. 1966.

U.S. Department of Defense U.S. Military Personnel Statistics. 1775-1973.

U.S. Department of Defense Dictionary of Military Terms. The Joint Chiefs of Staff. Arco. 1988.

The Hero Next Door Returns

U.S. Submarine Losses NAVPERS 15,784, 1949 Issue, World War II. U.S. Government Printing Office. Washington, D.C.

Unexplained Mysteries of World War II. William B. Breuer, John Wiley & Sons Inc. 1997.

The United States Marine Corps in W.W.II. Compiled and edited by S.E. Smith. Random House, New York. 1969.

The Victors, Stephen Ambrose, Simon & Schuster, 1998

Voices of the Wisconsin Past: Women Remember the War. Edited by Michael E. Stevens.

The Wall Chart of World War II: A Chronological Presentation of the War That Changed the World. Dorset Press. 1991.

What a Way to Spend a War: Navy Nurse POWs in the Philippines. Dorothy Still Danner. 1995

W.W. II Time-Life Books: The Air War In Europe. Ronald H. Bailey. Alexandria, Va.

World War II, Ivor Matanle. Quadrillion Publishing Ltd., 1989.

World War II Strange & Fascinating Facts. Don McCombs and Fred Worth. Greenwich House, 1983

The Writers Guide to Everyday Life From Prohibition through World War II. Marc McCutcheon. Writers Digest Books. 1995.

Author Interviews (all in 2000)
Baumgart, Earl, Wauwatosa, Wis.
Boerner, Gustav, Clinton, Wis.
Brenzel, Dave, Oregon, Wis.
Dorfmeister, Marion, Oconomowoc, Wis.
Durnford, George, Monona, Wis.
Fredrick, Marie, Oconomowoc, Wis.
Gutekunst, Martin, Oconomowoc, Wis.
Harrison, Richard, archives manager, Wisconsin Veterans Museum, Madison, Wis.
Hubbard, Norton, Middleton, Wis.

Sources

Kapus, Jeannette, Germantown, Wis.
Langeteig, Marvin, Evansville, Wis.
Meyer, Lavern, Madison, Wis.
Murphy, Virgil, Bowler, Wis.
Murphy, Ernestine, Bowler, Wis.
Murphy, Roger, Milwaukee, Wis.
Murphy, Dorothy, Milwaukee, Wis.
Orlowski, Art, Wisconsin Dells, Wis., and Leesburg, Fla.
Watson, George, Monona, Wis.

Oral Histories and Personal Memoirs
Confessions of a POW: 45 Months Between The Rock and The Hard Place. David G. Brenzel. Self-published. 1991

Interview of Native American Women. Kristina Ackley, State Historical Society of Wisconsin, 1992.

Submarine Journal: At last! Story of WWII submarine SS250 FLIER loss and amazing sea-land Odyssey of survivors. Alvin E. Jacobson, survivor. Self-published. Spring 1998.

Other Sources
Military, Vol. XVI, No. 3, The Press of Freedom. Aug. 1999, p. 14.

The Ozarks Newspaper. Aug. 12, 1985.

Paraglide, "Remembering D-Day," 82nd Airborne Division Association, Summer 1994.

"Men Against the Sea: The Loss of the USS Flier SS-250." Peter Amundrud, Central Region director of the U.S. Submarine Veterans. LaCrosse, Wis.

Saturday Evening Post. "D-Day. David Howarth. March 14, 1959.

SUBNET. Cyberspace Association of U.S. Submarines. www.subnet.com.

Tigers of the Sea: The Story of the U.S. Navy in W.W.II. Marathon Music & Video, Dastar Corp, Eugene, Ore. 1998.

The Hero Next Door Returns

The USS Franklin: The Ship That Wouldn't Die. Documentary narrated by Gene Kelly. (Re-released) NBC Television. 1990.

Wisconsin Department of Veterans Affairs, records department. Madison, Wis.

Wisconsin Veterans Museum archives. Madison, Wis.

World War II: The War in Europe. The History Channel Collector's Choice. A&E Television Network. 1983.

ABOUT THE AUTHOR

Kristin Gilpatrick Halverson was born in Edgerton, Wis., to educators Robert and Barbara Gilpatrick. A Cedarburg High School alumna, she graduated from the University of Wisconsin-Eau Claire in 1990 with a double major in journalism and Spanish, having studied a semester in Valladolid, Spain. In college, her life-long passion for writing and history blossomed into a love for telling the stories of the "everyday" people who made history.

Kristin Gilpatrick

She put that passion to paper as a reporter for newspapers in Illinois and Wisconsin, winning nine press association awards along the way. Since 1997, she's been a magazine editor for the Credit Union Executives Society, Madison, Wis.

For the past 13 years, she has also been a big sister to two girls in the Big Brothers/Big Sisters programs and is active in her church. She married her best friend Steven L. Halverson, an EdwardJones investment representative, Oct. 25, 1997. They live in Monona, Wis., where Gilpatrick is completing her next book *Destined to Live: The Story of W.W. II Airman William "Wild Bill" Scanlon* and working on her third book in the *Hero Next Door*™ series. (Visit *www.heronextdoor.org* for updates and details.)

MORE STORIES AVAILABLE

Meet more World War II heroes in Kristin Gilpatrick's first book, *The Hero Next Door*™, where she introduces readers to:

- **James Geach,** a paratrooper with the 82nd Airborne who began his combat service as the Nazis were fleeing Africa and saw his first combat as the Allies pushed into Italy.
- **James Church,** an infantryman engineer with Gen. Simpson's 9th Army who first saw combat in the hedgerows of France and survived the Battle of the Bulge.
- **Glen Hanusa,** a Navy intelligence petty officer who met President Franklin D. Roosevelt while serving in Adak, Alaska.
- **George Kinsler,** a PBY flying boat gunner who helped rescue downed pilots and wounded soldiers before returning stateside as a aircraft engineer and PBY trainer.
- **Russ Kohloff,** a 5th Division Marine who fought in the jungle islands of the Pacific and withstood the bloody sands of Iwo Jima.
- **Garvin Kowalke,** a B-29 bomber pilot who flew weather reconnaissance and radiation level testing missions for the atomic bombing of Hiroshima in a plane he named for his hometown, "The City of Baraboo."
- **Joe Reilly,** a paratrooper with the 101st Airborne who saw his first combat in the D-Day invasion of France and was among those nicknamed The Battered Bastards of Bastogne for their defense of the surrounded city in the Battle of the Bulge.
- **Brothers Archie Sanderson,** who slugged his way across the battlefields of Europe as part of the 294th Combat Engineers, and **Gerald Sanderson** who flew in the flak-torn skies above as a gunner for the 815th Bomb Squadron out of Italy.
- **Eugene Skaar,** a utility maintenance man for the

382nd Army Battalion who was stationed in New Guinea and who fought the Japanese in the Philippines.

• **Clyde Stephenson,** a Marine on the U.S.S. California battleship, who had a unique vantage point of the Japanese attack on Pearl Harbor from his temporary position at the Fleet Machine Gun School at the harbor entrance.

• **Ernie Tresch,** a bomber pilot with the 320 Bomb Group out of Africa and later Italy who returned stateside to become a pilot for the highest ranking military official of the war—and future president of the United States—General Dwight D. Eisenhower.

• **John Topolski,** a radar operator with the 20th Army Air Force out of India who survived 29 hours alone in the Indian Ocean after the B-24 he was riding in was shot down.

Please complete the following form and send a check or money order only (no CODs) for $14.95 per book, plus $3 shipping per order to:

```
                Badger Books Inc.
                  P.O. Box 192
                Oregon, WI 53575


    ____ copies of  The Hero Next Door™
    ____ copies of  The Hero Next Door™ Returns


  Name: _____
  Address: _____
  City: _____
     State/Zip: _____

  (Wisconsin residents please add 82 cents state and
 local sales tax per book.)
```